Taking Part

Introducing
Social Skills to Children
PreK~Grade 3

(SECOND EDITION)

Gwendolyn Cartledge • James Kleefeld

Research Press • 2612 North Mattis Avenue • Champaign, Illinois 61822 • (800) 519-2707
www.researchpress.com

Second edition © 2009 by Gwendolyn Cartledge and James Kleefeld.

5   4   3   2   1   09   10   11   12   13

First edition © 1991 by American Guidance Service.

Copies of this book may be ordered from Research Press at the address given on the title page.

Composition by Jeff Helgesen
Cover design by Linda Brown, Positive I.D. Graphic Design, Inc.
Printed by McNaughton & Gunn, Inc.

ISBN-13: 978-0-87822-613-9
Library of Congress Control Number 2008942195

CONTENTS

INTRODUCTION

Taking Part: Introducing Social Skills to Children is a training program in social skills for children in special and general education classrooms, preschool through grade three. Social skills—interacting positively with others, communicating effectively and assertively, cooperating in play and work, resolving conflicts—are extremely important to the developing child. Social competence enhances the overall quality of a child's life. Research shows positive correlations between social skills and academic achievement, particularly in such behaviors as paying attention, staying on task, volunteering, and asking instructionally relevant questions (Cartledge & Milburn, 1995). Other studies show that normally developing children tend to reject peers with poor social skills, particularly those who display aggression (Guevremont & Dumas, 1994). Children who fail to learn and refine appropriate social behavior often find themselves in conflict with others. Bullying, for example, usually involves a combination of children who are socially aggressive and children who do not respond assertively.

Social skills are typically learned informally. Most children learn how to behave around others by making mistakes that generate adult correction or reprimand. Traditionally, a significant portion of this learning was expected to take place in the home. There is good evidence, though, that classroom instruction can be effective in encouraging social skills development and in alleviating various adjustment problems (Walker, Ramsey, & Gresham, 2004).

Taking Part aims to provide teachers, clinicians, and other professionals with specific strategies for social skills instruction. The skills taught are those considered critical for the development of the young child; the techniques presented have been found most effective in helping children learn (Walker et al., 1997). The program attempts to address the behavioral, cognitive, and affective components of social skills. Only by considering all the facets of social interaction can children successfully learn to "take part."

DEVELOPMENT

The authors developed *Taking Part* after presenting several workshops on social skills instruction to teachers. In each, almost all the participants expressed a desire to teach social skills, but few had the materials or training for such instruction. To remedy this, the authors developed activities and conducted a field trial with local teachers of young children. Their feedback helped shape the program's content. A revised version of *Taking Part* was submitted for field testing at sites selected to represent a full range of ages, geographic locations, economic levels, and cultures. Field testers' responses helped shape the final version of the program.

THEORETICAL MODEL

Social skills can be taught much like other parts of the curriculum. Components of instruction are the following:

- Defining the behavior to be taught.
- Assessing the student's current proficiency in the behavior.
- Teaching the needed skills by presenting examples, asking questions, and providing feedback.
- Evaluating the results of teaching; teaching again when necessary.
- Providing opportunities for practice, generalization, and maintenance over time (Cartledge & Milburn, 1995).

These steps are consistent with those of other skills training procedures (e.g., McGinnis & Goldstein, 2003) and comprise the model employed in this curriculum.

DEFINING THE BEHAVIOR TO BE TAUGHT

Social skills are best presented as clearly defined behaviors, each as a sequence of steps involving thinking, feeling, and doing.

Teachers and students must know exactly what responses are expected and when the skills have been performed. Globally stated behaviors are not only confusing, they often do not result in the acquisition of skills. No two children interpret the statement "Be nice to each other" in the same way. A skill such as "speaking kindly and using courtesy words," however, can be specifically defined and practiced.

ASSESSING CURRENT PROFICIENCY

Social skills are typically assessed through some form of behavioral observation. You may wish to set up a situation that calls for a particular skill and watch children respond. For example, in assessing a student's skill in sharing materials, you might enlist a second child to help, directing the target student accordingly: "Sue, Derek is using the paste. What would you do if you wanted to use the paste, too?" When the child being assessed responds, you would evaluate the child's skill according to age appropriateness.

For most skills, you might simply observe students in natural classroom conditions. Direct observation may be done informally but should focus on a particular skill or set of skills. For example, if you are interested in developing or improving conversation skills, note the degree to which specific students contribute to classroom discussions and the relevance of their contributions. Students with significant deficiencies can be identified for further instruction.

You can also determine student competence by using a formal social skills assessment instrument, such as the Social Skills Rating System (Gresham & Elliott, 1990). The scores obtained from these ratings can be used to compare students and assign them to instructional groups.

TEACHING NEEDED SKILLS

As discussed later in this introduction, the skill lessons of *Taking Part* are taught in a sequence of motivation, practice, and maintenance activities. At each stage of instruction, students are given many examples of appropriate skill use, asked questions to enhance their understanding of skills, and provided with specific feedback as they practice skills. Appendix A includes a list of skill names and steps for handy reference. Appendixes B through D provide reproducible materials—puppet mask outlines, program posters, and blackline masters, respectively.

EVALUATING THE RESULTS OF TEACHING

In evaluating students' skills, look for spontaneity of response, completeness of response, and smoothness of performance. Because the use of social skills depends on particular social situations, evaluation of students' performance can be based largely on your own personal satisfaction with the response. Students who fail to meet your established standards should receive additional instruction. You may choose to present program activities again or to modify them based on your students' needs. In some cases, you may need only to provide additional practice activities; in others, you may need to review concepts as well.

PROVIDING FOR PRACTICE, GENERALIZATION, AND MAINTENANCE

Practice is essential to a child's understanding and internalization of any skill. Introductory and motivational activities may acquaint the child with the skill language and steps, but only the personal involvement of trying out the behavior can make it a learned, automatic response.

Maintenance refers to getting a behavior to persist over time, making sure children continue to perform the skill after they've finished the program. Ideally, the social skills you teach will become a permanent part of each student's repertoire, with gradual, appropriate changes as the child develops. Generalization occurs when a child performs the behavior across a variety of conditions and settings. For example, if a child learns to compliment others during your social skills instruction, the child should also give compliments during other times of the day and in places outside the classroom, such as home and playground.

REFERENCES

Cartledge, G., & Milburn, J. F. (1995). *Teaching social skills to children and youth: Innovative practices.* Boston: Allyn & Bacon.

Gresham, F. M., & Elliott, S. N. (1990). *Social skills rating system.* Circle Pines, MN: American Guidance Service.

Guevremont, D. C., & Dumas, M. C. (1994). Peer relationship problems and disruptive behavior disorders. *Journal of Emotional and Behavioral Disorders, 2,* 164–172.

McGinnis, E., & Goldstein, A. P. (2003). *Skillstreaming in early childhood: New strategies and perspectives for teaching social skills.* Champaign, IL: Research Press.

Walker, H., Ramsey, E., & Gresham, F. M. (2004). *Antisocial behavior in school: Evidence-based practice.* Belmont, CA: Wadsworth/Thomson Learning.

Walker, H. M., Stiller, B., Golly, A., Kavanagh, K., Severson, H., & Feil, E. (1997). *First step to success: Helping young children overcome antisocial behavior.* Longmont, CO: Sopris West.

TEACHING THE SKILLS

SKILLS PRESENTED IN THIS PROGRAM

Taking Part consists of six units:

- Making Conversation
- Communicating Feelings
- Expressing Oneself
- Cooperating with Peers
- Playing with Peers
- Responding to Aggression and Conflict

Each unit contains from five to seven specific skills—thirty-three skills in all. The skills are presented in developmental sequence. There is necessarily some overlapping of age appropriateness, but earlier units generally contain simpler skills, and skills within a unit grow increasingly more difficult.

Unit 1: Making Conversation

Greeting

Introducing Yourself

Listening

Joining a Conversation

Starting a Conversation

Unit 2: Communicating Feelings

Naming Feelings

Naming My Feelings

Naming Others' Feelings

Sending Messages

Controlling Temper

Unit 3: Expressing Oneself

Making Positive Self-Statements

Making Positive Statements to Others

Expressing Feelings

Speaking Kindly and Using Courtesy Words

Speaking Assertively

Unit 4: Cooperating with Peers

Respecting Others' Property

Sharing Materials

Accepting Individual Differences

Joining a Group Activity

Mediating Group Rules

Offering and Giving Help

Giving and Accepting Criticism

Unit 5: Playing with Peers

Taking Turns

Putting Materials Away

Playing Group Games

Helping Others Participate

Following Game Rules

Winning and Losing

Unit 6: Responding to Aggression and Conflict

Ignoring Aggression

Getting Away from Aggression

Asking for Help

Responding Defensively

Negotiating Conflicts

CHOOSING SKILLS TO TEACH

The skills included in this curriculum are considered critical to a child's social development. However, teachers will need to consider various factors in deciding which skills to teach.

One such consideration is relevance. If peers or important adults in your students' environment do not agree that a skill is important, it will not be reinforced, and children will have difficulty maintaining it. Similarly, if you don't feel a skill is significant for your students, you may want to skip it in favor of others you prize more highly. On the other hand, if you feel a skill is not highly prized in the immediate environment but is important to the students' academic and overall success, you might find it worthwhile to include it and to solicit the involvement and support of families or other individuals who will more directly influence the children to use the skill.

A second consideration is developmental level. Your expectations for a child will vary according to the child's age and ability. To illustrate, conversation skills such as greeting may be appropriate for your particular school setting, but different age levels or developmental disabilities among your students may necessitate different behavioral goals. Older children are inclined to engage class newcomers in conversation about their background (e.g., "Where did you go to school before this?") and to supply information about the new setting. Younger children, however, tend to offer assistance or ask the new student to do something with them. In teaching this skill to young children, then, the more developmentally appropriate response for them to learn would be how to offer assistance rather than how to engage a peer in the exchange of background information.

A third consideration relates to student need. Instead of presenting skills sequentially, you may choose to present them according to your students' particular needs. In one classroom, for example, the most urgent need may be responding to aggression; in another, the most immediate need may be play skills.

SIZE AND COMPOSITION OF GROUPS

Social skills are most effectively taught in small groups of no more than ten students. Some activities may be used with individual children, but because these skills require interaction with others, students need to practice with peers. Students in larger groups have fewer opportunities to practice skills and receive feedback, the most critical factors in their social skills development. If small-group instruction is impossible in your setting, you might increase the number of sessions allocated to each skill to allow for sufficient student practice.

To the extent possible, social skills groups need to include competent students as well as students with significant skill deficiencies. All children stand to benefit from social skills instruction. For some children, the focus will be on establishing an entirely new skill in their repertoire; others will be helped to refine existing skills; others, already proficient, will serve as models to aid in their peers' skill development. By including students with varying levels of proficiency, you avoid the possibility of stigmatizing children who have been targeted for instruction. Stigma can further be avoided by establishing rules within your social skills groups that help maintain mutual respect and a comfortable, encouraging classroom atmosphere. Children will also benefit from your modeling and reinforcing appropriate ways to prompt and encourage social skills performance.

TIME REQUIREMENTS

Taking Part will be most useful in classroom settings in which the instructor has regular, frequent contact with students. Activities are most effective when presented in regular, short instructional periods throughout the year. Alternative schedules, such as lengthy or combined and concentrated instructional periods, are possible but less effective. The more these skills can be incorporated into daily use with frequent practice, the more students will internalize and retain them. You may choose to present social skills instruction at specified times or to teach specific skills in response to students' needs. For example, you might teach or review the skill of sharing if an argument about using materials erupts. In general, it is best to watch, note, and respond to your students' social skills needs. You may want to plan lessons on a weekly basis, identifying the skills needed and the students who will be involved in the instruction.

Many activities will take 15 minutes or less. Frequency, rather than duration, is the key to competence. You will usually introduce a skill on the first day, review and allow for practice on the second and third days, and provide for maintenance for two or three subsequent days. After this, it's best to use periodic or intermittent reinforcement to help maintain the skill while you're introducing and practicing new skills. Intermittent reinforcement may be occurring for several skills at one time and should only take a few minutes of your day.

MATERIALS

Beyond typical classroom supplies, most of the materials called for in the *Taking Part* activities are provided here. Any materials required for an activity are listed; any preparation needed is described.

Lessons

The bulk of the book includes step-by-step descriptions of all lessons and activities. Also provided are an introduction to the program, teaching guidelines, and introductions to each unit.

Puppets

This program features six animal characters, each represented by a puppet. The puppets are used to present the motivational story for each skill, and they figure in various practice and maintenance activities. These puppets, included in Appendix B, are presented as full-page black line art. The art may be traced or photocopied onto heavy card stock, cut out, colored, and glued to a craft stick or tongue depressor. Another option is to attach a paper bag or a sock to the back of the puppet. They are large enough to be used as masks if your students enjoy or prefer role-playing (for example) as animal characters rather than as themselves or as human characters. You may wish to use commercial hand puppets that represent the six animal characters instead, and duplicate the puppet line art for use as classroom displays or activity reminders.

Skill Posters

Four posters, included in Appendix C, illustrate eye contact, facial expression, voice tone, and body language important for performing social skills, serving as cues for children as they practice skills. It is suggested that you introduce the appropriate skill posters during the motivational activities, as directed, keeping them displayed during the remaining activities as prompts and reminders.

Blackline Masters

Various activities call for material to be duplicated from the blackline masters provided in Appendix D. Included is a sample assessment form (Blackline Master 1, Individual Social Skills Checklist) that you can either adapt for your own use or photocopy for each student. Other blackline masters include badges, signs, charts, and display materials to use with specific activities.

Stickers

Practice and maintenance activities include specific suggestions for awarding stickers to reinforce students' performance of skill steps and use of skills in their daily lives. Stickers are common and inexpensive rewards that work well. Although using nontangible rewards such as recognition, praise, smiles, and hugs is more effective for long-term behavior change, such rewards are sometimes a less effective way of initiating change in young children. Often, they must be taught to recognize the value of nontangible rewards. On the other hand, using costly tangible rewards such as toys or candy sometimes leads to children's exhibiting behaviors only when a reward is imminent. Instead of internalizing the social skills, they begin to seek out situations in which a reward may be presented. Stickers are a tangible product, but when collected or charted, they also carry the connotation of nontangible praise. In essence, "I got a gold star!" means much more than "I received this shaped, colored piece of paper."

You may use any style of sticker you have available, or you may try to find stickers with pictures of squirrels, bluejays, frogs, and other animals represented in this curriculum. Most young children are fond of decorating their belongings and environment with stickers. You might suggest that students create *Taking Part* scrapbooks. They could also paste stickers on themselves, their clothing, or classroom displays. As appropriate, stickers can be used on record forms you find useful for this program. Blackline Master 2 (My *Taking Part* Sticker Collection), gives students a handy place to store the stickers they earn.

TEACHING SEQUENCE AND INSTRUCTIONAL GUIDELINES

Each skill lesson in this program is taught in a sequence of motivation, practice, and maintenance activities.

Motivation

Motivation activities help children understand why a particular social skill is important for them to learn and use. Even though students may be able to identify the appropriate social skill for a given situation, they might not use the skill unless they can appreciate its benefits (that is, the reward or payoff for using the skill). Taking another's bicycle, for example, might look like the most expedient way of satisfying a child's wishes, even though the negative consequences of the act will probably outweigh the benefits. The motivating activities in *Taking Part* attempt to put negative social acts in perspective for young children, helping them to name and describe desirable and undesirable behaviors and their corresponding outcomes.

The central motivation activity for each skill is a vignette involving various members of a cast of animal characters. In most vignettes, a character is shown to lack a particular skill and then to learn that skill from another character.

The vignettes, presented as dialogues between puppets, are interspersed with brief synopses of the scenes and with suggested discussion questions that invite children to consider the significance of events, predict outcomes, think about the feelings connected with social situations, and reflect on similar circumstances in their own lives. The concluding discussion focuses on the specific behavioral steps for the skill, the skill's relevance to the children's lives, any special vocabulary or issues connected with the skill, and the facial expression, tone of voice, and body language called for by the skill.

Before presenting the vignette, review and rehearse the script so you can present it without reading every word. Young children are more likely to listen to and understand puppet plays delivered smoothly and animatedly.

Puppets have great value in the teaching of social skills. Young children accept puppet characters as friendly and accessible and will frequently respond to them better than to peers or adults. Practice using the puppets so you can feel fluent and comfortable with them. The simple guidelines in the following two paragraphs may help alleviate any apprehensions you may have about "performing" with puppets.

Whether you use commercial hand puppets made of soft fur or hand-colored pictures glued to a stick handle, make the puppet entertaining by giving it the illusion of life. A simple rule to follow is that whenever the character is talking, move the puppet around; whenever the character is not talking, keep the puppet perfectly still. Look at the puppet when that character is talking. The students will look where you look. You do not have to be a professional ventriloquist to make it seem as if the characters are talking. If you are uncomfortable with students' seeing your mouth move, hold the puppet in front of your face while it is talking.

Once you are familiar with the script of a puppet vignette, use your full range of voice tone and inflection, facial expressions, and gestures to make the story as dramatic and interesting as possible. It will help if you read through the scenarios, think about the six characters before you begin, and decide on a voice tone for each character. You might decide, for instance, to make Benny Frog have a deep voice and Carla Bluejay have a squeaky voice. Keeping your voice tone consistent throughout the *Taking Part* program will help students identify with and learn from the character scenarios.

Because the motivational stories introduce skills, every effort should be made to engage students in the discussions that punctuate scenes. You might also ask children to hold puppets or take part in the vignette presentation in some way. Whatever strategies you employ, it is extremely important that children specify in their own words the target skill and why it is important. Elicit responses from each student to ensure that everyone understands.

At times, you may want to hold several class discussions of a skill, particularly when students' understanding of the skill is in doubt. Before proceeding to practice activities, you need to be satisfied that each child in the group understands the skill.

Practice

Once the importance of a social skill has become clear to children, they need opportunities to practice the skill. Each practice section begins with a role-play activity that allows children to act out the skill by reenacting the events of the motivational vignette. Other practice activities—games and further opportunities for role-play—encourage children to perform a social skill fluently, without extensive prompting. Children are further motivated to improve their skills by the reward of stickers and the process of collecting them.

Taking Part provides many opportunities for skill practice. You'll want to use as many activities and adaptations as your students require, personalizing lessons as much as possible for your particular group. To ensure skill acquisition and fluency, several sessions may be needed for the practice component of certain skills.

Guidelines for Role-Play

As children role-play, give corrective and reinforcing feedback about their presentations. This feedback needs to be highly specific—for example, "Ralph, the way you asked Sandra to help was good. Remember, you need to look at her and smile when you say it." General feedback such as "That was a good job" or "That wasn't right" isn't nearly as effective in helping a child learn a skill.

It's also helpful to encourage students to give each other positive feedback. The activities presented in such skills as Sending Messages, Making Positive Statements to Others, and Speaking Kindly and Using Courtesy Words can provide good practice for peer feedback. You may wish to present or review these skills because they can help students reinforce each other.

Maintenance

The third part of each skill lesson consists of activities to maintain the skill in the child's repertoire and to help the child generalize the behavior to other settings. Maintenance activities encourage children to use their skills in real-life situations.

Maintenance activities need not be confined to your designated social skills instruction periods. For the most part, they lend themselves to application throughout the school day. For example, a typical maintenance activity is structured so that children you observe displaying the target skill any time throughout the day earn the opportunity to have their names entered on a bulletin board display. When the display is completely filled in with names, the class achieves its goal and rewards itself.

In addition to the activities, a major component of the maintenance program is reinforcement of the behaviors when they occur in the natural classroom environment. Whenever you see a child performing a newly taught skill, take time to recognize and compliment that student, referring specifically to the skill performed: "Lucas, you are really improving at asking to join a group." Complimenting students publicly helps others recognize, label, and imitate specific skills and is reinforcing for the group. It also helps teach children the value of praise and nontangible rewards. Children are also encouraged to use skills by being rewarded with stickers. If appropriate for your group, you can ask the children themselves to tell you when they have used a skill. Those children can then be recognized and rewarded.

Reinforcement of Skills

Teachers need to alter reinforcement techniques so that, as children progress, greater emphasis is placed on social reinforcers and less on tangible rewards. The goal is for students to derive pleasure from the behavior itself. The child who learns to make friendly, appropriate greetings may find it naturally reinforcing to have the response reciprocated, thereby triggering further positive interactions. It's useful to couple tangible rewards with recognition and praise and to gradually decrease the use of tangible rewards as students become more internally motivated.

Teaching with Children's Literature

Each skill includes a maintenance activity suggesting the use of children's literature as a way to illustrate and encourage social skills. All maintenance activities provide a list of suggested books for use with the given skill. Titles reflect classic stories as well as more modern literature. A range of books is suggested for each skill so that you may use what is most readily available to you. These books have been previewed and, in most cases, were chosen for their specific message about an individual skill. For most literature, though, a children's book becomes classic because it has a deeper message or several levels of interpretation. You should always preview and become familiar with a suggested title so that you can choose how to present it to the class and keep it relevant to the social skill.

In addition to the individual titles suggested, several book series address social skills issues though the use of consistent characters and may provide excellent discussion starting points or valuable lessons in individual skills. Often the characters portray social situations in separate books or stories and present a desired moral or important life lesson in ways that are engaging and humorous. A character may put away materials in one book, join a play group in another book, and share toys in another. Reading a series of such books to students can have a positive and compound effect as students learn to identify with or emulate the characters. Such series include books featuring the Berenstain Bears by Stan and Jan Berenstain, Franklin the Turtle by Paulette Bourgeois, Little Critter by Mercer Mayer, and Arthur by Marc Brown, among others.

Activity Adaptations

The activities of *Taking Part* have been created for children from preschool through grade three in regular and mainstreamed classrooms. However, most of the skills are appropriate for children who are younger or older or who are in different classroom environments. To assist you in modifying material to meet your students' needs, many activities conclude with one or more adaptations that either extend or simplify the main activity. Use these adaptations based on your students' ages, developmental levels, interest levels, and learning requirements.

Encouraging Skill Use at Home

Children are helped immeasurably in using social skills when family members encourage them. Create a simple note home to parents that describes the skill being taught in school. You can further encourage children to use their new skills at home by giving simple home assignments. For example, after completing activities about making positive statements to others, you might ask children to compliment someone in their family. If time permits, conduct a brief classroom practice session on complimenting family members and follow up afterward with a discussion of how students' family members received the compliments.

Encouraging Skill Use in School

Children can also be asked to use the skills with a school friend or a teacher. You can assist by informing colleagues of the skills students are learning and asking them to note and encourage the use of those skills. This may be particularly effective if you have children who are mainstreamed into regular education classes or students who have regular contact with art, music, physical education, or other special subject teachers.

Children can also help each other maintain skills. Encourage students to notice and praise each other when they see social skills being performed. You can prompt this behavior by saying, for example, "Did you see George offer to help Jennifer? Please compliment him for using the skill." Or "Lisa is ignoring Peter's teasing. Maybe you could remind her of how important that is."

As mentioned, some maintenance activities ask children to work toward a group goal. Such cooperative activities encourage students to praise and shape each other's behavior. At times, you may need to model and monitor such peer reinforcement.

CULTURAL ISSUES IN TEACHING SOCIAL SKILLS

Social skills are culturally determined and situation specific. A culturally diverse society produces many behavioral differences among children. Teachers and other professionals need to differentiate cultural differences from behavioral deficits. For example, although the larger society values eye contact as a basic element in social communication, some cultural groups discourage children from making eye contact with adults. Significant differences may be found in such areas as socialization of the sexes, assertive and aggressive communication styles, and the specific social communication skills encouraged.

In some cases, it may be advisable for teachers to present certain social skills in this program as alternative ways to behave rather than as the preferred way to respond. On the other hand, in situations where a student's response repertoire is self-destructive and in conflict with the school's culture—for example, inappropriate responses to aggression—teachers may be obliged to encourage more adaptive behaviors.

ASSESSING STUDENTS' PROGRESS

Assessment is most useful when viewed as an ongoing process rather than an isolated event. A good record-keeping system with specific monitoring procedures can be helpful, allowing continual feedback on student progress. Individual performance standards need to be established for each child, taking into consideration developmental level, cultural factors, and need.

The Individual Social Skills Checklist included in the set of blackline masters can be useful for monitoring student progress. You can adapt this form or simply photocopy it, making a separate sheet for each child. In the spaces below the categories "Mastered," "Shows Some Competence," and "Needs Instruction," fill in the date the item was assessed. This makes it possible not only to record student progress but also to track how long the instruction took. Use the "Comments" section for any notes that seem useful.

This assessment form is an example of one kind of record keeping. Any system that can help you provide an ongoing assessment of your students' performance will help strengthen and validate your social skills instruction. You may wish to create your own form that identifies how group goals are progressing or the number of times a specific social skill was observed, for example. Some social skills lend themselves better to counting instances, while others are significant if they occur less often but at the appropriate time. For example, it may be significant to record that class participants said "thank you" a certain number of times, while the skills taught in Unit 6, "Responding to Aggression," may have only occurred once but at precisely the right moment.

Whether you use the Individual Social Skills Checklist as you deem appropriate, or create your own assessment form, keeping a record of student progress will help you and your students get the most out of *Taking Part*.

U N I T
1 MAKING CONVERSATION

Conversation skills are the foundation of interpersonal competence. Children who successfully interact with others can appropriately and accurately send and receive both verbal and nonverbal messages. Many children acquire conversation skills during their earliest years and systematically perfect them over time. Some children, particularly those with less guidance or those with special needs, fail to master the skills and may, even as adults, remain inadequate and awkward communicators.

Little direct instruction of informal social communication skills is provided in the classroom. Considering the critical impact of social communication skills on interpersonal, academic, and vocational competence, teachers can ill afford to ignore instruction in these skills.

In this unit, children will talk about and practice the steps for the following skills:

- Greeting
- Introducing Yourself
- Listening
- Joining a Conversation
- Starting a Conversation

Special Issues

As in each unit of *Taking Part*, skills in this unit are presented from least to most difficult. However, because conversation skills tend to develop simultaneously, prerequisite skills are not always obvious. The skill of Listening, for example, might profitably be taught before, rather than after, the skills of Greeting and Introducing Myself. All three can reasonably be considered prerequisites of Starting a Conversation.

As suggested with various skills, children need to be taught to discriminate among settings and circumstances when they make conversation. Greetings made on a playground will differ from those made in a classroom. Similarly, vocabulary may differ if the person being greeted is an adult rather than a peer. Practice activities allow children to switch and discriminate among social situations.

Taking Part stickers are used as incentives for skill step performance and skill use in practice and maintenance activities throughout this unit. You may wish to distribute copies of Blackline Master 2 (My Taking Part Sticker Collection), which gives students a handy place to store the stickers they earn.

S K I L L

1 GREETING

SKILL STEPS: GREETING

1. Look in the person's eyes.

2. Smile.

3. Say hello in a friendly voice.

MOTIVATION

Skill Presentation: Greetings from Carla

Materials

> Three puppets (Benny Frog, Carla Bluejay, Shelli Squirrel); Posters 1, 2, 3

Introduce the three puppets. Tell students that you're going to present a story about these characters called "Greetings from Carla." Ask the children to listen carefully.

Carla Bluejay doesn't know how to greet Benny Frog.

Benny Frog: Hello, Carla. How are you today?

Carla Bluejay: *(Head down, voice low.)* Okay.

Benny Frog: *(Shakes his head and turns toward students.)* That Carla Bluejay never says hello! She isn't very friendly! I'm going to stop talking to her when I see her.

Ask the children:

- Why do you think Benny said he isn't going to talk to Carla when he sees her?
- Why doesn't he think she's friendly? How did Carla make Benny feel? (As necessary, point out that the way Carla greeted Benny made him feel bad and think she's not interested.)

Shelli Squirrel tells Carla how to greet others.

Shelli Squirrel: Hi, Carla. It's nice to see you! What's new?

Carla Bluejay: *(Head down, voice low.)* Nothing.

Shelli Squirrel: You look kind of sad. Do you feel okay?

Carla Bluejay: Yeah. *(Starts to walk away.)*

Shelli Squirrel: Wait a minute. Don't you want to stay and talk?

Carla Bluejay: *(As if surprised.)* Okay! I like to talk. Nobody ever asks me to stay and talk.

Shelli Squirrel: Well, maybe that's because you don't act as if you want to talk. Just now when I talked to you, you didn't even greet me.

Carla Bluejay: What do you mean by "greet"?

Shelli Squirrel: Greeting people means looking in their eyes, smiling, and saying hello in a friendly voice. When you greet people nicely, they will be friendly to you, and you'll feel good.

Ask the children:

- What does Shelli tell Carla to do when she sees people she knows? (Greet them.)
- What does "greeting people" mean? (Be sure the steps of the skill are mentioned: look in the person's eyes, smile, say hello in a friendly voice.)
- Why does Shelli say Carla should greet people she knows? (So they will be friendly to her, so she will feel good.)

Carla practices greeting Shelli and then greets Benny correctly.

Carla Bluejay: I'd like to try greeting someone.

Shelli Squirrel: Okay, I'll pretend I'm walking down the street. You come up and greet me.

Carla Bluejay: *(Head down, voice low.)* Hello.

Shelli Squirrel: You said, "Hello," Carla, but I think you need to try it again.

Ask the children:

- Why does Shelli tell Carla to try her greeting again? (She didn't look in Shelli's eyes, smile, or use a friendly voice.)

Shelli Squirrel: This time, look in my eyes, smile, and use a friendly voice.

Carla Bluejay: *(Looking up and speaking brightly.)* Hello.

Shelli Squirrel: Great, Carla! Now you could ask, "How are you?"

Carla Bluejay: How are you?

Shelli Squirrel: I'm fine, thank you. How are you?

Carla Bluejay: I'm fine. This is fun! I'd like to try greeting someone else.

Shelli Squirrel: Here's your chance. Benny Frog is coming.

Carla Bluejay: Hello, Benny. How are you?

Benny Frog: Hi, Carla. What a nice greeting!

Carla Bluejay: Thank you. I just learned how to greet people, and I'm trying it out.

Shelli Squirrel: You did fine, Carla. You greeted Benny very nicely.

Carla Bluejay: Thanks, Shelli. You were right. Greeting people makes me feel good.

Ask the children:

- How did Carla Bluejay feel when she learned to greet her friends nicely?
- What steps did Shelli teach Carla?

Review the skill steps, asking the children to repeat each one:

1. Look in the person's eyes.

2. Smile.

3. Say hello in a friendly voice.

As appropriate, discuss what else Carla and Shelli did in their greetings—for example, they asked, "How are you?" Encourage children to mention other things they hear or see when people greet each other—for example, "How's it going?" or gestures such as handshakes and waves.

Invite the children to tell about times when they've greeted someone or wanted to greet someone but didn't know what to do or say.

Present Posters 1, 2, and 3, one at a time. Use Poster 1 to emphasize the importance of looking in the person's eyes—for example, to let the person you are greeting see that you are talking to him or her. For Posters 2 and 3, ask children how they would feel if someone who greeted them looked or sounded angry or unfriendly. Display the posters during the remaining activities to prompt or cue children as needed.

PRACTICE

Greetings from Carla Role Play

Materials

Three puppets (Benny Frog, Carla Bluejay, Shelli Squirrel)

Give the puppets to three children and have them take turns greeting each other. For example, Carla Bluejay greets Shelli Squirrel; Shelli responds with an appropriate greeting and then greets Benny Frog. Benny responds and greets Carla Bluejay. Prompt and cue students as necessary.

Following the role play, discuss how the skill was presented, then give the puppets to three other children. As time permits, allow each child to practice with a puppet. When all of the students have participated, have various children role-play greeting someone, this time without using the puppets. Encourage the class to offer the players feedback on the way they presented the skill.

Meet Me, Greet Me

Materials

Stickers

Have students role-play greetings in the situations listed below or in others they suggest. Before beginning, remind children of the skill steps and tell them to watch for the steps in the role plays. After each role play, discuss how the skill was performed. During discussion, emphasize that the words we use to greet a friend may be different from the words we use to greet an adult. Our greetings on the playground may be different from our greetings in the classroom. Suggest that children keep in mind whom they are greeting and the circumstances. You might ask students how they would greet specific people (the school principal, a younger child they don't know, a peer).

Give a sticker to each student who performs the skill steps adequately. Tell students who do not earn stickers that they will have other opportunities to practice the steps and receive stickers.

Sample situations

1. You see Roy, the new boy in your class, playing in his yard.
2. You answer the door when your parents' friends, Mr. and Mrs. Nolan, come to visit.
3. You meet your teacher, Ms. Berlin, in the hall at school.
4. You see your friend Renee on the playground.
5. Your cousin Tonisha has come to your house to play.

Adaptations

1. Rather than asking students to discriminate among situations and people, have them focus only on making eye contact and saying hello.
2. Ask children to move beyond greeting to asking the person a question or saying something about themselves.

The Hello Game

Materials

Stickers

Tell children they will practice greeting by playing The Hello Game. Have them form two lines. The children in one line file past and greet each person in the other line. Remind the students to look the other person in the eye, smile, say hello, and say the person's name ("Hello, Tasha"). Repeat, having the students in the second line greet each person in the first line.

Ask the children how they felt when the other person used their name in a greeting. Emphasize that remembering and saying a person's name makes the greeting more personal. Encourage children to identify a person whose greeting they particularly liked and to tell why they liked that greeting.

As appropriate, repeat the activity, having students ask questions or make statements with their greetings.

Give a sticker to each student who performs the skill steps adequately. Tell students who do not earn stickers that they will have other opportunities to practice the steps and receive stickers.

Adaptation

Introduce children to the game in groups of two or four. Gradually have them form longer lines.

MAINTENANCE

Greetings Every Day

Materials

Stickers; Blackline Master 1 (Individual Social Skills Checklist, optional)

Observe students daily for opportunities to recognize and compliment those who greet others. As appropriate, ask the children to tell you when they have used the skill and to describe what they said and did. Give a sticker to each student who uses the skill.

You may wish to use Individual Social Skills Checklist to record students' progress in this unit's skills.

Greetings in Literature

Materials

Classroom books and stories such as these:

Keats, Ezra Jack. *Apartment Three.* New York: Macmillan, 1986.

Scarry, Richard. *Richard Scarry's Please and Thank You Book.* New York: Random House, 1978.

Stojic, Manya. *Hello World! Greetings in 42 Languages Around the World.* New York: Cartwheel Publishers, 2002.

Select stories that discuss or feature characters greeting each other. After the children have read or listened to a story, discuss the ways that greetings were important to the characters.

Greeting Can

Materials

One-pound coffee can with plastic lid or other suitable container; label for the container; tokens, such as checkers, coins, or small pieces of paper

Preparation

Make a slot in the plastic lid. Label the can "Greeting Can" or draw an appropriate picture for the label. You may want to decorate the can.

Explain that you have a Greeting Can for encouraging students to greet each other. Tell them that each time you see a student greet another person correctly, you'll drop a token into the can. At the end of the week, you'll open the can and count all the tokens the class has earned.

As appropriate, help children set a goal (number of tokens) for the class. If they meet or exceed the goal, celebrate or reward the group with extra free time, a short movie, lunch in the class-room, or some other privilege.

Adaptations

1. Some children might need the encouragement of your standing by the door as a reminder to greet others. For some, your initiating a greeting to them may be a necessary reminder.

2. Encourage continued use of the skill by making a monthly chart and comparing each week's total.

3. Have individual children set goals. Use special tokens for each child, such as small pieces of paper with the child's name on them.

How Are You? Day

Materials

Blackline Master 3 (How Are You?)

Preparation

Use the blackline master to make enough "How Are You?" tags for each student to have at least three.

Distribute the tags. Explain that this is How Are You? Day, and that the class is going to play a game. Tell students that during transitions or free time, whenever two students pass each other, one is to say, "Hello. How are you?" The other is to respond with "Hello. I'm fine, thank you." After the verbal exchange, they are to present each other with a tag. Ask students to prompt each other as needed to perform the skill correctly; every encounter should result in an exchange of tags.

At the end of the day, discuss the skill steps. Invite children to take their tags home as a reminder of the day.

Adaptation

Give each child a single tag.

2 INTRODUCING YOURSELF

SKILL STEPS: INTRODUCING YOURSELF

1. Look in the person's eyes.
2. Smile.
3. Say hello and tell your name.
4. Ask the person's name.

MOTIVATION

Skill Presentation: Will Introduces Himself

Materials

> Three puppets (Hank Hawk, Will Rabbit, Felicia Fox); Posters 1, 2, 3

Introduce the three puppets. Tell students that you're going to present a story about these characters called "Will Introduces Himself." Ask the children to listen carefully.

Hank Hawk tells Will Rabbit how to introduce himself.

Hank Hawk: Hi. I'm Hank. What's your name?

Will Rabbit: (*Head down, voice low.*) Will.

Hank Hawk: Did you say "Will"? I could hardly hear you. Why are you so sad, Will?

Will Rabbit: I'm new in this school, and nobody wants to play with me. I hate it here.

Hank Hawk: Have you introduced yourself to anyone?

Will Rabbit: What do you mean?

Hank Hawk: Introducing yourself means letting people know who you are. When you introduce yourself, you look in the person's eyes, smile, say hello, tell the person your name, and then ask the person's name. I introduced myself to you just now.

Will Rabbit: Why should I introduce myself?

Hank Hawk: Introducing yourself helps you make friends and get along with people. You'll start feeling good about your new school.

Ask the children:

- Why is Will Rabbit sad? (He is new in school, has no one to play with.)

- What does Hank Hawk tell Will to do when he sees a classmate he doesn't know? (Introduce himself.)

- What does "introducing yourself" mean? (Be sure the steps of the skill are mentioned: look in the person's eyes, smile, say hello and tell your name, ask the person's name.)

- Why does Hank say Will should introduce himself? (To make friends and get along, to feel good.)

Will practices introducing himself and then introduces himself to Felicia Fox.

Will Rabbit: That makes sense, Hank. Can I practice with you?

Hank Hawk: Sure. Let's pretend we don't know each other.

Will Rabbit: Hello. My name's Will. What's yours?

Hank Hawk: That was good. Remember to look in the person's eyes and smile to show you are friendly.

Will Rabbit: Okay.

Ask the children:

- Why does Hank remind Will to look in the person's eyes and smile when he introduces himself? (To show he is friendly.)

Hank Hawk: Here comes Felicia Fox. Go ahead and introduce yourself to her. I'll listen.

Will Rabbit: Okay. *(Pause.)* Hi. My name is Will. What's yours?

Felicia Fox: I'm Felicia. I saw you here yesterday, but I didn't know who you were. Do you want to play ball with me?

Will Rabbit: Sure. Be there in just a minute.

Ask the children:

- What happened when Will introduced himself to Felicia? (She was friendly to him.)

Hank Hawk: That was great, Will!

Will Rabbit: I'm really glad you told me about introducing myself, Hank. Now I have friends to play with.

Ask the children:

- What happened after Will learned to introduce himself to others? How did he feel?
- What steps did Hank teach Will?

Review the skill steps, asking the children to repeat each one:

1. Look in the person's eyes.
2. Smile.
3. Say hello and tell your name.
4. Ask the person's name.

Ask the children to tell about times they've introduced themselves to someone and about times when they wanted to introduce themselves but didn't know what to do or say.

Display Posters 1, 2, and 3. Relate the posters to the skill steps and ask students how looking in the other person's eyes and having a friendly face and voice help when you introduce yourself to someone. Display the posters during the remaining activities, using them to prompt or cue children as needed.

PRACTICE

Will Introduces Himself Role Play

Materials

Three puppets (Hank Hawk, Will Rabbit, Felicia Fox)

Give the puppets to three children and have them take turns introducing themselves. For example, Hank Hawk introduces himself to Will Rabbit. Will responds appropriately and then introduces himself to Felicia Fox. Felicia responds and then introduces herself to Hank. Prompt and cue students as necessary.

Following the role play, discuss how the skill was presented. Review the skill steps as needed, then give the puppets to three other children. As time permits, allow each child to practice with a puppet. When all have participated, have various children role-play introducing themselves, this time without using the puppets. Encourage the group to offer the players feedback on the way they presented the skill.

Let Me Introduce Myself

Materials

Stickers

Have students role-play introducing themselves in the situations listed below or in others they suggest. Before beginning, remind students of the skill steps and tell them to watch for the steps in the role plays. Prompt students as needed. After each role play, discuss how the skill was performed. During discussion, emphasize that the words they use to introduce themselves to a peer may be different from the words they use to introduce themselves to an adult. Suggest that children keep in mind who it is they are introducing themselves to, and under what circumstances.

Give a sticker to each student who performs the skill steps adequately. Tell students who do not earn stickers that they will have other opportunities to practice the steps and receive stickers.

Sample situations

1. Buster is at a cousin's birthday party. He doesn't know any of the children there except his cousin.

2. Liz is new in school. She doesn't know anyone in her class.

3. Derek just moved into a new apartment. He goes outside and sees three children walking to the soccer field.

4. Louanne is waiting for her mother to pick her up from the day care center. A child Louanne doesn't know is waiting to be picked up, too.

5. Michael is at the library waiting for story time to begin. He's sitting next to a child he doesn't know.

Adaptations

1. Have daily sessions, role-playing and discussing one situation each time.

2. Take a role yourself and have students introduce themselves to you.

3. Record students' ideas about introducing themselves and present them in a language experience chart or class story-book.

Meet Me on My Travels

Materials

Small suitcase or traveling bag; objects such as flowers, play money, puzzle pieces, crayons

Tell students they'll be practicing introducing themselves by playing a game. Ask four students to play the roles of North, South, East, and West. Give each child an object and direct each to stand in the appropriate corner of the room. Give a fifth student the suitcase or traveling bag. This student is to go on a trip around the room, introducing himself or herself to each of the other four students. Each of the four is to respond with an appropriate greeting—for example, "Hello. I'm Jeffrey from the East." Then Jeffrey gives the traveling student an object to put in the suitcase or bag. When all the objects are collected, assign five new students to play.

Adaptation

Choose various popular characters and provide (or have children make) objects appropriate for them. You may want to use a story such as "The Wizard of Oz" or "The Gingerbread Man," in which various characters are successively introduced.

Meet Me in School

Materials

Stickers

Preparation

Arrange to take your class into another teacher's room to practice introductions. Preferably, students should be about two grades apart so they are more likely to be strangers. If appropriate, ask your colleague to prepare her or his class for the activity.

Explain to your students that they are going to meet some other children and will practice introducing themselves. Take the class to your colleague's room and have each of your students choose someone she or he doesn't know for the practice. Whatever the responses of your colleague's students, praise your students when they follow the skill steps.

When you return to your room, give a sticker to each student who performed the skill steps adequately. Tell students who did not earn stickers that they will have other opportunities to practice the steps and receive stickers.

Adaptation

Have just a few of your students at a time practice introducing themselves to students in another room.

Guess Who I'll Meet

Materials

Jar, box, or other small container; blank label; slips of paper; stickers

Preparation

Label the container "Guess Who I'll Meet" or draw an appropriate picture for the label. On the slips of paper, write names or draw pictures of familiar story characters. Put these in the container.

Take turns having two students each draw a slip of paper from the container. They are to introduce themselves to each other as the various story characters.

Give a sticker to each student who performs the skill steps adequately. Tell students who do not earn stickers that they will have other opportunities to practice the steps and receive stickers.

Adaptations

1. Instead of story characters, use people in current events, historical figures, or animals.

2. Have two containers. In one, place story characters; in the other, names or pictures of real people, current or historical. Students may enjoy introducing Cinderella to Abraham Lincoln, for example.

MAINTENANCE

Introducing Yourself Every Day

Materials

Stickers

Observe students daily for opportunities to recognize and compliment those who introduce themselves. As appropriate, ask the children to tell you when they have used the skill and to describe what they said and did. Give a sticker to each student who uses the skill.

Introducing Yourself in Literature

Materials

Classroom books and stories such as these:

Carle, Eric. *The Grouchy Ladybug*. New York: HarperTrophy, 1996.

Carle, Eric. *The Lonely Firefly*. New York: Philomel, 1995.

Keats, Ezra Jack. *Apartment Three*. New York: Macmillan, 1986.

Udry, Janice May. *What Mary Jo Shared*. New York: Scholastic, 1991.

Select stories that discuss or feature characters introducing themselves. After the children have read or listened to a story, discuss ways that the introductions were important to the characters.

Introductions Honor Roll

Materials

Manila folder; blank label; stickers

Preparation

On a sheet of paper, write the names of all your students as a list, leaving space between each name. Staple this paper to the inside of a folder. Label the folder "Introductions Honor Roll"; if you wish, decorate it.

Show children your Introductions Honor Roll, where you'll keep a record of their introductions. Tell them you will place a sticker by the name of each student you see making a correct introduction. Explain that you will also put stickers by the names of students who tell you about introductions they accomplished.

To offer students special opportunities to introduce themselves, for several weeks invite guests into your room. You may want to ask guests to visit for a specific purpose—such as to read a story or tell about their job. Explain that your students will be practicing introductions; mention the skill steps students have been taught. Allow time for children to introduce themselves individually.

As the children accumulate stickers by their names, periodically share this honor roll with the group. As necessary, lead a short review discussion on the introducing skill.

Adaptation

Prepare children in advance and cue them to introduce themselves.

S K I L L

3   LISTENING

MOTIVATION

Skill Presentation: Planning a Party

Materials

> Three puppets (Carla Bluejay, Will Rabbit, Shelli Squirrel); Posters 1, 3

Introduce the three puppets. Tell students that you're going to present a story about these characters called "Planning a Party." Ask the children to listen carefully.

Characters can't plan a party because they interrupt each other and talk about other things.

Carla Bluejay: Hi, Shelli. Hi, Will. Now that we're all here, let's plan our party.

Will Rabbit: I almost didn't make it! This great big wind blew up and . . .

Shelli Squirrel: Oh, boy! Talk about wind! I remember a really windy day when I . . .

Will Rabbit: Let me finish my story. This big gust of wind . . .

Shelli Squirrel: Hey! I was telling you about a day when . . .

Carla Bluejay: Wait a minute! We're not here to tell wind stories!

Ask the children:

- What does Carla Bluejay mean? What are the animals together to do? (Plan a party.)
- Why haven't they started planning yet? (They're too busy talking about other things.)

(Characters start to bicker.)

Shelli Squirrel: Well, I was just going to tell you about . . .

Will Rabbit: About what? I can't remember what you were saying.

Shelli Squirrel: That's because you don't listen, Will!

Will Rabbit: Oh, yeah? Well, neither do you!

Carla Bluejay: Neither of you listens! And no one is listening to me! We're supposed to be planning our party!

Ask the children:

- How do you think Carla feels about no one listening to her? (Bad, angry.)
- How do Shelli and Will feel? (Bad, angry.)
- What happens when people don't listen to one another? (Bad feelings, lack of understanding of what was said, no attention to task.)
- What do you think might happen in this story if no one starts listening? (Fighting, end of friendship, no party plans.)

Carla tells the others about listening skills.

Will Rabbit: She's right, Shelli. We haven't even started to talk about the party yet.

Shelli Squirrel: I know. What happened?

Carla Bluejay: We didn't listen to each other. When we listen, we understand what others say. We don't get angry at each other. I think we all need to follow the three steps of listening.

Shelli Squirrel: What do you mean?

Carla Bluejay: First, we look in the person's eyes. Second, we think about what the person is saying. Third, we repeat what the person said, to show we understand.

Ask the children:

- What does Carla say they should do to get their party planned? (Follow the three steps of listening.)
- What are the three steps? (Be sure the skill steps are mentioned: look at the person, think about what the person is saying, repeat what the person says.)

Will Rabbit: That makes sense, Carla. I know how to look in someone's eyes. But it's harder to think about what someone is saying.

Carla Bluejay: Yes, it is, Will. But we'll know we're good listeners when we can repeat what someone says. Do you want to try it, Shelli? What did I just say about listening?

Shelli Squirrel: You said that we'll know we're good listeners when we can repeat what someone said.

Carla Bluejay: Great, Shelli! Now let's plan our party!

Ask the children:

- What did these characters need to learn before they could plan? (How to listen to each other.)
- What happened when they didn't listen? How did they feel?
- What steps did Carla teach Shelli and Will?

Review the skill steps, asking the children to repeat each one:

1. Look in the person's eyes.
2. Think about what the person is saying.
3. Repeat what the person has said.

Invite the children to tell about problems they've had because they didn't listen at home, at school, with friends.

Present Posters 1 and 3. Use Poster 1 to emphasize the importance of eye contact when listening to what someone else is saying. For Poster 3, ask the students how using a pleasant tone of voice fits into the listening skill steps (repeating what the person has said). Use the posters during the remaining activities to prompt or cue children as needed.

> *Note: The emphasis in the following activities should be on listening skills, not on precise verbal memory. Let students know that it's fine to paraphrase what someone says as long as the meaning is conveyed.*

PRACTICE

Planning a Party Role Play

Materials

Three puppets (Carla Bluejay, Will Rabbit, Shelli Squirrel)

Ask three students to hold the puppets. Carla Bluejay says one sentence about planning their party (for example: "Now let's plan our party!"). Shelli Squirrel repeats what Carla said, then coaches Shelli to say something else about the party (for example: "We're planning our party. What shall we have to eat?"). Continue by having Will Rabbit repeat Shelli's question and then tell what he'd like to eat.

When all three children have practiced listening and repeating, discuss how the characters performed the skill. Then ask three other children to role-play with the puppets. Prompt as needed. When all have participated, have various children role-play listening skills without using the puppets. At this point, you might propose another topic for discussion—for example, something that happened at school today. Encourage the group to offer the players feedback on the way they performed the skill.

The Parrot Game

Materials

Stickers

Choose a familiar topic students can use to practice listening— for example, favorite foods, activities, subjects, colors; what they did last weekend; pets; school events.

Have the class sit in a circle for the Parrot Game. Explain that you are going to say one sentence about a topic—for example, favorite foods. You will then call on a student in the circle. That student must follow the Parrot Rules. This means that the person must first repeat what you said. Then the person is to say another sentence about favorite foods. That person is to call on another student, who in turn repeats the new sentence, adds another, calls on a classmate, and so on around the circle. Supply hints or cues as needed for the sentences students are to add.

Give a sticker to each student who follows the Parrot Rules. Tell students who do not earn stickers that they will have other opportunities to practice the steps and receive stickers.

Adaptations

1. Play this game several times, gradually increasing the difficulty by moving from familiar, personal topics like favorite foods to more difficult ones—for example, topics being covered in various school subjects.

2. After some exposure to the format, when the children have begun to demonstrate competence in listening and repeating, have students repeat the previous two comments they heard. You might also have several students give comments consecutively and then call on one student to repeat all the comments.

3. Have students play the Parrot Game in small groups. Supply them with topics or ask them to select their own.

The Roving Reporter

Materials

Blackline Master 4 (Badges); real or toy microphone or object to represent one (for example, the wooden end of a jump-rope)

Preparation

Use the blackline master to make a badge by writing "Roving Reporter" on it or drawing a picture. Attach double-stick tape or a safety pin to the back.

Ask the children to choose something—a recent drawing or other project, an article of clothing, some other personal item—they'd like to tell the group about. Then have them sit in a circle. Explain that they'll be playing a game to practice listening skills. Ask one student to be the first Roving Reporter; give that student the badge and microphone.

Explain the game: the Roving Reporter pretends to interview another student about the object that student is holding or has selected, asking, "Please tell us about that." The person being interviewed tells the reporter two things about the object. The reporter repeats the two statements. The person being interviewed then becomes the Roving Reporter and interviews someone else.

Have the next reporter begin. Continue around the circle until every student has had a chance to be the reporter and to be interviewed.

Adaptations

1. Ask that children say and repeat only one thing about the objects; if needed, supply or suggest what they are to say.

2. Change the topic of the interviews and vary the number of sentences said and repeated.

3. Immediately after completing the activity, ask the children to write brief descriptions of one or two of the objects and what was said about them.

MAINTENANCE

Listening Every Day

Materials

Stickers

Observe students daily for opportunities to recognize and compliment those who listen well. As appropriate, ask the children to tell you when they have used the skill and to describe what they said and did. Give a sticker to each student who uses the skill.

Listening in Literature

Materials

Classroom books and stories such as these:

Keats, Ezra Jack. *Louie*. New York: Puffin, 2004.

Lionni, Leo. *Frederick*. New York: Knopf, 1990.

Seuss, Dr. *Horton Hears a Who Pop-up*. New York: Robin Corey Books, 2008.

Wiseman, Bernard. *Morris and Boris at the Circus*. New York: HarperTrophy, 1990.

Wiseman, Bernard. *Morris Tells Boris Mother Moose Stories and Rhymes*. New York: Putnam Publishing Group, 1975.

Select stories that discuss or feature characters listening to each other. After the children have read or listened to a story, discuss the ways that listening was important to the characters.

We're All Ears

Materials

Blackline Masters 5a, 5b (We're All Ears)

Preparation

Prepare a bulletin board display for rewarding listening skills. Reproduce the face with large ears from Blackline Master 5a and the small faces and ears from Blackline Master 5b. Title the bulletin board "We're All Ears" and post the face with large ears in the center. Place the smaller faces around the large face; have the small ears available.

Explain to the children that all this week you'll be watching for good listening skills. Each time you notice a good listener, you'll write that child's name on a paper ear and pin it to one of the faces on the bulletin board display.

During the week, as you do this, also recognize and compliment the children who listened. Be sure to include children making attempts to be good listeners. You may want to recognize younger students for how well they listen to you during classroom activities and older students for how well they listen to peers. At the end of each day, mention all the children whose names were added to the board.

Adaptations

1. For further practice, as convenient, pause intermittently during your teaching and ask a student to repeat the last thing you said. Compliment successful listening or a good

attempt, write the child's name on a paper ear, and pin the ear on the board.

2. If you have students able to reward their peers' listening, choose a student each day to watch classmates for good listening and to place the paper ears on the bulletin board (or to tell you to do so). Remind the student to reward classmates fairly and to include children making attempts to listen successfully.

3. As an alternative to the use of ears, post a picture of a treasure chest and surround it with cutout gold pieces large enough to write a name on.

SKILL
4 JOINING A CONVERSATION

SKILL STEPS: JOINING A CONVERSATION

1. Listen to what people say.
2. Wait for your turn to talk.
3. Say what you think.

MOTIVATION

Skill Presentation: Shelli Joins a Conversation

Materials

> Four puppets (Shelli Squirrel, Benny Frog, Carla Bluejay, Hank Hawk); Posters 1, 2, 3

Introduce the four puppets. Tell students that you're going to present a story about these characters called "Shelli Joins a Conversation." Ask the children to listen carefully.

Shelli Squirrel doesn't know how to join a conversation.

Benny Frog: Hi, Shelli. How are you today?

Shelli Squirrel: Oh, hi, Benny. I'm okay, I guess.

Benny Frog: What's the matter?

Shelli Squirrel: Oh, I'm mad at myself!

Benny Frog: About what?

Shelli Squirrel: In school today, my teacher read us this great story about a family of woodchucks!

Benny Frog: We read that story, too. I liked it.

Shelli Squirrel: So did I, but then my teacher asked us questions about the story, and I didn't say a single thing!

Benny Frog: Well, why didn't you?

Shelli Squirrel: I didn't know how to start. I wanted to talk, but I didn't know what to say.

Ask the children:

- Why is Shelli Squirrel unhappy? (She didn't know how to join a conversation at school.)
- Do you ever wish you were better at talking during conversation?

Benny Frog tells Shelli how to join a conversation.

Benny Frog: You know, I used to have that problem. Then my teacher showed me how to join a conversation. He said joining a conversation means listening to what people say, waiting for your turn to talk, and saying what you think. Since I learned to join a conversation, school is a lot more fun. I also learn more.

Ask the children:

- What does Benny say Shelli should do when she wants to talk in class? (Join a conversation.)
- What does "joining a conversation" mean? (Be sure the skill steps are mentioned: listening, waiting for your turn, saying what you think.)
- What does Benny say happened after he learned to join conversations? (School became more fun, he learns more.)

Shelli and her friends practice joining a conversation.

Shelli Squirrel: Can you show me?

Benny Frog: Sure. Here come Carla Bluejay and Hank Hawk. I'll ask them to help. *(Pause.)* Hi, Carla! Hi, Hank! I'm going to show Shelli how to join a conversation. Will you pretend to be her classmates? I'll pretend to be your teacher, and we'll talk about that story about woodchucks we all read today.

Carla Bluejay: Sure, Benny! I could use some practice joining a conversation, too.

Hank Hawk: Boy, so could I! I'm not too good at that, either.

Benny Frog: Okay, let's get started. Who can tell me how the story started? *(Pause.)* Well, who can tell me how it ended? *(Pause.)* Who remembers the name of the main character? *(Pause.)* Now, class, we can't have a conversation unless you talk. Someone help by answering a question. Who liked the story we read?

Carla Bluejay: I liked it a lot.

Benny Frog: Good, Carla. What was your favorite part?

Carla Bluejay: I liked when the littlest woodchuck ran away from home.

Benny Frog: Okay. Who else had a favorite part?

Carla Bluejay: I also liked when the little woodchuck met the wren building its nest.

Benny Frog: Thanks, Carla. Anyone else? *(Pause.)* We still don't have a conversation here because Shelli and Hank haven't said anything. In a conversation, everyone gets to take a turn and say something.

Ask the children:

- Why does Benny say they still don't have a conversation? (Shelli and Hank haven't contributed.)
- What happens in a conversation? (Everyone gets a turn to talk.)

Carla Bluejay: I liked the part about the wren, too.

Benny Frog: Thanks, Carla. You told us what you thought. Who'd like to talk next?

Shelli Squirrel: I didn't understand why the little woodchuck was afraid of the bear.

> **Hank Hawk:** I think the little woodchuck was afraid because the bear was so much bigger than she was.
>
> **Carla Bluejay:** Yes, I think that was it. She was also afraid because she did not know the bear, and her mother told her not to talk to strangers.
>
> **Shelli Squirrel:** At first I couldn't understand how she could be afraid of the bear! Now I see why.
>
> **Benny Frog:** You're all doing a good job listening and talking. Listening to each other during a conversation helps give you something to say when it's your turn.

Ask the children:

- Why does Benny say the conversation is going well? (Everyone is listening and talking.)

- Why is listening important during a conversation? (So we can think of something to say when it's our turn.)

> **Benny Frog:** Shelli, do you understand how to join a conversation now?
>
> **Shelli Squirrel:** Yes, I do, Benny. You're all great friends to help me.

Ask the children:

- How did Shelli feel after she learned to join a conversation?
- What steps did Benny teach Shelli?

Review the skill steps, asking the children to repeat each one:

1. Listen to what people say.

2. Wait for your turn to talk.

3. Say what you think.

Invite the children to tell about times when they have felt awkward about joining a conversation or discussion.

Explain that joining a conversation and joining a class discussion are much the same. Point out that most of us participate in discussions or conversations every day, at home and in school.

Present Posters 1, 2, and 3, one at a time. Emphasize the fact that the skills the students learned for greeting people, introducing themselves, and listening (eye contact, friendly facial expression, and a pleasant tone of voice) are also important in starting and participating in a discussion. Display the posters during the remaining activities, using them to prompt or cue students as needed.

PRACTICE

Shelli Joins a Conversation Role Play

Materials

> Four puppets (Shelli Squirrel, Benny Frog, Carla Bluejay, Hank Hawk)

Give the puppets to four children and ask them to sit in a circle. Benny Frog begins a conversation (you may want to suggest a topic or supply an opening sentence or question). Shelli Squirrel, Hank Hawk, and Carla Bluejay are to join the conversation in turn; prompt or cue children as necessary.

After the role play, discuss how the characters performed the skill. Go over the skill steps as needed, then give the puppets to four other children and repeat the role play. As time permits, allow each child to take a turn with a puppet. When all have participated, have various children role-play joining a conversation, this time without using the puppets. Encourage the group to offer the players feedback on the way they performed the skill.

Fruit Store

Materials

> Pictures of fruit (or any set of pictures showing objects within a single category, such as vehicles, clothing, household utensils, tools); stickers

Ask the children to form groups of three to six students. Explain that they will practice joining conversations by playing a game called "Fruit Store." Give one child in each group a picture. The child with the picture is to say, "I'm going to the fruit store to buy a _____," naming the fruit and holding up the picture. The other students in the group are to take turns asking or saying something about the fruit or about someone else's statement or question.

Prompt children as necessary, perhaps supplying model sentences and questions, such as "What color is the fruit?" "Why are you buying that fruit?" "What will you do with the fruit?" "How much does the fruit cost?" or "I first tasted that fruit when..."

Encourage each child to take part in the conversation. After everyone has participated, have the groups repeat the activity with new pictures. You might also repeat the activity with different sets of pictures or objects.

Give a sticker to each student who performs the skill steps adequately. Tell students who do not earn stickers that they will have other opportunities to practice the steps and receive stickers.

Adaptation

Follow up this activity by writing a cooperative story. In a small group, one student begins by dictating a sentence to someone else—for example, "I'm going to the fruit store to buy a..." The student who recorded the sentence then passes the paper to someone else and dictates another sentence or question. Group members continue taking turns writing and speaking until everyone agrees that the story is finished.

Story Pictures

Materials

Pictures of familiar places, people, or things; stickers

Arrange the pictures face down. Tell the class that you are going to choose a picture and start a story about it. Then you'll pause and call someone's name. The student named is to select another picture and continue the story with a sentence or question relating the second picture to the first one. Coach or cue the children as needed.

For example, suppose you pick a picture of a trumpet. You could begin a story by saying, "I know a girl named Margaret who liked to toot on her trumpet. Luther?"

Luther picks another picture and continues the story. If he selects a picture of a tree, for example, he might say, "One day Margaret took her trumpet up a tree."

Provide an appropriate ending to the story once you have run out of cards or participants. During the activity, emphasize that contributing to the story is the main objective, no matter how the story turns out.

Give a sticker to each student who performs the skill steps adequately. Tell students who do not earn stickers that they will have other opportunities to practice the steps and receive stickers.

Puzzle-Talking

Materials

Several puzzles; stickers

Select the first puzzle. Give one puzzle piece to each child. Have the puzzle board handy. Introduce the game by explaining that the group will have a discussion. Every time someone makes a contribution to the conversation, that person may bring a puzzle piece to the board and place it in the appropriate spot.

Begin a conversation on a topic of interest to the class.

As the conversation continues and children add pieces to the puzzle, the picture will begin to be recognizable. Have students keep the conversation going until the picture is complete (or nearly so). If necessary, encourage students to help each other make contributions. Repeat the activity using another puzzle.

Give a sticker to each student who performs the skill steps adequately. Tell students who do not earn stickers that they will have other opportunities to practice the steps and receive stickers.

Adaptations

1. As appropriate, choose a more complicated puzzle and give two or more pieces to each student.

2. Instead of a puzzle, use a large picture with places for students to fasten additions; for example, a tree with places for leaves, a train with spaces for cargo, a tiger with room for stripes, a clown with space for polka-dots.

MAINTENANCE

Joining a Conversation Every Day

Materials

Stickers

Observe students daily for opportunities to recognize and compliment those who contribute to a conversation. As appropriate, ask the children to tell you when they have used the skill and to describe what they said and did. Give a sticker to each student who uses the skill.

Joining a Conversation in Literature

Materials

Classroom books and stories such as these:

Cohen, Miriam. *Will I Have a Friend?* New York: Macmillan, 1989.

Keats, Ezra Jack. *Apartment Three.* New York: Macmillan, 1986.

Wiseman, Bernard. *Morris and Boris at the Circus.* New York: HarperTrophy, 1990.

Wright, Dare. *The Lonely Doll.* New York: Doubleday, 1985.

Select stories that discuss or feature characters contributing to a conversation. After the children have read or listened to a story, discuss the ways that joining a conversation was important to the characters.

Conversation Bank

Materials

Child's bank or slotted box (such as a tissue box); coins (real or play money); blank label

Preparation

Write "Conversation Bank" on the label and fasten it to the bank or box.

Show the children the Conversation Bank, saying that joining a discussion is like saving money in a bank: The more you put into it, the more valuable it becomes. Explain that whenever someone contributes to this week's class conversation or discussion, you will add a coin to the bank. Use the Conversation Bank throughout the week to increase student interest and involvement in class discussions.

Encourage involvement by recognizing and soliciting contributions: "Good idea, Tom. I'm glad you added to our discussion." "Bess, how do you feel about that?" After each discussion, count the coins and reiterate the value of contributing to conversations.

SKILL
5
STARTING A CONVERSATION

> ### SKILL STEPS: STARTING A CONVERSATION
> 1. Go up to the person.
> 2. Smile and say hello.
> 3. Ask about what the person is doing or tell about what you are doing.
> 4. Listen to the person's answer.
> 5. Say something else.

MOTIVATION

Skill Presentation: Hank Starts a Conversation

Materials

Three puppets (Benny Frog, Hank Hawk, Felicia Fox); Posters 1, 2, 3

Introduce the three puppets. Tell students that you're going to present a story about these characters called "Hank Starts a Conversation." Ask the children to listen carefully.

Hank Hawk doesn't know how to start a conversation.

Benny Frog: Hi, Hank. I see you're working on your art project.

Hank Hawk: *(Sounding dejected.)* Yeah.

Benny Frog: You don't sound too happy about it.

Hank Hawk: It's boring. I wish I had someone to work with.

Benny Frog: I just passed Felicia Fox working on her art project. Maybe you could work with her.

Hank Hawk: I was working next to her for a while, but I left. I was bored. It was too quiet.

Benny Frog: Did you talk to Felicia about your project or about hers?

Hank Hawk: No, I just colored. I didn't say anything.

Ask the children:

- Why do you think Hank was bored working next to Felicia? (Neither person said anything.)
- How is Hank feeling now? (Sad, bored.)

Benny Frog tells Hank about starting a conversation.

Benny Frog: Maybe if you started a conversation with Felicia, you wouldn't be bored.

Hank Hawk: Start a conversation? What does that mean?

Benny Frog: Starting a conversation means that when you see someone you'd like to talk to, you go up to the person, smile, and say hello. Then you think of something nice to say. You could ask about what the person is doing or tell about what you've been doing. When the person answers you, you listen to the answer. Then you say something else to keep the conversation going.

Hank Hawk: Do you mean it's all right to come up to someone and talk, even if the person isn't a teacher?

Benny Frog: Of course, it's all right. You can start a conversation with anyone.

Hank Hawk: What if I can't think of anything to say?

Benny Frog: You can always ask, "Can I play with you?" or "What are you doing?" Those questions can help anyone start a conversation.

Hank Hawk: What if Felicia won't talk to me?

Benny Frog: I'll bet she will. Having conversations makes what you're doing a lot more fun.

Ask the children:

- What does Benny tell Hank to do so he won't be bored? (Start a conversation with Felicia.)
- What does "starting a conversation" mean? (Be sure the skill steps are mentioned: go up to the person; smile; say hello and ask about what the person is doing or tell about what you're doing; listen to the person's answer; say something else.)
- Why does Benny say Hank should start a conversation with Felicia? (So he'll have more fun.)

Hank starts a conversation with Felicia.

Hank Hawk: Hmmm. I suppose I could try it. I really hate working by myself.

Benny Frog: There's Felicia. Go over and start a conversation with her. I'll listen and tell you how you did.

Hank Hawk: Okay. *(Pause.)* Hi, Felicia. Are you done with your art project?

Felicia Fox: Oh, hi, Hank. I still need to decide what colors to use.

Hank Hawk: I need to do that, too. Do you think these two blues go together?

Felicia Fox: Yes, I do. What do you think of my green and gold?

Hank Hawk: I like it.

Felicia Fox: Why don't you stay and work here, Hank? It's more fun when you have someone to talk to.

Hank Hawk: It sure is. I'll get my stuff and be right back.

Ask the children:

- How do we know that Hank started a conversation with Felicia? (She responded to him, she invited him to work with her.)

- How do you think Hank feels now?

Hank Hawk: How did I do, Benny?

Benny Frog: You did great, Hank! You started a conversation with Felicia, and now you have someone to work with.

Hank Hawk: I'll finally have some fun doing this project! I feel a lot better. Thanks for starting a conversation with me, Benny! You really helped.

Benny Frog: No problem!

Ask the children:

- How did Hank feel when Benny first saw him? How did he feel after his conversation with Felicia?
- What steps did Benny teach Hank?

Review the skill steps, asking the children to repeat each one:

1. Go up to the person.
2. Smile and say hello.
3. Ask about what the person is doing or tell about what you are doing.
4. Listen to the person's answer.
5. Say something else.

Invite the children to tell about times they've started conversations with others and about times they've wanted to start conversations but didn't know how.

Present Posters 1, 2, and 3, one at a time. Use these posters to illustrate that starting a conversation involves many of the same steps (making eye contact, having a friendly facial expression, and using a pleasant tone of voice) as the skills they have already learned. Display the posters during the remaining activities to prompt or cue children as needed.

In the following activities, be sure students understand that a conversation is when two or more people talk to each other. Help the children see that starting a conversation is friendly and helpful and that it often makes playing or working more enjoyable. Discuss how conversation also helps us learn about others and lets us practice various *Taking Part* skills (such as greeting, introducing ourselves, and listening).

Monitor the exchanges and encourage short, pleasant conversations. Recognize and compliment students who initiate conversations and students who respond positively, regardless of the degree of language skill used in the conversations.

PRACTICE

Hank Starts a Conversation Role Play

Materials

Three puppets (Benny Frog, Hank Hawk, Felicia Fox)

Give the puppets to three children and ask them to role-play the events in the story: Hank Hawk complains to Benny Frog about being bored and wanting someone to work with. Benny tells Hank about starting a conversation. Hank goes to Felicia Fox and starts a conversation with her. Felicia responds by inviting Hank to work with her. Coach and prompt the children as necessary.

After the role play, discuss how the skill was presented, asking students to comment on the characters' greeting and listening skills as well as their conversing skills. Then have the players exchange puppets and role-play again. As time permits, allow each child to take a turn with a puppet. When all have participated, have various children role-play starting a conversation, this time without using the puppets. Encourage the group to offer the players feedback on the way they presented the skill.

Say, Say, Say

Materials

Stickers

Have students role-play starting conversations in the situations listed below or in others they suggest. Before beginning, remind students of the skill steps and tell them to watch for the steps in the role plays. After each role play, discuss how the skill was performed.

Give a sticker to each student who performs the skill steps adequately. Tell students who do not earn stickers that they will have other opportunities to practice the steps and receive stickers.

Sample situations

1. You see Joni, a new student in your class, sitting by herself in the lunchroom.
2. When you go to the playground, you see your friend Ray.
3. Eliza, your neighbor, is sitting on her porch when you come outside.
4. Michelle, a classmate, is on the school bus when you get on.
5. Your father is fixing the kitchen sink when you get home from school.

Adaptations

1. Rather than presenting situations, ask children to role-play starting a conversation with another student in the class. Refer to the skill steps, prompting students to ask about the other person and to tell something about themselves.
2. Encourage children to extend their role-played conversations beyond initiation and to make them as believable as possible.

Conversations with Lonnie

Materials

Blackline Master 4 (Badges); stickers

Preparation

Use the blackline master to make a badge. Write "Lonnie of the Day" on it or draw a picture. Attach double-stick tape or a safety pin to the back.

Tell students that they will practice starting conversations with a person named Lonnie, who is lonely for people to talk with. Each day, a child will be "Lonnie of the Day," and everyone else will take turns starting conversations with Lonnie.

Choose a capable student to be the first Lonnie, and give him or her the badge. Demonstrate the activity by starting a conversation with this child. For example, say, "Hello, Lonnie. I like your shirt." As necessary, prompt "Lonnie" to say, "Thank you." Continue the conversation by saying, "You're welcome. What are you having for lunch today?" Again, prompt Lonnie to answer, as needed. Instruct the other children to come up to today's

"Lonnie" during free time and start a conversation. Lonnie is to respond to what others say or ask.

Continue the activity, choosing a "Lonnie of the Day" to wear the badge until every child has played Lonnie.

Give a sticker to each student who performs the skill steps adequately. Tell students who do not earn stickers that they will have other opportunities to practice the steps and receive stickers.

Adaptation

Instead of having a student play Lonnie, supply a character such as a stuffed animal or a picture or poster of someone. Place this picture or toy on a table or study carrel. Audiorecord statements Lonnie might say in response to students who start a conversation. Tell students what responses you've recorded and help them adjust their conversation accordingly. For example, if you have recorded the statements "I'm fine. How are you?" and "I played with my truck. What did you do yesterday?" you could suggest that students ask questions such as "Hi, Lonnie. How are you today?" and "What did you do yesterday?"

MAINTENANCE

Starting a Conversation Every Day

Materials

Stickers

Observe students daily for opportunities to recognize and compliment those who initiate conversations. As appropriate, ask the children to tell you when they have used the skill and to describe what they said and did. Give a sticker to each student who uses the skill.

Starting a Conversation in Literature

Materials

Classroom books and stories such as these:

Cohen, Miriam. *Second Grade Friends*. New York: Scholastic, 1993.

Udry, Janice May. *What Mary Jo Shared*. New York: Scholastic, 1991.

Wiseman, Bernard. *Morris and Boris at the Circus*. New York: HarperTrophy, 1990.

Select stories that discuss or feature characters beginning conversations. After the children have read or listened to a story, discuss the ways that starting conversations was important to the characters.

The Talk-Starter Bug

Materials

Blackline Master 6 (Talk-Starter Bugs)

Preparation

Use the blackline master to make several "Talk-Starter Bug" badges. Attach double-stick tape or a safety pin to the back of each badge.

Display the badges and tell students that when the Talk-Starter Bug bites, people want to start conversations. Ask several students to wear the badges; choose more capable students at first. Explain that during free time or other special times during the day, these students will watch for opportunities to start conversations—for example, when they see someone who has finished a task or is sitting alone. As needed, allow time for the selected students to practice initiating a conversation with someone in the group. Then get back to your regular academic schedule.

Retrieve the Talk-Starter Bug badges at the end of the day. Select several new students to wear them each day, and review the rules for the activity. Continue until everyone has had some experience initiating conversations.

UNIT

2 COMMUNICATING FEELINGS

Much of the information we communicate to others, particularly information about feelings, is transmitted nonverbally. Facial expressions, postures, gestures, and voice tone all provide clues about the message being sent. To communicate effectively, children must accurately interpret and use these nonverbal signals.

Related to nonverbal communication is the concept of empathy. *Empathy* is typically defined as one's ability to interpret the emotions of others and to be emotionally responsive to these emotions. Empathy is considered to be a critical factor for prosocial behavior. Children who understand how others are feeling and are able to relate compassionately to those feelings are more likely to respond in socially appropriate ways. Through direct instruction, children can be helped to become more empathic.

In this unit, students will discuss and practice the following skills:

- Naming Feelings
- Naming My Feelings
- Naming Others' Feelings
- Sending Messages
- Controlling Temper

Special Issues

Because a significant portion of nonverbal communications conveys emotions, this unit focuses on the basic emotions of happiness, sadness, anger, and fear. As presented in the first three skills, children first practice distinguishing these four emotions by labeling each; then they identify these emotions in themselves; and finally they practice interpreting these emotions in others. The emphasis is on identification of feelings rather than behavioral steps. Children discuss and practice the body language and behavior typical of each emotion. In Skills 4 and 5, children learn behavioral steps for communicating their feelings to others nonverbally and for controlling temper through nonverbal calming techniques.

Young children often label feelings as either "good" or "bad." They may have particular difficulty with the distinctions between sadness, anger, and fear. Depending on your group, it may be useful at first to focus activities on the two most basic emotions, happiness and sadness, gradually introducing the emotion of fear, and finally anger. It helps to explain to the children that all feelings are acceptable; none is "bad." The important thing is to recognize one's own and others' feelings so that misunderstandings can be avoided. As emphasized in these activities, children can be helped to identify emotions by learning characteristic body language and typical actions for each. For example, a sad person may have a turned-down mouth and teary eyes; the person may not want to play. A happy person may smile and welcome a playmate. Angry people may strike out at others.

Part of the focus of this unit is on alternatives to aggressive expressions of temper. It's often helpful to acknowledge that the urge to hit or otherwise strike out at others is a normal response to anger but that there are safer, more productive ways to communicate. When appropriate, ask children to brainstorm various nonviolent ways they could express anger and control temper. Ask, "If this happened to you, what would you do?" Explain that anger is not "good" or "bad"; it is a normal human emotion that children can learn to express appropriately.

Taking Part stickers are used as incentives for skill step performance and skill use in practice and maintenance activities throughout this unit. You may wish to distribute copies of Blackline Master 2 (My Taking Part Sticker Collection), which gives students a handy place to store the stickers they earn.

SKILL

1 NAMING FEELINGS

SKILL STEPS: NAMING FEELINGS

1. Remember that "happy" is how you feel when something really good happens.

2. Remember that "angry" is how you feel when someone is mean or unfair.

3. Remember that "afraid" is how you feel when you want to get away.

4. Remember that "sad" is how you feel when you lose something or do something wrong.

MOTIVATION

Skill Presentation: Will Learns about Feelings

Materials

> Four puppets (Will Rabbit, Shelli Squirrel, Felicia Fox, Benny Frog); Posters 1, 2, 3, 4

Introduce the four puppets. Tell students that you're going to present a story about these characters called "Will Learns about Feelings." Ask the children to listen carefully.

Will Rabbit and Shelli Squirrel observe and name their friends' feelings.

> **Will Rabbit:** I like when you stay with me while my mother's working, Shelli. You know such good stories! Will you tell me one now?

Shelli Squirrel: Sure, Will. We can sit on this tree stump. *(Pause.)* Why, there's Felicia Fox. Hi, Felicia!

Will Rabbit: Felicia's not answering. She's too busy stuffing bubble gum into her mouth with one hand and rubbing her tummy with the other. Look at her big smile!

Shelli Squirrel: How are you doing today, Felicia?

Felicia Fox: Mmm! Mmm! Mmm!

Shelli Squirrel: Is that all you can say? Tell us, how do you feel?

Ask the children:

- How do you think Felicia Fox feels? (Good, happy.)
- Why do you think she feels happy? (Likes chewing bubble gum.)
- How does Felicia show her feelings? (Rubs her tummy, smiles, says "Mmm!")
- When have you felt happy? How did you show it?

Will Rabbit: I think Felicia feels good, Shelli.

Shelli Squirrel: Yes, Will, I think you're right. When someone feels as good as Felicia feels, we say she's happy. Felicia's happy because she loves to chew bubble gum.

Will Rabbit: I feel happy when I'm eating carrots and lettuce.

Shelli Squirrel: Of course you do, Will. *(Pause.)* Why, who's that croaking? Oh, it's you, Benny Frog. How are you today?

Benny Frog: Someone took my bubble gum! I left it right here on this stump, and now it's gone. Wait until I find who took my gum! Boy, will they be sorry!

Will Rabbit: I don't think Benny is happy, like Felicia is. He's frowning and stamping his foot.

Shelli Squirrel: You're right, Will. Someone has been mean to Benny. Someone has taken his bubble gum!

Ask the children:

- How do you think Benny Frog feels? (Angry, bad.)

- Why do you think he feels angry and bad? (Someone took his bubble gum.)
- How does Benny show his feelings? (Frowns, stamps his foot, uses angry language.)
- When have you felt angry? How did you show it?

Will and Shelli continue to observe and name their friends' feelings.

Will Rabbit: I think Benny feels mad inside. I think he's angry.

Shelli Squirrel: I think you're right. Have you ever been angry, Will?

Will Rabbit: I was angry when Hank Hawk took some of my carrots.

Shelli Squirrel: I remember that. You were as angry then as Benny looks right now. And I think Benny just found out who took his bubble gum. Listen to the way he's croaking at Felicia!

Will Rabbit: Yes, and Felicia is running toward the lake, holding her paws over her ears and yelling. She must not be happy anymore. She must feel bad.

Shelli Squirrel: Benny's loud croaking must be hurting Felicia's ears. She's afraid of loud noises.

Will Rabbit: I was afraid once when Benny Frog was chasing me.

Felicia Fox: Felicia's probably afraid Benny will hurt her. When we think we might be hurt, we feel afraid.

Ask the children:

- How does Shelli say Felicia feels now? (Afraid.)
- Why does Felicia feel afraid? (Afraid of loud noises, afraid Benny might hurt her.)
- How does Felicia show her feelings? (Runs away, covers her ears, yells.)
- When have you felt afraid? How did you show it?

Shelli Squirrel: Here comes Felicia. She looks like she wants someone to talk to. Hello, Felicia. How do you feel?

Felicia Fox: I feel bad on the outside and bad on the inside. Benny Frog scared me. I guess I shouldn't have taken his bubble gum. I knew it didn't belong to me.

Shelli Squirrel: Yes, taking other's things almost always makes them angry, Felicia. I hope you feel better soon.

Will Rabbit: So do I. 'Bye, Felicia. (*Pause.*) You know, Shelli, I think Felicia has another feeling besides "afraid." She's shaking her head and walking slowly. Her head is down.

Shelli Squirrel: You're right, Will. Felicia also feels sad because she took Benny's bubble gum. Sometimes doing things we're not supposed to do makes us sorry and sad.

Ask the children:

- How does Shelli say Felicia feels now? (Sad, sorry.)
- Why does Felicia feel sad? (Sorry she took Benny's gum, sorry she did something she wasn't supposed to do.)
- How does Felicia show her feelings? (Shakes head, walks slowly with head down.)
- When have you felt sad? How did you show it?

Will and Shelli discuss feelings.

Will Rabbit: I know about that feeling, too! When I cheated at tag and everyone left the game, I felt sad. When I decided to play fairly, I felt better. I was happy again.

Shelli Squirrel: Maybe Felicia will feel happy again when she decides not to take someone else's things.

Will Rabbit: I hope so.

Shelli Squirrel: I think Felicia learned her lesson. And I think you learned about feeling happy, angry, afraid, and sad. When you know about feelings, you understand yourself and others better. You'll know what to do when people have feelings.

Ask the children:

- Why does Shelli say it's important to know about feelings? (So you'll understand yourself and others better, so you'll know what to do when people have feelings.)

> **Will Rabbit:** That's true. And now, Shelli, please tell me a story!

Shelli Squirrel: Okay!

Ask the children:

- What different feelings did Felicia Fox have in this story? (Happiness, fear, sadness.)
- How did Benny Frog feel in the story? (Angry.)
- How did the characters show these feelings?

In your discussion, emphasize that emotions are normal—everyone has them, and it is important to know what people are feeling so we will know how to behave around them.

Invite the children to recall examples of each feeling from their own experience. Then ask them to repeat the following:

Some things we should remember about feelings are . . .

1. "Happy" is how you feel when something really good happens.
2. "Angry" is how you feel when someone is mean or unfair.
3. "Afraid" is how you feel when you want to get away.
4. "Sad" is how you feel when you lose something or do something wrong.

Display Posters 1, 2, 3, and 4, using them to illustrate the nonverbal signals that someone is happy (making eye contact, pleasant facial expression and voice, friendly posture). Contrast these with some of the visual clues that someone is upset, as illustrated by the story (looking down, a sad or angry expression or voice, unfriendly posture such as turning away or hanging your head).

> *In the following activities, emphasize to the children that all their feelings are acceptable; none is wrong. A child who felt happy when Grandfather left home may*

have had difficulties with that relationship, and a child who was sad when the family went on vacation may have disliked being away from home. It may be helpful to have children explain their situations and feelings if they express any that initially seem inappropriate.

PRACTICE

Will Learns about Feelings Role Play

Materials

> Four puppets (Will Rabbit, Shelli Squirrel, Felicia Fox, Benny Frog)

Give the puppets to four children. Ask Felicia Fox and Benny Frog to pantomime the events of the story: Felicia happily chews bubble gum; Benny enters, discovers the missing gum, and shows anger; Benny directs his anger toward Felicia, who responds with fear. As each emotion is portrayed, Will Rabbit and Shelli Squirrel describe what's happening and name each feeling. Coach the children as necessary.

After the role play, discuss how the characters portrayed and named each feeling. Then have the children exchange roles and role-play again. As time permits, allow each child to take a turn with a puppet. When all have participated, have various children role-play the four feelings again, this time without using puppets. They can use either the story events or another story that you or they devise. Encourage the group to offer the players feedback on the way they portrayed and named their feelings.

Feelings Circle

Materials

> Blackline Master 7 (How Do Feelings Look?); stickers

Preparation

> Use the blackline master to make enough "How Do Feelings Look?" handouts for each student.

Ask the children to sit in a "Feelings Circle." Remind them that we show our feelings not only in words but in the ways we look and behave. Ask them to recall and repeat the four feelings discussed in the story: happiness, anger, fear, and sadness. Tell them they'll be playing a game in which one student will pantomime a feeling and another student will guess which feeling is being portrayed.

Pick two children to stand in the middle of the circle. Take one child aside and narrate an emotional situation to pantomime (for suggestions, see following sample situations). The second child is to say which feeling is being portrayed. Coach or prompt as necessary, helping the pantomiming child use body language to convey feelings. Afterward, ask the group whether they agree with the feeling guessed, and why. Then give the second child an emotional situation to pantomime for the first child to guess. Select other pairs of children and continue until all students have had a turn to pantomime and to guess a feeling.

If children have difficulty discriminating between, say, sadness and anger, help them understand that by considering the person's behavior, they can conclude that the person feels bad. Suggest that they think about what a person would probably do in reaction to an event, such as crying to express sadness, or hitting or yelling to express anger. What a person does can help us identify his or her feelings.

There are no "right" or "wrong" feelings to portray. Children may pantomime any feeling they consider appropriate to the situation.

After the pantomimes, distribute the worksheet "How Do Feelings Look?" Discuss with the children the body language associated with the four feelings. Suggest that students keep their worksheet and use it throughout this unit as a reminder and reference.

Give a sticker to each student who correctly names a feeling. Tell students who do not earn stickers that they will have other opportunities to name feelings and receive stickers.

Sample situations

1. You are eating an ice cream cone.
2. You are being chased by a barking dog.
3. You see someone take your pencil and break it.
4. You tear your new shirt.

5. You are having a birthday party.

6. You are startled by someone wearing a mask.

7. You hear someone call you a bad name.

8. You find out that your pet has run away.

9. You win a game.

10. You see your best friend coming to play with you.

Adaptations

1. Limit the situations to those involving only happiness and sadness.

2. Have children describe, rather than role-play, a given situation; have their partners tell which emotion would likely be felt.

3. After sufficient practice, add situations involving other feelings, such as jealousy, frustration, loneliness, or greed.

Reading Emotions

Materials

Stickers

Ask the children to listen carefully as you read several brief stories. They are to decide from your verbal and nonverbal clues which feelings you are describing. After each story, have students identify the emotion first, then share similar experiences. Ask questions to help the children better understand and recognize the components of each emotion. For example, if happiness was the emotion identified:

- What did you hear in the story that told you I felt happy?
- What words made you think of happiness?
- How did my voice tell you that I felt happy?
- What changes did you see in my face? How did my mouth look? How did my mouth change? How did my eyes look? How did my eyes change? How did my eyebrows look? How did my eyebrows change?

Give a sticker to each student who correctly names a feeling. Tell students who do not earn stickers that they will have other opportunities to name feelings and receive stickers.

As expressively as possible, read the following four stories (or four others you create). Let your intonation and inflection clearly represent the emotion you're depicting. Also use postures, gestures, and facial expressions to convey feelings. Pause after each reading.

Happiness: I'm going with my mom to the playground tomorrow! We'll go across the hanging bars and slide down the wiggly slide. I can play in a giant sandbox and steer the fire engine. The playground has a climbing net and steps and ramps and a balance beam! We'll take fruit juice and crackers! I just can't wait! I feel . . .

Sadness: My dog, Feiffer, is dead. He was playing in the yard, and then he ran out into the street. A car was coming and couldn't stop in time. I played with Feiffer every day. Now I won't ever see him again. I feel . . .

Anger: That boy from down the street is always stomping on everyone's flowers. Just now I went outside, and he was throwing garbage at the side of my house. He yelled a bad word and ran away. Now the whole wall looks terrible, and it will take Aunt Ida and me hours to clean it up. I wish he would move and never come around here again! I feel . . .

Fear: I'm watching this horrible movie about a monster. Nobody knows where this monster is hiding. It keeps creeping around corners and jumping out of the dark. I'm home alone, and I know I should turn the TV off. I don't know why, but I keep watching. What's that sound on the stairs? I feel . . .

Adaptations

1. To accompany your reading, show pictures of people feeling each emotion.

2. Ask children to create and present brief stories that express one of the four emotions (or others you consider appropriate). Have classmates guess what is being portrayed.

3. As appropriate, discuss other feelings that situations might evoke, such as excitement or frustration.

MAINTENANCE

Naming Feelings Every Day

Materials

Stickers; Blackline Master 1 (Individual Social Skills Checklist, optional)

Observe students daily for opportunities to recognize and compliment those who correctly name feelings. As appropriate, ask the children to tell you when they have named a feeling and to describe the circumstances. Give a sticker to each student who uses the skill.

You may wish to use the Individual Social Skills Checklist to record students' progress in this unit's skills.

Naming Feelings in Literature

Materials

Classroom books and stories such as these:

Aliki. *Feelings.* New York: HarperTrophy, 1986.

Allen, Jonathan. *"I'm Not Scared."* New York: Hyperion Books, 2008.

Cain, Janann. *The Way I Feel.* Seattle: Parenting Press, 2000.

Select stories that discuss or feature characters identifying emotions. After the children have read or listened to a story, discuss how naming feelings was important to the characters.

Feelings Board

Preparation

Create a bulletin board divided into four sections with the headings "Happiness is . . .," "Anger is . . .," "Fear is . . .,"and "Sadness is . . .".

Divide the class into four groups and assign each group one of the feelings. Distribute art supplies and have each group member draw a picture to illustrate the emotion. Display the pictures on the board.

Keep the board long enough for you to rotate the groups, giving every child an opportunity to draw each emotion.

Adaptations

1. Have the children write or dictate captions for their pictures. If your students write, you may wish to substitute a written description of an emotional experience for the drawn one.

2. Do the activity as a cooperative project, with each group producing one large picture to illustrate the emotion.

SKILL

2 NAMING MY FEELINGS

> ### SKILL STEPS: NAMING MY FEELINGS
>
> 1. Think about what just happened.
> 2. Think about how you feel about what happened.
> 3. Remember the emotion words.
> 4. Choose one of the emotion words.

MOTIVATION

Skill Presentation: Shelli Names Her Feelings

Materials

> Two puppets (Felicia Fox, Shelli Squirrel); Posters 2, 3, 4

Introduce the two puppets. Tell students that you're going to present a story about these characters called "Shelli Names Her Feelings." Ask the children to listen carefully.

Shelli Squirrel shows fear and tells Felicia Fox about it.

> **Felicia Fox:** Oh, Shelli, there you are again, sleeping on the floor near me! I read you all those bedtime stories and tucked you in tight. You promised to sleep in your bed all night.

> **Shelli Squirrel:** I know. But I just couldn't.

> **Felicia Fox:** This has been happening every night, Shelli! Your father won't want me to babysit anymore.

I just can't read you stories all night. What's the matter?

Shelli Squirrel: I don't know.

Felicia Fox: Can you tell me why you always leave your room?

Shelli Squirrel: Do you promise you won't laugh?

Felicia Fox: I promise.

Shelli Squirrel: Well, it's because of the little people.

Felicia Fox: Little people?

Shelli Squirrel: As soon as you turn out the light, I see little people coming to get me! They won't go away, even when I close my eyes.

Felicia Fox: I see. And you're shaking and staying close to me. Do you know what you're feeling, Shelli?

Ask the children:

- What do you think Shelli is feeling?
- Why do you think so?

Shelli Squirrel: I think I'm afraid, Felicia.

Felicia Fox: Yes, I think you are, Shelli. That would explain why you leave your bed and want to sleep right next to me. Let me help.

Shelli Squirrel: Can you, Felicia?

Felicia Fox: Yes. Now that you've told me what you're feeling, I know what to do.

Ask the children:

- What clues helped Shelli know she was feeling afraid? (Leaving her bed, trembling, staying close to Felicia, telling about "little people" coming to get her.)
- When have you felt afraid but didn't tell anyone about it?
- How did you feel when no one knew you were afraid?

Felicia Helps Shelli overcome her fear.

Felicia Fox: Tonight after your story, I will have something special for you, Shelli—something that will help.

(*Pause to show passage of time.*) Time for bed, Shelli. I'm going to turn off the light. You watch.

Shelli Squirrel: Why, I see a little light glowing in the corner.

Felicia Fox: This is your new night-light. It used to be your father's when he was little. When I told him you were afraid to go to sleep, he gave me this for you. It's not bright enough to keep you awake, just bright enough to chase away those little people.

Shelli Squirrel: I hope so, Felicia!

Felicia Fox: Just to be sure, I'll check on you a few times tonight.

Shelli Squirrel: I think it's going to work, Felicia! I love my little light—and my warm bed!

Felicia Fox: Hmmm, I think your feelings about going to bed have changed now, Shelli. You're smiling and relaxed, and I'll bet you'll sleep in your bed all night. Can you tell me what you're feeling now?

Ask the children:

- What do you think Shelli is feeling now?
- Why do you think so?

Shelli Squirrel: I'm happy! I feel safe! I'm not scared anymore! I'm glad I told you what was bothering me.

Felicia Fox: I'm glad you did, too, Shelli. Until I knew you felt afraid, I didn't know how to help you. When you tell someone how you feel, you usually start feeling better.

Shelli Squirrel: Oh, yes. Good night, Felicia!

Ask the children:

- How did Felicia help solve Shelli's problem? (Gave her a night-light.)
- How did Shelli feel after telling Felicia what was bothering her? (Better, glad.)
- Why does Felicia say she needed to know what Shelli was feeling? (So she could help.)

- Have you ever told someone about your feelings? What happened? How did you feel after you told?

Discuss with the children why it's important to let others know how we feel. Emphasize that telling how we feel can get us help if we need it. Sharing our feelings brings us closer to our friends and can make us feel better.

Although the story focused on the feeling of fear, remind the class about all four important feelings people often have: happiness, anger, fear, and sadness. Mention that these feelings are sometimes shown without using words—Shelli showed her fear by leaving her bed each night. Ask the children to repeat the following:

I can name my feelings when I . . .

1. Think about what just happened.
2. Think about how you feel about what happened.
3. Remember the emotion words.
4. Choose one of the emotion words.

Show children Posters 2, 3, and 4. Ask children what feeling they think the person in each picture shows. Emphasize that a person's face, voice, and posture can show the person's feelings just as much as words can. Ask children what kind of facial expressions, voice, and posture show someone is sad, afraid, or angry.

PRACTICE

Shelli Names Her Feelings Role Play

Materials

Two puppets (Felicia Fox, Shelli Squirrel)

Give the puppets to two children and ask them to role-play the events in the story: Shelli Squirrel shows her fear by getting out of bed, trembling, and going to sleep near Felicia Fox. Felicia asks Shelli what she's feeling when she leaves her bed each night. Shelli replies that she feels afraid. Felicia gives Shelli a night-light, and Shelli responds by showing she feels happy and safe. Felicia asks Shelli what she's feeling now. Shelli replies that she feels happy and safe. Coach the children as needed.

After the role play, discuss how the feelings were presented. Then ask the players to exchange roles and role-play again. As time permits, allow each child to take a turn with a puppet. When all have participated, have various children role-play naming their feelings, this time without using the puppets. They can use the story or suggest other situations. Encourage the group to offer the players feedback on the way they showed and described their feelings.

Will Rabbit Talks about Feelings

Materials

Puppet (Will Rabbit); stickers

Introduce Will Rabbit. Tell students that Will is going to talk to them about feelings. Will Rabbit says, "Everyone always says they can't tell how I'm feeling. They never know if I'm happy, sad, angry, or afraid. Well, maybe that's because I don't make my face show how I feel. I'm going to practice that now. Will you help me?"

(Pause for the class to respond.)

Will Rabbit: Thanks! Let's see. First, I'll pretend that my mother made my favorite dessert—carrot cake. Now how would I feel if I came home from school and saw my favorite cake?

(Pause for the class to respond.)

Will Rabbit: That's right, happy. Who can show me how to have a happy face?

(Pause for the class to respond.)

Will Rabbit: Oh, of course! I'd have a great big smile, and my eyes would shine. Then my mother would know I felt happy about the cake. Please help me with another feeling. Suppose I was drinking from my favorite cup, the one my grandfather gave me, and it fell and broke. I would feel . . . how?

(Pause for the class to respond.)

Will Rabbit: Right. I would feel very sad. Who can show me a sad face?

(Pause for the class to respond.)

Will Rabbit: Yes, I see. My mouth would be down in a frown, and so would my eyebrows. I would hang my head low. Tears might start coming out of my eyes. People would know right away that I was sad. Now, what if my little brother threw my cup down on purpose and broke it? Then I would feel . . . how?

(Pause for the class to respond.)

Will Rabbit: That's right. I would be angry. Can you show me an angry face?

(Pause for the class to respond.)

Will Rabbit: Yes, of course. My mouth and forehead would be scrunched up, my eyebrows would be way down, and my teeth would be tight together. That would make me look really angry. Let's practice one more feeling. Suppose some bigger rabbits started to call me names and chase me. I would feel . . . how?

(Pause for the class to respond.)

Will Rabbit: Right. I would be afraid. How would my face look?

(Pause for the class to respond.)

Will Rabbit: Okay! I might open my eyes wide and raise my eyebrows. My mouth would be frowning or maybe wide open and yelling for help. Everyone would know I felt afraid. Thanks for helping me practice showing my feelings. Who can remember the feeling I liked best?

(Pause for the class to respond.)

Will Rabbit: Yes, I liked feeling happy about the carrot cake. How did I feel about breaking my cup?

(Pause for the class to respond.)

Will Rabbit: Right, I felt sad. When my brother broke the cup on purpose, how did I feel?

(Pause for the class to respond.)

Will Rabbit: Yes, I felt angry with him. And do you remember the big rabbits chasing me? How did I feel?

(Pause for the class to respond.)

Will Rabbit: Yes. I was afraid. Thanks again for showing me how all those feelings look.

Discuss Will Rabbit's descriptions of emotions. Invite children to talk about emotional incidents from their own lives. Emphasize their physical reactions to each: how their body felt, how their face looked.

Give a sticker to each student who correctly portrays Will's feelings. Tell students who do not earn stickers that they will have other opportunities to practice the skill and receive stickers.

Adaptation

Present this material in two sessions.

Face Voting

Materials

Blackline Master 8 (Feelings Faces); craft sticks or tongue depressors, two for each child

Preparation

Use the blackline master to supply each child with four "feelings faces"—one happy, one sad, one angry, one afraid. Have children make their own happy–sad sticks and angry–afraid sticks, or prepare them in advance. Glue a happy face and a sad face to each side of one stick; glue an angry face and a fearful face to each side of another stick. You might also color (or have children color) the happy faces one color, perhaps yellow, and the sad faces another, perhaps blue; the angry faces could be red and the fearful faces green.

Begin by giving each child a happy–sad stick. Present various familiar situations, asking students to raise their sticks with either the sad face or the happy face showing, according to how the situation would make them feel. Emphasize to the children that no answer is wrong. They are to vote, or show the face they choose, based on individual feelings.

Sample situations

1. You lose your new ball.
2. You find your favorite sandwich in your lunch bag.
3. You just made a new friend.
4. The family next door moves away.
5. You get a book for your birthday.
6. Your teacher asks you to put away the art supplies.
7. Your aunt comes for a long visit.
8. Your mother says you cannot watch television.
9. Someone calls you names.

As appropriate, discuss with the children why certain situations can make one person happy, yet make another person sad. Then distribute the angry–afraid sticks and repeat the activity.

Sample situations

1. An older child threatens to tattle on you.
2. You break the radio you borrowed from your uncle.
3. A dog barks at you.
4. Someone throws your book bag in a puddle.
5. You get lost going to a friend's house.
6. Your teacher asks you to stay after school.
7. It's late, and your father hasn't come home from work yet.
8. Your older sister is yelling at you.
9. A bully threatens to fight you.

Encourage children to keep their sticks and use them any time during the week to express their feelings.

Adaptations

1. Restrict the activity to happy and sad situations only.

2. Give students both sticks at the same time. Present all the situations and have them decide among all four emotions.

MAINTENANCE

Naming My Feelings Every Day

Materials

Stickers

Observe students daily for opportunities to recognize and compliment those who label or describe their own emotions. As appropriate, ask the children to tell you when they have named their feelings and to describe the circumstances. Give a sticker to each student who uses the skill.

Naming My Feelings in Literature

Materials

Classroom books and stories such as these:

Aliki. *Feelings.* New York: HarperTrophy, 1986.

Allen, Jonathan. *"I'm Not Scared."* New York: Hyperion Books, 2008.

Cain, Janann. *The Way I Feel.* Seattle: Parenting Press, 2000.

Carle, Eric. *The Grouchy Ladybug.* New York: HarperTrophy, 1996.

Cosgrove, Stephen. *Catundra.* Los Angeles: Price Stern Sloan, 1978.

Curtis, Jamie Lee. *Today I Feel Silly and Other Moods That Make My Day.* New York: Joanna Cotler, 1998.

Select stories that discuss or feature characters identifying their own emotions. After the children have read or listened to a story, discuss how identifying feelings was important to the characters.

Feelings Mobiles

Materials

Blackline Master 8 (Feelings Faces); four blank labels; four wire coat hangers; string

Preparation

Use the blackline master to make four "feelings faces." On the labels, write or illustrate the following four topics (or others you devise):

1. Things that make me happy
2. Things that make me angry
3. Things that frighten me
4. Things that make me sad

Attach a label and the corresponding face to the top or center of each coat hanger.

Organize students into four groups. Give each group a labeled hanger and distribute one or two small pieces of drawing paper to each child. Assign each group one of the topics.

Each child is to draw a picture showing activities or people that illustrate the group's topic. Check to be sure children understand the emotion words being depicted.

After the groups have finished, use string to fasten the pictures from each group to the coat hangers, as space permits. Hang the completed mobiles in the room. Each week, remove one mobile from display and use it for a class discussion of the particular topic. Encourage students to talk about the mobile pictures and then to add their own ideas and opinions about the topic. When appropriate, ask the creators of any unusual pictures to discuss or explain why they illustrated the topic the way they did. If necessary, remind students that no pictures and no feelings are "wrong"; all reflect individual experiences.

Keep this activity ongoing by having drawing paper, string, and coat hangers available in an art or project center. Encourage students to make new individual or group feelings-mobiles, sometimes based on daily school experiences.

Adaptations

1. Ask children to illustrate only happy and sad feelings.
2. Invite children to illustrate more complicated emotions, such as surprise, relief, jealousy, frustration, disappointment.

3. Ask children to explain or discuss their contributions before fastening them to the mobile.

4. Ask children to write about their drawings. Hang the written work on the mobiles or post it nearby.

3 NAMING OTHERS' FEELINGS

SKILL STEPS: NAMING OTHERS' FEELINGS

1. Look at the other person's face.

2. Look at the person's body posture.

3. Listen to the person's words.

4. Listen to the person's tone of voice.

MOTIVATION

Skill Presentation: Will Learns about Feelings

Materials

    Two puppets (Will Rabbit, Carla Bluejay); Posters 2, 3, 4

Introduce the two puppets. Tell students that you're going to present a story about these characters called "Will Learns about Feelings." Ask the children to listen carefully.

Will Rabbit tells Carla Bluejay that Felicia Fox and Benny Frog don't like him.

Carla Bluejay: Hi, Will! How's it going?

Will Rabbit: *(Glumly.)* Oh, hello, Carla. Okay, I guess.

Carla Bluejay: You don't sound very happy. I just passed Felicia Fox and Benny Frog playing ball. Let's go play with them. That will cheer you up!

Will Rabbit: Oh, no, it won't! I've tried playing with them, but it never works out. They don't like me.

Carla Bluejay: Of course they like you, Will.

Will Rabbit: They do not! Last week I told them they could ride my bike, but they ignored me. They wouldn't stop yelling at each other—something about whose turn it was to put away toys.

Ask the children:

- Why does Will say Felicia and Benny don't like him? (Ignored his offer of a bike ride, were too busy yelling at each other.)
- If Felicia and Benny really do like Will, as Carla says, why do you think they ignored him? (If necessary, suggest that Felicia and Benny were angry at each other and so were in no mood to play.)

Will tells Carla about other times Felicia and Benny wouldn't play with him.

Carla Bluejay: Hmmm. Tell me more.

Will Rabbit: Well, another time they told me not to bother them. All they were doing was looking for Felicia's ball—the one she got from her brother and liked so much. Felicia was crying, and Benny looked like he was about to start!

Ask the children:

- Why do you think Felicia and Benny told Will not to bother them while they were looking for Felicia's favorite ball? How were they feeling then? (Sad.)

Carla Bluejay: Go on.

Will Rabbit: I tried one more time, and they just turned and walked away from me.

Carla Bluejay: Were they talking about anything?

Will Rabbit: Benny said something about losing the book their teacher gave them to use for their science project. That time it looked like both of them were about to cry.

Ask the children:

- Why do you think Benny and Felicia walked away from Will and kept talking about the book they lost?
- How did they feel then? (Scared.)

Carla Bluejay: I think I'm getting the picture, Will. Did anything else happen?

Will Rabbit: Last week I saw them smiling, but I walked right by them without saying anything. I thought they were mad at me. They called me and said I should have come over to play with them. I never know what they're going to do.

Ask the children:

- How could Will have known whether Felicia and Benny wanted to play with him this time? (They were smiling and happy.)

Carla tells Will about identifying others' feelings.

Carla Bluejay: You know, Will, it sounds to me as if Felicia and Benny want to be friends with you.

Will Rabbit: What? Then why do they treat me differently every time they see me? Sometimes they like me, and sometimes they don't.

Carla Bluejay: I think they like you all the time, Will. When they were happy, they wanted to play with you. But they don't always feel the same way. Everyone has lots of different feelings.

Will Rabbit: What do you mean?

Carla Bluejay: People may not want to play with anyone when they're sad or angry or afraid. When Felicia and Benny were arguing, they felt angry at each other—that's why they didn't want to ride your bike. When Felicia's ball was lost, they felt sad. When they thought they lost their teacher's book, they felt afraid. Those weren't good times to ask them to play. Most other times would be fine—like the time you saw them smiling.

Ask the children:

- Why does Carla say Felicia and Benny really do want to be friends with Will? (When they were happy, they wanted to play with him.)
- What does Carla say happens when people feel angry, sad, or afraid? (They don't want to play.)

Carla tells Will about watching for the different ways people look.

> **Will Rabbit:** But how can I tell when it's a good time to ask them to play?
>
> **Carla Bluejay:** You need to use your eyes.
>
> **Will Rabbit:** My eyes?
>
> **Carla Bluejay:** Yes. The way people's faces and bodies look can help you know how they're feeling.

Ask the children:

- Why does Carla say Will needs to use his eyes to know how people feel? (Facial expressions, postures, and gestures help us know how people are feeling.)
- Do you usually know how your friends are feeling?

> **Will Rabbit:** Tell me more, Carla.
>
> **Carla Bluejay:** When people feel angry, their mouth and forehead are scrunched up, their eyebrows are down, their teeth are tight together. Their bodies usually look stiff.
>
> **Will Rabbit:** Yes, Felicia and Benny looked like that when they were arguing.
>
> **Carla Bluejay:** How did they look when they were afraid they'd lost their teacher's book?
>
> **Will Rabbit:** Their eyes were wide and their eyebrows were raised. They huddled together.
>
> **Carla Bluejay:** Sure. And when they felt sad about losing Felicia's ball, I'll bet they frowned and held their heads low. You said they looked like they were about to cry.

Will Rabbit: They did look pretty upset.

Carla Bluejay: But when you passed them that time without speaking, they were smiling and happy.

Will Rabbit: They were. But I didn't know that meant they would play with me.

Carla Bluejay: Sometimes people don't say how they feel. You have to look at them to tell.

Ask the children:

- How does Carla say people look when they're angry? Afraid? Sad? Happy?

- How can knowing this help Will? How can it help you?

> **Will Rabbit:** Well, Carla, I understand what you mean. Right now I can see Felicia and Benny smiling. That means they're probably happy.

Carla Bluejay: Right, Will!

> **Will Rabbit:** Then let's go play with them! No telling how long this will last!

Ask the children:

- Why was Will confused about when Felicia and Benny wanted to play with him? (He didn't know how to interpret their feelings.)

- Why is it important to know how others are feeling? (So we'll know how to behave with people.)

- How do people look when they're happy? Sad? Angry? Afraid?

As appropriate, mention that body language, particularly facial expression, is not always a reliable guide to people's feelings. Sometimes we need to notice what people are doing or saying: arguing, playing a game, looking for something. Explain that sometimes people try to hide how they feel by changing their facial expression. They may smile when they do not want anyone to know that they are unhappy, for example. Remind students that they may need to watch for and read other kinds of body language in addition to facial expressions.

A further point you might make is that we are not always responsible for the ways others behave or respond. As the story illustrates, sometimes people treat others according to how they feel at the moment. You may wish to give other examples of this: A parent upset by an event at work may yell at a child at home, even though the child has done nothing wrong. A usually friendly peer may not want to play one day if the person feels sad about some personal incident. A grandparent may be preoccupied by a health problem and so be inattentive to a child.

Help the children recall what made Felicia Fox and Benny Frog feel angry, sad, and afraid, and how they looked and behaved when they felt like that. Invite them to share their own experiences of realizing or failing to realize how other people were feeling. Then ask them to repeat the following:

When you want to know how others feel . . .

1. Look at the other person's face.

2. Look at the person's body posture.

3. Listen to the person's words.

4. Listen to the person's tone of voice.

Display Posters 2, 3, and 4. Explain that to understand how people feel, it is necessary to consider how they look and what they do as well as what they say. Emphasize that if students learn to identify these nonverbal clues (such as whether or not someone is using the skills illustrated in the posters), they will have fewer misunderstandings with others.

PRACTICE

Will Learns about Feelings Role Play

Materials

Four puppets (Will Rabbit, Carla Bluejay, Felicia Fox, Benny Frog)

Give the puppets to four children and ask them to role-play the events of the story: First, Felicia Fox and Benny Frog angrily argue about whose turn it is to put away toys; when Will tries to play with them, they ignore him. Next, Felicia and Benny sadly search for Felicia's favorite ball; when Will tries to play, they tell him not to bother them. Next, Felicia and Benny fearfully discuss the teacher's book they lost; when Will tries to play, they walk away from him. Finally, Felicia and Benny happily play; Will walks past them, and they call to him to join them. Coach or prompt as needed.

After each encounter, Will and Carla Bluejay discuss what Felicia and Benny were feeling and why they did or didn't want to play. Be sure each feeling is named.

Afterward, discuss with the group how the characters portrayed and named each feeling. Then have the children exchange puppets and role-play again. As time permits, allow each child to take a turn with a puppet. When all have participated, have various children role-play the four feelings again, this time without using puppets. They can use either the story events or another story that you or they devise. Encourage the group to offer the players feedback on the way they portrayed and named their feelings.

Juan's Changing Face

Materials

Blackline Master 9 (Changing Faces)

Preparation

Use the blackline master to make enough "Changing Faces" handouts for each student.

Distribute the "Changing Faces" sheets. Tell the class that you're going to tell a story about a student, Juan, who has many feelings. After each section of the story, you'll ask students to discuss how Juan is feeling and to draw Juan's face as they think it would look in response to events.

Pause after each section of the story to have the children name and draw the feelings involved.

Juan's Changing Face: Part 1

Juan's teacher, Mr. Maguire, is teaching the class to play kickball. Juan is not a good kickball player, and no one wants him on their team. When Mr. Maguire puts Juan on the Blue Team, the team members groan and complain. Juan offers to sit and watch, but Mr. Maguire says he has to play on the Blue Team.

Face-Change 1

> Ask the students to decide how Juan is feeling. Help them conclude that Juan is probably feeling sad. Ask them to draw a sad face.

Juan's Changing Face: Part 2

The game starts. Juan tries his best, but he just can't kick the ball well. He either misses or doesn't kick hard enough. Each time, he makes an out.

Face-Change 2

> Discuss Juan's feelings about not doing well during the game. Help students conclude that Juan probably feels angry. Have them draw an angry face.

Juan's Changing Face: Part 3

The last time Juan played, he got hit by a ball. It hurt. Now Juan sees a ball coming straight at him, kicked by the strongest player in the game.

Face-Change 3

> Discuss how Juan feels when he sees the ball coming at him. Help the students conclude that Juan would feel afraid. Have them draw a fearful face.

Juan's Changing Face: Part 4

Juan manages to get out of the way of the ball. Then another ball comes right to him, and Juan decides not to be afraid of it. He kicks this ball so hard that he falls down and lands right on top of it. Everyone laughs. They all start calling him "Plop-Down Juan."

Face-Change 4

> Discuss Juan's feelings at being teased. Explain that constant teasing is called "bullying" and makes the victim feel very bad. Help them conclude that a person in that situation would

probably feel either sad or angry. Have them draw either a sad or an angry face, depending on which they think Juan feels.

Juan's Changing Face: Part 5

Juan feels so bad about being teased that he runs after the ball and kicks it as hard as he can. It zooms past the other team and into the home-run space. Juan has made the winning point for his team. Everyone cheers and congratulates Juan. Mr. Maguire says Juan is turning into a good kickball player.

Face-Change 5

Have the students discuss Juan's feelings after his winning kick. Help them conclude that he'd be happy. Have them draw a happy face.

Briefly review the five parts of the story and the feeling depicted in each. Ask the children to name each feeling again and to show their drawings. Remind the children that we all have these same emotions of happiness, sadness, anger, and fear. Review with them the importance of knowing how others are feeling. Say that one way we accomplish this is by looking at faces.

Adaptations

1. Concentrate on the sections of the story that depict sadness and happiness.

2. In addition to having the children draw the faces, ask volunteers to pantomime the character's postures and gestures.

3. Encourage the children to depict a wider range of emotions than the four focused on previously—for example, surprise, shame, pride, jealousy, embarrassment.

Pictured Feelings

Materials

Stickers; Blackline Master 7 (How Do Feelings Look?)

Preparation

Secure pictures of people expressing feelings through facial expression, posture, and gesture. You may wish to draw the pictures, or you can cut some from magazines or discarded library books. Have available the "How Do Feelings Look?" sheets.

Show the pictures to the class. Ask or point out which aspect of nonverbal communication is most prominent in each: facial expression, posture, or gesture. Invite the children to describe times when they had specific feelings and can remember their own facial or body expressions.

After discussing each picture, assemble the children in a circle and select a pair to come to the center. Give one child a picture to pantomime; ask the second child to guess the feeling. If the guess is incorrect, give the second student the same illustration to portray, and have the first name the feeling for the group. If the guess is correct, give the second student a new picture to portray. Continue until all children have pantomimed and guessed a feeling.

Give a sticker to each student who correctly connects feelings with body language and facial expression. Tell students who do not earn stickers that they will have other opportunities to practice the skill and receive stickers.

Adaptations

1. Rather than have children guess the emotion being portrayed, you name it, have a child perform it, and then ask the class to repeat the name.

2. Concentrate on one or two simple emotions and repeat the enactments as necessary.

Save the pictures for use in the next activity.

Body–Face Match

Materials

Pictures from previous activity; stickers

Preparation

Cut out the faces from each picture so you have one set of body postures and one set of facial expressions.

As necessary, review the ways each of the four emotions can be shown by facial expression, posture, and gesture. Have children give examples of situations producing those emotions and how their body and face might look in those situations.

Next, show the children the set of facial expressions. Ask them to say which feeling seems to be expressed by each face. Then show the set of body postures. Ask for volunteers to match faces to bodies. Discuss how facial expression, posture, and gesture together express feelings.

If students are quick to label each emotion or feeling as "good" or "bad," help to expand their vocabulary and emotional concepts by accepting those labels as general terms and then helping students define them more precisely.

Give a sticker to each student who correctly connects feelings with body language and facial expression. Tell students who do not earn stickers that they will have other opportunities to practice the skill and receive stickers.

Adaptations

1. Provide magazines or discarded library books and ask students to locate good examples of people expressing emotions.

2. Distribute a set of body illustrations and have the students draw faces with appropriate expressions.

MAINTENANCE

Naming Others' Feelings Every Day

Materials

Stickers

Observe students daily for opportunities to recognize and compliment those who identify and label the emotions of others. As appropriate, ask the children to tell you when they have named someone's feeling and to describe the circumstances. Give a sticker to each student who uses the skill.

Naming Others' Feelings in Literature

Materials

Classroom books and stories such as these:

Aliki. *Feelings*. New York: HarperTrophy, 1986.

Cosgrove, Stephen. *Serendipity: The Gnome from Nome*. Los Angeles: Price Stern Sloan, 2003.

Crary, Elizabeth. *I Want It* (2nd edition). Seattle: Parenting Press, 1996.

Select stories that discuss or feature characters identifying others' feelings. After the children have read or listened to a story, discuss how identifying others' feelings was important to the characters.

Feelings on Television

Characters in some comedy and dramatic series television programs are often sharply drawn and make good subjects for discussing the expression of feelings. Select a popular program and discuss with your students the characters and their usual emotions. Ask the children about the characters' actions, facial expressions, vocabulary, tone of voice, and postures as they express various feelings.

Adaptations

1. Assign students to watch specific television shows for the purpose of identifying the characters' emotions in discussions the following day.

2. Record a program and show it (or part of it) in class so the students can discuss it with each other.

How Do They Feel?

Materials

Magazines, newspapers, discarded picture books

Preparation

Create a bulletin board divided into four sections labeled "Happy People," "Angry People," "Scared People," and "Sad People."

Divide the class into four groups and assign each group to a particular emotion. Have group members look through magazines, newspapers, or discarded picture books for pictures illustrating the emotion that they can cut out and display. Encourage them to look at facial expressions, gestures, and postures.

Adaptations

1. Ask children to write or dictate captions for the illustrations they find.

2. Have group members work cooperatively on collages illustrating their assigned emotion.

4 SENDING MESSAGES

SKILL STEPS: SENDING MESSAGES

1. Think of the message you want to send.
2. Think how your face should look.
3. Think how your hands and body should look.
4. Send your message.

MOTIVATION

Skill Presentation: Will's Ice Cream Hat

Materials

   Two puppets (Will Rabbit, Shelli Squirrel); Posters 2, 3, 4

Introduce the two puppets. Tell students that you're going to present a story about these characters called "Will's Ice Cream Hat." Ask the children to listen carefully.

Will Rabbit knocks Shelli Squirrel down, trying to say, "I like you" with a hug.

Will Rabbit: Why, there's my good friend Shelli walking home from school. How can she carry all those books and papers in one hand? I guess her other hand's busy, holding that yummy-looking ice cream cone. Shelli is such a good friend. I'm going to give her a hug.

Shelli Squirrel: Will Rabbit, what are you trying to do? You knocked me down, got my clothes dirty, and made us both drop all our papers and books. And my ice cream cone is now on your head! You have an ice cream hat!

Will Rabbit: Oh, Shelli, I'm sorry. I was only trying to say, "I like you" with a hug.

Ask the children:

- Why did Will Rabbit knock Shelli Squirrel down? (Trying to hug her.)

- Do you think this was a good time for Will to hug Shelli?

Shelli tells Will about other ways to say, "I like you."

Shelli Squirrel: It isn't a good idea to run up and hug someone when their arms are full and they can't hug you back. Just look at the mess you made.

Will Rabbit: But I like to hug!

Shelli Squirrel: A hug is a good way to say, "I like you." But if you want to hug someone, wait until their arms are empty. Then hold out your arms to offer a hug.

Will Rabbit: But your arms were full. Does that mean I shouldn't hug you?

Shelli Squirrel: If someone has full arms, you should wait for a better time to hug. Or you could use a different way to show you like them.

Will Rabbit: Like what?

Ask the children:

- What else do you think Will could have done to show he liked Shelli?

Shelli and Will discuss appropriate and inappropriate ways to show feelings.

Shelli Squirrel: You could have shown me you like me by offering to help me, or waving, or patting me nicely on the shoulder.

Will Rabbit: How can I tell what to do? Should I hug, or help, or wave, or pat?

Shelli Squirrel: You have to look and pay attention to what the other person is doing. You know, Will, this isn't the first time you've used the wrong way to show your feelings.

Will Rabbit: I know, I know.

Shelli Squirrel: Like yesterday in class when the teacher asked if you wanted to collect the milk money. You shook your head no. But you didn't mean it.

Will Rabbit: I meant to nod yes. I love to collect money!

Shelli Squirrel: And why did you wave goodbye to Shelli Squirrel when you wanted her to come get her toy that you found?

Will Rabbit: I don't know; I did want her to come.

Shelli Squirrel: And I couldn't understand why you were frowning during our song time. I thought you liked singing.

Will Rabbit: I do. I meant to smile. I just get all mixed up sometimes. Nobody understands what I mean.

Ask the children:

- What happens to Will when he uses the wrong way of showing his feelings? (No one understands what he means.)

- Do you ever have this problem? Do your friends always understand what you mean?

Shelli tells Will how to send accurate messages.

Shelli Squirrel: Will Rabbit, I think you need to learn how to send messages!

Will Rabbit: Messages? You mean like when we play "Telegraph"?

Shelli Squirrel: Sort of. You need to be sure your face and body are saying what you mean.

Will Rabbit: But how can I be sure?

Shelli Squirrel: First, think of the message you want to send.

Will Rabbit: "I like you"?

Shelli Squirrel: Yes. Then think of how your face, hands, and body should look when you send your message. Then send the message.

Will Rabbit: Lots of thinking! But I'd sure like it if my friends understood what I was feeling.

Shelli Squirrel: We all want to send the right messages about our feelings. We all need to think first.

Ask the children:

- How does Shelli say Will can learn to send the right messages about his feelings? (Be sure the steps of the skill are mentioned: think of the message you want to send, think how your face should look, think how your hands and body should look, send your message.)

- Why does Shelli say we need to think before we send messages about our feelings? (To decide how our face, hands, and body should look; so people will understand what we're feeling.)

Will Rabbit: Good advice, Shelli. Maybe if I see you with your arms full again, I'll wave.

Shelli Squirrel: That would be fine, Will. Now please help me pick up these books and papers.

Will Rabbit: Okay. Then we could go get ice cream cones together.

Shelli Squirrel: Maybe tomorrow. But first, now that our arms are empty—how about a nice hug!

Ask the children:

- Why did Will Rabbit have trouble showing how he felt? (He didn't know how to send messages.)
- How did this problem make Will feel?
- What steps did Shelli teach Will?

Review the skill steps, asking the children to repeat each one:

1. Think of the message you want to send.
2. Think how your face should look.

3. Think how your hands and body should look.

4. Use your face and body to send your message.

Ask the children to tell about situations in which they didn't know how to show their feelings.

Display Posters 2, 3, and 4. Explain that to send accurate messages, students need to think about how their face, hands, and body should look and how their voice should sound. Display the posters during the remaining activities, using them to prompt or cue children as needed.

PRACTICE

Will's Ice Cream Hat Role Play

Materials

Two puppets (Will Rabbit, Shelli Squirrel)

Give the puppets to two children and have them role-play the events of the story: Will Rabbit runs to hug Shelli Squirrel while her arms are full; he knocks her down; she expresses her feelings about what he's done and suggests some other ways he could show he likes her; he asks how he can tell which message to send; she gives him the skill steps. Coach and prompt the children as necessary.

After the role play, discuss how the players presented the story. Then have the two actors exchange roles and role-play again. As time permits, allow each child to take a turn with a puppet. When all have participated, have various children role-play sending messages, this time without using puppets. They can use either the story events or another story that you or they devise. Encourage the group to offer the players feedback on the way they presented the skill.

Saying without Talking

Materials

Stickers

Explain that the group will practice sending messages without talking. Demonstrate saying, "I like you" by giving someone a hug. Then present various messages and have the children convey each nonverbally. After practicing as a group, ask individual children to respond.

Give a sticker to each student who sends an accurate message. Tell students who do not earn stickers that they will have other opportunities to practice the steps and receive stickers.

Suggested messages:

1. Hello or goodbye
2. Yes or no
3. I'm happy or I'm sad
4. Come here or go away
5. Ouch!
6. Stop!
7. I don't know
8. Maybe or maybe not
9. I'm sleepy
10. I'm surprised

Adaptations

1. Ask children to express messages, first verbally, then nonverbally.
2. Ask children to create their own list of messages as an independent activity and later share their nonverbal communication ideas with the rest of the class.

Signing Time

Make your students aware of a commonly used method of nonverbal communication by inviting a teacher of children with hearing impairments into your class to teach some simple signing.

MAINTENANCE

Sending Messages Every Day

Materials

Stickers

Observe students daily for opportunities to recognize and compliment those who use appropriate nonverbal communication. As appropriate, ask the children to tell you when they have used the skill and to describe what they did. Give a sticker to each student who uses the skill.

Sending Messages in Literature

Materials

Classroom books and stories such as these:

Ashman, Linda. *M Is for Mischief.* New York: Dutton, 2008.

Ets, Marie Hall. *Just Me.* New York: Penguin, 1978.

Henkes, Kevin. *Lilly's Purple Plastic Purse.* New York: Greenwillow, 1996.

Keats, Ezra Jack. *Whistle for Willie.* New York: Penguin, 1977.

Verdick, Elizabeth. *Teeth Are Not for Biting.* Minneapolis: Free Spirit Publishing, 2004.

Select stories that discuss or feature characters using nonverbal communication. After the children have read or listened to a story, discuss how nonverbal communication was important to the characters.

Message Time

Preparation

Make a portable sign that says "Message Time" or that illustrates the concept. Decide when during the day you will conduct this activity. You may wish to vary the time each day so that children get a variety of nonverbal communication experiences.

Show students the Message Time sign. Explain that every day when you post this sign, the class will begin Message Time. During Message Time, you will set aside about 15 minutes during which all regular activities will be conducted using only nonverbal communication. Explain that everyone, including you, will express their messages without talking. If you are teaching, you will do so by pointing, writing, showing pictures, and making gestures. If students have questions, they may write or pantomime them.

After each Message Time, conduct a brief discussion about the messages sent and received.

Adaptation

Shorten Message Time to 5 or 10 minutes. Provide frequent reminders that Message Time is in effect. Couple the Message Time notice with an audible signal such as a bell or buzzer.

Class Signals

Preparation

Title a bulletin board "Class Signals."

Help the children devise nonverbal signals that the class can use for specific messages and activities. Some signals might be relatively universal, such as raising a hand to signal a desire to talk. Others might be unique to your class. Holding a pencil straight up, for example, may be designated to mean "I need to sharpen my pencil," and holding a pencil sideways might mean "I am finished with my seat work." Once various signals are agreed upon, list and perhaps illustrate them on the bulletin board. Encourage students to use the class signals whenever possible.

Adaptations

1. Provide frequent reminders of the signals and lots of practice using them.
2. Have the children make a Class Signals chart as a group project.

SKILL
5 CONTROLLING TEMPER

SKILL STEPS: CONTROLLING TEMPER
1. Stop what you are doing.
2. Take five deep breaths.
3. Count to 10.
4. Think about the right thing to do.
5. Do the right thing.

MOTIVATION

Skill Presentation: Benny Frog Gets Cool

Materials

Three puppets (Benny Frog, Will Rabbit, Hank Hawk)

Introduce the three puppets. Tell students that you're going to present a story about these characters called "Benny Frog Gets Cool." Ask the children to listen carefully.

Benny Frog gets angry during a game of tag.

Benny Frog: You ninny! You clumsy birdbrain!

Will Rabbit: I'm sorry, Benny. Since I'm "It," I was reaching out to tag you, but I tripped and fell on you instead. I didn't mean to hurt you.

Benny Frog: Well, it did hurt. Why don't you watch what you're doing? You're always wrecking my games. I hate playing tag with you!

Will Rabbit: Benny!

Benny Frog: Featherhead! Furry buffoon! Nincompoop! (*Pause.*) Hey, where are you going, Will? Come back!

Ask the children:

- How is Benny Frog feeling? (Angry.)
- How is he showing his anger? (Yelling, calling Will Rabbit names.)
- How do you think Will Rabbit feels when Benny calls him names? What does Will do? (He leaves.)
- What do you do when you're angry? What happens when you do this?

Hank Hawk tells Benny that he's hurt Will's feelings.

Hank Hawk: Hello, Benny. What's all the racket?

Benny Frog: Hi, Hank. Do you know where Will Rabbit went? I want to play tag with him.

Hank Hawk: Yes, I've seen him, Benny. But I don't think he wants to play with you now.

Benny Frog: Oh, I'm not mad at him now. I was mad before, but now I'm not.

Hank Hawk: Will doesn't know that. And he probably won't play with you for a while.

Benny Frog: Why not?

Hank Hawk: Because when you got mad, you called him names and hurt his feelings. When you hurt someone's feelings they can stay hurt for a long time. That's why you should learn to "get cool."

Ask the children:

- Why does Hank Hawk say that Will doesn't want to play with Benny? (Benny hurt Will's feelings.)

- What do you think Hank means when he tells Benny to "get cool"?

Hank tells Benny what it means to "get cool."

> **Benny Frog:** "Get cool"? What does that mean?
>
> **Hank Hawk:** It means that when you're angry, you need to take time to cool off.
>
> **Benny Frog:** Is getting angry bad? I get angry a lot!
>
> **Hank Hawk:** No, getting angry isn't bad. But when you get angry, you need to learn not to hurt anyone, including yourself. You need to control your strong feelings.

Ask the children:

- Does Hank say it's bad that Benny gets angry? (No.)
- What does Benny need to learn? (Not to hurt anyone when he's angry, to control his strong feelings.)

Hank teaches Benny the first steps of controlling his temper, and Benny practices.

> **Benny Frog:** How can I learn to control my temper?
>
> **Hank Hawk:** When something makes you angry, first stop what you're doing. Then take five deep breaths and count to 10.
>
> **Benny Frog:** Why should I do that?
>
> **Hank Hawk:** Because it will help you relax and think about what to do.

Ask the children:

- What does Hank say is the first step in "getting cool"? (Stop what you're doing.)
- Then what? (Take five deep breaths and count to 10.)
- Why does Hank say Benny should do this? (To help him relax and think about what to do.)

> **Hank Hawk:** Why don't you try it now?

Benny Frog: Okay. Like this? *(Takes five deep breaths.)* And this? 1, 2, 3, 4, 5, 6, 7, 8, 9, 10.

Hank Hawk: Yes. Then, after you do that, think about the right thing to do. What would have been the right thing to do when you were angry with Will?

Benny Frog: Well, he did say he was sorry. I guess he really didn't mean to fall on me.

Hank Hawk: So what should you have done?

Benny Frog: Is this the time to "get cool?"

Hank Hawk: Yes.

Benny Frog: Then I should have taken five breaths and counted to 10 and tried to think of the right thing to do.

Hank Hawk: Yes. After you think about the right thing to do, you do the right thing. What might have happened if you'd done the right thing with Will?

Benny Frog: I wouldn't have hurt Will's feelings. We'd still be playing tag.

Ask the children:

- What does Hank say Benny should do after he counts to 10? (Think about the right thing to do.)
- Then what? (Do the right thing.)
- What might have happened if Benny had done the right thing with Will? (He wouldn't have hurt Will's feelings, and they would still be playing together.)

Benny apologizes to Will and promises to use his new skill.

Benny Frog: What do I do now? I still want to play tag with Will.

Hank Hawk: Maybe you need to tell him you're sorry. There he is, sitting by himself.

Benny Frog: I'll try. *(Pause.)* Hello, Will. I'm really sorry about yelling at you.

Will Rabbit: You hurt my feelings!

Benny Frog: I know. Hank Hawk explained it to me. He's been showing me how to control my temper.

Will Rabbit: That's something you need to learn.

Benny Frog: Will you play tag with me again so I can practice the steps? I'm sure to get mad at least once!

Will Rabbit: Well, okay. But this is your last chance.

Benny Frog: Thanks, Will. I'm ready. Now . . . you're "It"!

Ask the children:

- How did Will Rabbit feel after Benny Frog couldn't control his temper and yelled at him? Do you think Benny wanted Will to feel this way?
- What steps did Hank teach Benny?

Review the skill steps, asking the children to repeat each one:

1. Stop what you are doing.
2. Take five deep breaths.
3. Count to 10.
4. Think about the right thing to do.
5. Do the right thing.

As appropriate, conduct a brief discussion on "doing the right thing." Explain that this means we don't hurt anyone, we don't say mean things to anyone, and we try to be fair. Illustrate with a simple example: Suppose someone takes your ball. What would be the right thing to do? You might ask the person to return the ball, ask the person to play with you, tell the person why you're angry, or tell the teacher (if necessary). Help students understand that each of these options fulfills the criteria of "the right thing."

Make sure students understand that there's nothing wrong with getting angry. It is important, however, not to hurt anyone or anything when we're angry. Ask the children to tell about situations in which they got angry and hurt someone else's feelings. Discuss how else they might have shown their anger.

PRACTICE

Benny Frog Gets Cool Role Play

Materials

Three puppets (Benny Frog, Will Rabbit, Hank Hawk)

Give the puppets to three children and ask them to role-play the events of the story: Benny Frog and Will Rabbit play tag. Will trips and falls on Benny. Benny has a temper tantrum. Will leaves. Hank Hawk enters and tells Benny to "get cool." He explains the steps of controlling temper, and Benny practices each step. Then Benny apologizes to Will. Coach and prompt the children as necessary. If you prefer not to have children role-play inappropriate behavior, take the role of Benny Frog yourself.

After the role play, discuss how the characters portrayed the scene. Then have the children exchange puppets and role-play again. As time permits, allow each child to take a turn with a puppet. When all have participated, have various children role-play controlling their temper, this time without using puppets. They can use either the story events or another story that you or they devise. Encourage the group to offer the players feedback on the way they performed the skill.

Let Me Get Cool

Materials

Stickers

Have students role-play controlling their temper in the following situations or in others they suggest. Before beginning, remind children of the skill steps and tell them to watch for the steps in the role plays. After each role play, discuss how the skill was performed.

Give a sticker to each student who performs the skill steps adequately. Tell students who do not earn stickers that they will have other opportunities to practice the steps and receive stickers.

Sample situations

1. Someone bumps into you accidentally.

2. A classmate throws a pencil to someone, and it hits you instead.

3. Your brother throws away your homework, mistakenly thinking it's rubbish.

4. While you're painting a picture, a classmate takes the jar of yellow paint.

5. Your teacher says you'll have to stay inside during recess to finish your work.

6. An older student takes your dessert every day at lunch.

High Tower

Materials

Stackable blocks; stickers

Assemble the students in a circle, either on the floor or around a table, with the blocks in the middle. Explain that they're going to play a game to help them practice controlling their tempers. They are to use the blocks to make as tall a tower as they can without any blocks falling. Tell them that if something happens to make the tower fall, they are to go through the steps of controlling their temper (even if they aren't really angry). Demonstrate by building a tower, asking a student to knock it down, and then going through the skill steps yourself.

As the children build towers, move about the group, bumping the table, blocks, or students' arms if the towers aren't falling on their own. Prompt the children to practice the steps of controlling their tempers.

Give a sticker to each student who performs the skill steps adequately. Tell students who do not earn stickers that they will have other opportunities to practice the steps and receive stickers.

Adaptation

To make the tower-building more challenging, use irregularly shaped blocks or designate that only the smallest block can be used for the base.

MAINTENANCE

Controlling Temper Every Day

Materials

Stickers

Observe students daily for opportunities to recognize and compliment those who control their temper. As appropriate, ask the children to tell you when they have used the skill and to describe what they said and did. Give a sticker to each student who uses the skill.

Controlling Temper in Literature

Materials

Classroom books and stories such as these:

Blaine, Marge. *The Terrible Thing That Happened at Our House.* New York: Scholastic, 1983.

Curtis, Jamie Lee. *It's Hard to Be Five.* New York: Joanna Cotler, 2004.

Riley, Susan. *Angry (Thoughts and Feelings).* Elgin, IL: Child's World, 1999.

Sharmat, Marjorie Weinman. *Walter the Wolf.* New York: Holiday House, 1996.

Verdick, Elizabeth. *Feet Are Not for Kicking.* Minneapolis: Free Spirit Publishing, 2004.

Wiseman, Bernard. *Morris and Boris.* New York: Putnam Publishing Group, 1979.

Select stories that discuss or feature characters controlling their temper. After the children have read or listened to a story, discuss how controlling temper was important to the characters.

Temper Control Helpers

Materials

Blackline Master 4 (Badges)

Preparation

Use the blackline master to make several badges. Write "Temper Control Helper" or draw a picture on each. Attach double-stick tape or safety pins to the backs.

Select several capable children to be the first Temper Control Helpers. Give them badges. Tell the class that these helpers will be looking for opportunities to help people control their tempers. When a helper sees someone who appears to be losing control, she or he will take the angry student through the steps of the skill.

At this point, review the skill steps for everyone. Mention that the helpers will help angry students decide on the right thing to do (Step 5). As necessary, allow the helpers to role-play what they will say and do.

Monitor and assist the helpers as needed. At the end of the day, discuss with the children how well the skill was practiced; review the skill steps. Then designate several new helpers for the next day—preferably, children who successfully controlled their tempers today.

Adaptation

Have helpers call you over as soon as they see someone who needs to practice anger control. Coach both helper and angry student as needed.

UNIT
3

EXPRESSING ONESELF

As children develop, they need to recognize their own and others' emotions, understand that feelings are universal and valid, and learn ways to express their feelings appropriately. Children who fail to learn appropriate means for expressing their feelings often find themselves in conflict with others. Expressing anger, for example, in aggressive and abusive ways tends to be both counterproductive and self-defeating.

Telling others how we feel is often difficult; however, such expression offers the benefits of releasing pent-up emotions and frustrations, making way for renewed relationships and experiences. Many children are not encouraged to express themselves, nor have their feelings been accepted by the significant people in their lives. They may either keep their feelings inside or express themselves in nonproductive or antisocial ways. Even children who have been encouraged to express themselves verbally can find themselves in conflict with peers if their expressions are often aggressive. Children rarely learn appropriate, nonaggressive expression of feelings "accidentally"; they need specific instruction in assertive, constructive verbal and nonverbal communication.

Skills taught in this unit include the following:

- Making Positive Self-Statements
- Making Positive Statements to Others
- Expressing Feelings
- Speaking Kindly and Using Courtesy Words
- Speaking Assertively

Special Issues

In addition to avoiding conflict, appropriate self-expressions can help to establish and improve personal relationships. Positive communication, which includes pleasant greetings, compliments, and the use of courtesy words, is useful in evoking positive responses in others, thereby leading to a positive interaction cycle. Children can be helped to identify the statements made by others that make them feel warm and happy, and, in turn, children can learn to make similar expressions under the appropriate circumstances.

The ultimate goal is for children to understand that positive relationships, which are much more productive in helping us achieve socially appropriate objectives, can be attained and fostered most easily through appropriate social communication skills. The activities in this unit provide practice in these important skills.

> *Taking Part stickers are used as incentives for skill step performance and skill use in practice and maintenance activities throughout this unit. You may wish to distribute copies of Blackline Master 2 (My Taking Part Sticker Collection), which gives students a handy place to store the stickers they earn.*

SKILL

1 MAKING POSITIVE SELF-STATEMENTS

> ### SKILL STEPS:
> ### MAKING POSITIVE SELF-STATEMENTS
>
> 1. Think of what you like to do.
> 2. Think of what you can do well.
> 3. Tell someone.

MOTIVATION

Skill Presentation: Benny's Special Croak

Materials

> Four puppets (Hank Hawk, Benny Frog, Will Rabbit, Carla Bluejay)

Introduce the four puppets. Tell students that you're going to present a story about these characters called "Benny's Special Croak." Ask the children to listen carefully.

Hank Hawk tells Benny Frog he isn't important because all he does is croak.

> **Hank Hawk:** Hey, Benny, don't you ever do anything except croak?
>
> **Benny Frog:** Nope. Croaking is what I do best.
>
> **Hank Hawk:** Well, croaking isn't very important. Look at me. I fly high, and I can see everything. That is very important. You should learn how to fly like me.

Benny Frog: I would like to be more important. Can you teach me how to fly?

Hank Hawk: Sure. Climb onto this high rock, stretch out your legs, and jump.

Benny Frog: Ouch! Hank, this hurts too much. I don't think I can learn to fly.

Hank Hawk: Well, if you don't want to be important, I can't help you. *(Leaves.)*

Benny Frog: Ouch, I'm so sore! What I like to do and what I do well is croak! That's enough for me!

Ask the children:

- Why does Hank Hawk say Benny Frog isn't important? (All he does is croak.)
- Why does Benny ask Hank to teach him to fly? (So he'll be important.)
- Have you ever wished you could do something someone else can do? If you couldn't do it, how did you feel?
- What does Benny tell himself after Hank leaves? (Croaking is good enough for him.)

Will Rabbit says Benny Frog isn't special because all he does is croak.

Will Rabbit: Hey, Benny, croaking is all you ever do. That's not special. Why don't you learn to hop fast like I can? I can get anywhere in a flash. That is special.

Benny Frog: Hmmm. I would like to be special. Can you teach me how to hop fast?

Will Rabbit: Sure. Just follow me.

Benny Frog: *(Gasping.)* I can't do this anymore. I have to get back to the pond.

Will Rabbit: Well, if you don't want to be special, I can't help you. *(Leaves.)*

Benny Frog: Why did I try to be someone I'm not? I like to croak, and I'm good at croaking, and that's good enough for me!

Ask the children:

- Why does Will Rabbit say Benny Frog isn't special? (All he does is croak.)
- Why does Benny ask Will to teach him to hop fast? (So he'll be special.)
- What does Benny tell himself after Will leaves? (Croaking is good enough for him.)

Benny Frog's loud croaking saves Carla Bluejay.

Benny Frog: What's that big splash I just heard? Oh, no! Carla Bluejay has fallen out of her nest into the pond! *(Croaks loudly.)*

Carla Bluejay: Help! Help! I can't swim!

Will Rabbit: I heard you croaking, Benny. What's wrong!

Benny Frog: Carla's fallen in the water! Quick, go get Hank!

Will Rabbit: I'll be back in a flash! *(Will Rabbit leaves but quickly returns with Hank Hawk.)*

Benny Frog: Hank, quick! Save Carla!

Hank Hawk: Here I go!

Carla Bluejay: Oh, thank you, Hank. You saved my life.

Hank Hawk: You're welcome. But you should also thank Will. He came hopping to get me.

Carla Bluejay: Thank you, Will, thank you! Thank you for hopping to get Hank.

Will Rabbit: You're welcome, Carla. But most of all, you should thank Benny. He croaked so loudly that I came running to see what was the matter.

Carla Bluejay: Well, Benny, I guess you are the most important, most special animal of all. It was your croaking that really saved me. Thank you so much.

Hank Hawk: Yes, Benny. That was great croaking. I guess you don't have to hop fast or fly to be important and special.

Will Rabbit: Hank's right, Benny. But I have a feeling you always knew what you were really good at.

Benny Frog: I did. You and Hank made me sad when you said I wasn't important or special. But I told myself something that made me feel better.

Ask the children:

- How does Benny say he felt when Hank and Will told him he wasn't important or special? (Sad.)

- What did Benny tell himself that made him feel better? (He likes croaking, he's good at croaking.)

- What could you tell yourself about what you like to do? How would saying that help you feel better?

Benny tells his friends about positive self-statements.

Will Rabbit: Sounds like you have something to teach us. How can we make ourselves feel good about what we do well?

Benny Frog: You can think about what you like to do, think about what you do well, and tell someone about it. I like to croak, I'm good at croaking, and I want everyone to know it!

Ask the children:

- What does Benny say the others could do to help themselves feel good? (Be sure the steps of the skill are mentioned: think about what you like to do, think about what you can do well, tell someone.)

Will Rabbit: Good for you and for all of us, Benny Frog!

Benny Frog: Croak!

Ask the children:

- What did Benny Frog do to make himself feel good? (Told himself what he does well.)

- What steps did he teach his friends?

Review the skill steps, asking the children to repeat each one:

1. Think of what you like to do.

2. Think of what you can do well.

3. Tell someone.

As appropriate, discuss with the children the value of knowing how to make yourself feel good, especially when others say you aren't important or special. Point out that everyone has something he or she does well and can be proud of; it's not necessary to be like everyone else.

You may wish to mention that the difference between bragging and making positive self-statements is intent. The intent of bragging is usually to act superior to others as a way of making them feel bad. The intent of positive self-statements is self-affirmation and self-awareness. Children need to understand that they can be proud of the things they do well without demeaning others.

Invite the children to tell about times others made them feel bad or unimportant. Ask them how this skill might have helped them feel better about themselves.

PRACTICE

Benny's Special Croak Role Play

Materials

Four puppets (Hank Hawk, Benny Frog, Will Rabbit, Carla Bluejay)

Give the puppets to four children and ask them to role-play the events of the story: Hank Hawk and Will Rabbit each tell Benny Frog he isn't important or special. Then Carla Bluejay falls in the pond and Benny croaks loudly to get Will's attention. Will runs to get Hank, who saves Carla. Then Benny tells the others about positive self-statements. Coach or prompt the children as needed.

After the role play, discuss how the skill was presented. Then ask the children to exchange puppets and role-play again. As time permits, allow each child to take a turn with a puppet. When all have participated, have various children role-play making positive self-statements, this time without using puppets. They can use either the story events or another story that you or they devise. Encourage the group to offer the players feedback on the way they performed the skill.

PRACTICE

I'm Okay on the Phone

Materials

> Two real or toy telephones, or two drawn or cut-out pictures of telephones and two pieces of heavy cardboard; stickers

Preparation

> If you're using pictures of phones, glue each to heavy cardboard.

Ask the children to form two lines, Line A and Line B, and have each line stand near a telephone. Explain that students in each line will take turns "calling" each other to say something positive about themselves.

Explain the procedure: The first person in Line A (Player A) calls the first person in Line B (Player B) and says, "Hello, ____. How are you today?" Player B answers, "I'm okay because . . ." completing the sentence with a positive self-statement. For example, ". . . because I'm a good dancer."

Player A then echoes Player B's positive self-statement and adds a positive self-statement: "I'm glad you're okay because you're a good dancer. I'm okay because I can draw a cow." Player B then echoes Player A's self-statement: "I'm glad you're okay because you can draw a cow."

Player B then hands the phone to the person next in line, who calls the person next in line behind Player A, and so on. Repeat the activity until each student has made a positive self-statement and repeated someone else's statement.

Help students with their self-statements by asking such questions as "Who is a good runner?" "Who can make cookies?" "Who helps take care of a younger brother or sister?" "Who does well in math?" "Who always gets homework in on time?"

Give a sticker to each student who makes a positive self-statement. Tell students who do not earn stickers that they will have other opportunities to practice the steps and receive stickers.

Adaptations

1. Decrease the dialogue requirements by, for example, having the first player call and ask for a classmate, who answers with a "hello" and a single positive statement.

2. Work with students to write "I'm Okay on the Phone" scripts, including several positive self-statements they can use when repeating the activity.

3. When you repeat the activity, focus on a specific topic or skill area. Personal appearance, school subjects, hobbies, interpersonal skills, and athletics are all appropriate topics for positive self-statements.

I'm a Star

Materials

Real or toy microphone or object to represent one (such as the wooden end of a jump-rope); stickers

Using the microphone, introduce each student individually as a "star" of television, recordings, or movies, using the student's own name. Then ask the "star" to make one or two positive self-statements. For example: "I'd like to introduce Pam, world-famous television star, who's here to tell us why she's so famous. Pam, can you tell us two good things about yourself?" Pass the microphone to the student. After the positive self-statements, have the class applaud. Continue with another student until every child has had a turn.

Give a sticker to each student who makes a positive self-statement. Tell students who do not earn stickers that they will have other opportunities to practice the steps and receive stickers.

Adaptation

Help students write "I'm a Star" scripts, including several positive self-statements they can use in the activity.

Something I Do Well

Materials

Stickers

Arrange students in a circle so they can speak easily to each other. Tell them you're going to give them some ideas for good things they can say about themselves. Present various familiar activities. For each, have one or more students give a positive self-statement.

Possible activities:

1. Riding a bicycle

2. Finishing a book

3. Learning a new song

4. Helping your family

5. Helping your teacher

6. Helping a friend

7. Making a friend

Give a sticker to each student who makes a positive self-statement. Tell students who do not earn stickers that they will have other opportunities to practice the steps and receive stickers.

Adaptations

1. Concentrate on activities from that day.

2. Have children draw pictures of their activities and then write or dictate a positive self-statement about their drawing.

3. For each topic, encourage children to recall several things about which they are justifiably proud. Ask them to share these experiences with their peers as well as with you. You may want to assign a brief essay about a given topic.

Let My Friends Know

Arrange students in a circle. Present an easy, familiar academic task, such as identifying numerals, letters, or sight words. Tell students that they are each going to give a positive statement about themselves after they respond to your questions.

Ask each student something you're sure he or she will be able to answer; coach as needed. Direct the student to answer and then to make a positive statement about being right. You might suggest general statements, such as "I'm good at math," or ask each student to think of an original self-statement.

After each self-statement, lead the rest of the group in a "silent cheer." For example, have everyone wave their hands, give a thumbs-up salute, or clasp their hands and shake them above their heads.

MAINTENANCE

Making Positive Self-Statements Every Day

Materials

Stickers; Blackline Master 1 (Individual Social Skills Checklist, optional)

Observe students daily for opportunities to recognize and compliment those who make positive statements about themselves. As appropriate, ask the children to tell you when they have used the skill and to describe what they said. Give a sticker to each student who uses the skill.

You may wish to use the Individual Social Skills Checklist to record students' progress in this unit's skills.

Making Positive Self-Statements in Literature

Materials

Classroom books and stories such as these:

Appelt, Kathi. *Incredible Me!* New York: HarperCollins, 2003.

Cosgrove, Stephen. *Flutterby.* Los Angeles: Price Stern Sloan, 1995.

Cosgrove, Stephen. *Leo the Lop: Tail Two.* Los Angeles: Price Stern Sloan, 2002.

Curtis, Jamie Lee. *Today I Feel Silly and Other Moods That Make My Day.* New York: Joanna Cotler, 1998.

Murelle, Diane. *Oliver Onion: The Onion Who Learns to Accept.* Shawnees Mission, KS: Autism Asperger Publishing, 2004.

Sharmat, Marjorie Weinman. *I'm Terrific.* New York: Holiday House, 1992.

Select stories that discuss or feature characters making positive self-statements. After the children have read or listened to a story, discuss how making positive self-statements was important to the characters.

Something to Croak About

Materials

Puppet (Benny Frog)

Introduce the puppet and remind students of the story "Benny's Special Croak." Tell them they'll each get a chance to "croak" about something, as Benny Frog did. Ask them to think about one accomplishment of which they are particularly proud. It may or may not have happened that day.

Pass the puppet around the group and have each student take a turn using it as a mask and telling about an achievement. Tell students to use the form, "I have something to croak about. Once I . . ." (If your students seem fearful of or intimidated by using the puppet as a mask, have them simply hold up the puppet.)

Help with self-statements by modeling them or by supplying hints to students based on what you know about them.

Repeat the activity every day, involving either the whole group or several students at a time.

Adaptation

After the activity, reinforce the positive self-statements by creating a bulletin board entitled "I Have Something to Croak About." Display the puppet and leave room for index cards to be posted nearby. Distribute cards and ask each child to write a self-statement, sign it, and display it near the puppet. Children may also draw pictures or dictate their statements.

Graphically Great

Preparation

Set up a bulletin board called "Graphically Great," with space for four or five bar graphs. Across the bottom, label four or five activities pertinent to your class. You might choose academic skills that most students are near mastering or nonacademic activities such as bike riding, fun with friends, fun with family, helping. Make paper rectangles with students' names on them and double-stick tape on the back, several for each student.

Ask each child to make a positive self-statement about one of the topics on the board. As children make their statements, add their rectangles to the categories they choose, thus forming the bars. Repeat the process at other times and watch the graph grow.

SKILL

2 MAKING POSITIVE STATEMENTS TO OTHERS

> ### SKILL STEPS: MAKING POSITIVE STATEMENTS TO OTHERS
>
> 1. Look at the person.
> 2. Find something nice about how the person looks or what the person is doing.
> 3. Tell the person.

MOTIVATION

Skill Presentation: Felicia Learns to Be Positive

Materials

> Four puppets (Shelli Squirrel, Felicia Fox, Hank Hawk, Carla Bluejay); Posters 1, 2, 3

Introduce the four puppets. Tell students that you're going to present a story about these characters called "Felicia Learns to Be Positive." Ask the children to listen carefully.

Felicia Fox says mean things to Shelli Squirrel and Hank Hawk.

Shelli Squirrel: Hi, Felicia. On your way to school?

> **Felicia Fox:** Yes, and I hope I get there quick. It looks like rain, and I'm wearing new clothes.

Shelli Squirrel: I see that. You look very nice.

Felicia Fox: I do, don't I? But your shirt really looks dumb. Why didn't you put on a new shirt?

Shelli Squirrel: I . . . I . . . Oh, go away, Felicia!

Felicia Fox: What's the matter with her? (*Pause.*) Hank, what happened to your shoes? Don't you have new ones? Those are so old and ugly.

Hank Hawk: I . . . I . . . You be quiet, Felicia!

Felicia Fox: What's the matter?

Hank Hawk: Stay away from me!

Ask the children:

- Why do Shelli Squirrel and Hank Hawk tell Felicia to get away from them? (She says mean things, she hurts their feelings.)

- How do Shelli and Hank feel when Felicia is mean to them? (Angry, hurt, sad.)

- Do you ever make your friends angry or hurt when you talk to them?

Felicia is mean to Carla Bluejay, who tells her about making positive statements to others.

Carla Bluejay: Hello, Felicia.

Felicia Fox: Oh, hello, Carla. Is that your art project? I have mine, too. Look!

Carla Bluejay: That's pretty, Felicia.

Felicia Fox: Yours sure isn't, Carla! Those colors are ugly, and that duck looks more like a pig!

Carla Bluejay: You are the meanest fox I've ever met, Felicia! I'm not going to walk with you!

Felicia Fox: (*Crying.*) Oh, everyone hates me! You won't walk with me. Shelli won't walk with me. Hank won't walk with me. No one in school will even talk to me!

Carla Bluejay: Well, what do you expect, Felicia Fox? You say nasty things to people and make them feel bad.

Felicia Fox: What do you mean, Carla? I only said what I thought.

Carla Bluejay: But what you said wasn't nice, Carla. It hurt my feelings. If you want to get along with others, you'd better learn how to say nice things to people so they'll feel good.

Ask the children:

- How does Felicia feel about the way people treat her? (Sad.)
- What does Carla Bluejay tell Felicia she needs to learn? (How to say nice things to people so they will feel good.)
- Why is it important to say nice things to others?

Felicia Fox: What am I doing wrong?

Carla Bluejay: How do people usually look when you say things to them?

Felicia Fox: They look sad. Or angry.

Carla Bluejay: Yes. And what do they do?

Felicia Fox: They either yell at me or go away from me.

Carla Bluejay: Right. But when you say nice things to people, they feel good. They look happy. They want to be around you.

Ask the children:

- How does Felicia say her friends look when she says unkind things to them? (Sad, angry.)
- What do her friends do? (Yell at her, go away from her.)
- What does Carla say will happen if Felicia learns to say nice things to people? (They'll feel good, they'll look happy, they'll want to be around her.)

Carla Tells Felicia how to make positive statements to others.

Felicia Fox: I see what you mean. How can I make people feel good?

Carla Bluejay: By looking for things that people do well and telling them about those things—not about things you don't like. You feel good when someone says something nice to you, don't you?

Felicia Fox: Yes, I liked when Shelli said I looked nice and you said my art project was pretty.

Carla Bluejay: See? If you say nice things to others, they'll feel good, too. They'll be friends with you.

Felicia Fox: How can I learn to say nice things?

Carla Bluejay: You can look at the person, find something nice about how the person looks or what the person is doing, and tell the person.

Ask the children:

- How does Carla say Felicia can make people feel good? (Be sure the steps of the skill are mentioned: look at the person, find something nice about how the person looks or what the person is doing, tell the person.)

Felicia practices the skill.

Felicia Fox: Do you think if I did that with Hank and Shelli, they'd want to walk with me again?

Carla Bluejay: It's worth a try.

Felicia Fox: Okay. You listen and tell me how I do.

Carla Bluejay: I will.

Felicia Fox: Hello, Shelli. I saw you swim across the brook just now. You are a great swimmer!

Shelli Squirrel: Thanks, Felicia. That's the first nice thing you've said to me in a long time.

Felicia Fox: I know, Shelli. But Carla Bluejay's been helping me learn to make people feel good, instead of bad.

Shelli Squirrel: That's something you needed to learn, Felicia. Here's Hank. Maybe you should practice saying something nice to him, too.

Felicia Fox: Hi, Hank. I'll bet you'll do just great in the spelling contest today. You are the best speller in class!

Hank Hawk: I didn't think you ever noticed me doing something good, Felicia.

Felicia Fox: Carla Bluejay has been showing me how to make people feel good, Hank.

Hank Hawk: It's about time! You seem to have learned a lot already. Would you like to walk to school with Shelli and me tomorrow?

Felicia Fox: I sure would! See you then!

Ask the children:

- How can Felicia tell she has made her friends feel good? (They are friendly to her.)

Carla Bluejay: You did very well, Felicia. You told Shelli and Hank what they do well and made them feel good.

Felicia Fox: Yes, and now they'll walk to school with me again. You've been a big help.

Carla Bluejay: That was a nice thing to say, Felicia!

Ask the children:

- What did Felicia need to learn? (How to say nice things to others.)
- Why was it important for Felicia to say nice things and make others feel good?
- What steps did Carla teach Felicia?

Review the skill steps, asking the children to repeat each one:

1. Look at the person.
2. Find something nice about how the person looks or what the person is doing.
3. Tell the person.

Invite the children to tell about situations in which they were mean to others or others were mean to them. Ask them to discuss the value of knowing how to be positive with people.

As appropriate, use Posters 1, 2, and 3 to prompt discussion of the importance of eye contact, friendly facial expression, and pleasant tone of voice when saying something nice to another person.

PRACTICE

Felicia Learns to Be Positive Role Play

Materials

>   Four puppets (Shelli Squirrel, Felicia Fox, Hank Hawk, Carla Bluejay)

Give the puppets to four children and ask them to role-play the story: Felicia Fox says something complimentary to Shelli Squirrel. Shelli responds with something complimentary about Felicia. Then Felicia says something complimentary to Hank Hawk, who responds with something complimentary about her. Finally, Felicia says something complimentary about Carla, who responds with something complimentary about her. Coach and cue the children as needed.

After the role play, discuss how the characters performed the skill. Then have the players exchange puppets and role-play again. As time permits, allow each child to take a turn with a puppet. When all have participated, have various children role-play making positive statements to others, this time without using the puppets. Encourage the group to offer the players feedback on the way they performed the skill.

Friendly Felicia

Materials

>   Puppet (Felicia Fox); stickers

Tell the children that because Felicia Fox has learned how to say nice things to others, she'll help them practice the skill. Begin by demonstrating: Hold the puppet and have Felicia compliment one of the students. Make your compliment appropriate for that particular student—for example, "George, you drew a very nice picture of a horse today" or "Melissa, your shoes are a pretty shade of blue."

Next, hand the puppet to the child you complimented, who is to select another student for Felicia to compliment. The second child is to thank Felicia, then take the puppet and compliment the first child. Continue until everyone has had a turn.

As appropriate, discuss the meaning of "compliment." If necessary, supply the compliment or a topic for the compliment—preferably, something appropriate to the child.

Give a sticker to each student who makes a positive statement about someone else. Tell students who do not earn stickers that they will have other opportunities to practice the steps and receive stickers.

Possible topics:

1. Sharing toys or materials
2. An art project
3. Good running
4. Nice singing voice
5. Attentive listening
6. Playing cooperatively
7. A bright smile
8. Working quietly

Adaptations

1. Have students generate a list of topics about which they could compliment the members of the class.
2. Follow up this activity by asking students to draw themselves giving a compliment to someone, write thank-you notes to peers who complimented them, or list some potential compliments to give to their family members.

Nice Notes Box

Materials

Box with slotted top (like a tissue box); blank labels; index cards; stickers

Preparation

Label the box "Nice Notes Box."

Display the Nice Notes Box and select a student to be the Nice Notes recipient of the day or week. Write that student's name on a label and fasten it to the box. (If your class is large, you may wish to have two or three Nice Notes Boxes and selected students.)

Distribute index cards to the other children. Explain that they are to write, draw, or dictate to you a compliment about the selected student and place it in the box. At the end of the day, take time to read the notes aloud or to show the pictures. Then allow the selected student to take the cards home. Repeat until all children have been complimented.

If necessary, help students with compliments by asking them what they are proud of and prompting others to compliment them on those things. Encourage statements about either positive traits (good sense of humor) or specific abilities (nice singing voice).

Give a sticker to each student who makes a positive statement about someone else. Tell students who do not earn stickers that they will have other opportunities to practice the steps and receive stickers.

Adaptation

Each time you repeat the activity, focus on a specific topic for compliments. Personal traits, school subjects, hobbies, and physical skills are all appropriate.

MAINTENANCE

Making Positive Statements to Others Every Day

Materials

Stickers

Observe students daily for opportunities to recognize and praise those who compliment others. As appropriate, ask the children to tell you when they have used the skill and to describe what they said and did. Give a sticker to each student who uses the skill.

Making Positive Statements to Others in Literature

Materials

Classroom books and stories such as these:

Sharmat, Marjorie Weinman. *Walter the Wolf.* New York: Holiday House, 1989.

Zolotow, Charlotte. *Do You Know What I'll Do?* New York: Collins, 2000.

Select stories that discuss or feature characters complimenting others. After the children have read or listened to a story, discuss how complimenting others was important to the characters.

Compliment Team

Materials

Blackline Master 4 (Badges)

Preparation

Use the blackline master to make badges. Write "Compliment Team" or draw a picture on each. Attach double-stick tape or safety pins to the backs. Select a few of the more capable students to be the first Compliment Team.

Explain that you have selected this week's Compliment Team of students who will compliment others in the class. Mention that eventually everyone will have a turn to be a team member. Distribute the badges. Remind classmates to thank the Compliment Team members for compliments.

The first day, assign each team member a classmate to compliment; also, tell each team member what to say. On the second day, again assign students to be complimented and give the topic of the compliments, but allow team members to phrase their compliments any way they choose. On the third day, assign students to be complimented but allow team members to choose both the topic and the phrasing of the compliments. On the fourth and fifth days of the week, have the team members select the students, the topics, and the phrasing.

Your directions for a week might resemble these:

First day: Suzanne, please return this paper to Bill and tell him his writing is much neater today.

Second day: Gerald, will you please say something nice to Harriet about her math homework?

Third day: Libby, I think Todd could use a friendly compliment today.

Fourth and fifth days: Todd, please look through these projects and compliment someone who did a good job.

Be sure to monitor students' compliments and give feedback. Continue until every student has served on a Compliment Team.

EXPRESSING FEELINGS

SKILL STEPS: EXPRESSING FEELINGS

1. Think about how you feel.
2. Think about who needs to know your feelings.
3. Tell the person how you feel.

MOTIVATION

Skill Presentation: Benny and Felicia Tell Their Feelings

Materials

Two puppets (Felicia Fox, Benny Frog)

Introduce the two puppets. Tell students that you're going to present a story about these characters called "Benny and Felicia Tell Their Feelings." Ask the children to listen carefully.

Benny Frog thinks Felicia Fox is angry at him.

Felicia Fox: Playing catch with you is fun, Benny. I'm glad you came over. I don't have a ball like this—catch it!

Benny Frog: Got it! Now you catch this!

Felicia Fox: Got it! This is great! Uh-oh, look out! Here comes a high fly!

Benny Frog: Ow! Ow-ow-ow! You hit me! I'm going home.

Felicia Fox: Wait, Benny! I didn't mean to hit you. Come back and play. I'm sorry. *(Pause.)* Boy, that Benny Frog! Why did he run off like that? It was an accident! Maybe I'll go over to his house.

Ask the children:

- Why do you think Benny ran off after Felicia hit him with the ball? What else could he have done?
- How did Felicia feel when Benny ran away?

Felicia Tells Benny about expressing feelings.

Felicia Fox: Hey, Benny! Are you in there? Let's play some more.

Benny Frog: No! I don't want to play with you if you're mad at me.

Felicia Fox: I'm not mad at you. I want to play catch.

Benny Frog: You must be mad. You hit me with the ball.

Felicia Fox: It was an accident. I didn't hit you on purpose.

Benny Frog: You didn't?

Felicia Fox: Of course not! I tried to tell you I was sorry, but you ran away.

Benny Frog: I ran away because I thought you were mad. Then I got mad at you. I didn't want to play with you anymore.

Felicia Fox: Well, I wasn't mad. I was having fun. If you had told me how you felt, we'd still be playing. You made me feel bad.

Benny Frog: Sometimes it's hard to tell someone how you feel.

Felicia Fox: I know. But all you need to do is think about how you feel, think about who needs to know how you feel, and then tell that person. You needed to tell me, instead of running home.

Ask the children:

- Why did Benny run away from Felicia? (He thought she was mad at him, he got mad at her.)

- How does Felicia say Benny could have told her how he feels? (Be sure the steps of the skill are mentioned: think about how you feel, think about who needs to know, tell that person.)

    Felicia Fox: It's especially important to say how you feel when you're angry or upset.

    Benny Frog: Why is it so important?

Ask the children:

- Why do you think Felicia says it's important to tell someone when you're angry or upset?
- Has someone been upset with you, and you didn't know why?
- Have you been upset with someone, but you didn't tell them why?

    Felicia Fox: When you tell someone how you feel instead of holding your feelings inside, you feel better. You get more done and have more fun when you don't waste time feeling bad. You help people understand you—and people treat you better when they know how you feel.

Ask the children:

- Why does Felicia say it's important to tell others how we feel? (To feel better, to get more done, to have more fun, to help people understand us and so treat us better.)

    Benny Frog: Yes, I see. Look at all the time we've spent feeling bad and not understanding each other. We could have played a lot more catch!

    Felicia Fox: Yes. So now that we do understand, let's go play some more.

    Benny Frog: I'm ready! Here's the ball. Let's go.

Ask the children:

- What happened when Benny Frog didn't tell Felicia Fox how he felt?
- What steps did Felicia teach Benny?

Review the skill steps, asking the children to repeat each one:

1. Think about how you feel.
2. Think about who needs to know your feelings.
3. Tell the person how you feel.

Help students understand that when we fail to express ourselves, we often create misunderstandings. Ask the children to mention some times when they found it hard to tell others how they felt. Ask if anyone has had a bad experience from not confiding feelings. Give examples of situations involving unexpressed feelings and ask the students to predict what might happen.

Sample situations

1. You think your parents will be angry with you for coming home late from school, so you run to your room and hide without telling them you are home.
2. You stop speaking to your grandmother because you're hurt that she didn't get you a birthday present.
3. Because your friend is playing with someone else, you think she is mad at you and you start ignoring her.

In the following activities, accept any response that sounds reasonable to the situation. In some circumstances children could be, for example, either embarrassed or afraid. If a response doesn't seem to make sense, have the student explain or expand on it.

You may need to help with descriptive language for emotions. Embarrassment, for example, is often experienced by children before they can label it; children may know how they feel but lack the words to say, "I was embarrassed."

PRACTICE

Benny and Felicia Tell Their Feelings Role Play

Materials

Two puppets (Felicia Fox, Benny Frog)

Give the puppets to two children and ask them to role-play the events in the story: Benny Frog and Felicia Fox play catch. Benny gets hit by a ball and leaves the game without telling Felicia how he feels. Felicia explains to Benny how to express feelings and why it is important to do so. Coach and prompt the children as needed.

After the role play, discuss how the characters portrayed the skill. Then have the children exchange puppets and role-play again. As time permits, allow each child to take a turn with a puppet. When all have participated, have various children role-play expressing their feelings, this time without using puppets. They can use either the story events or another story that you or they devise. Encourage the group to offer the players feedback on the way they presented the skill.

Tell Us Your Feelings

Materials

Stickers

Preparation

Have ready a set of emotion-laden incidents involving children, with slight variations between similar incidents that would change the feelings evoked.

Sample situations

1. You get a new toy.
2. You break your new toy.
3. You pet a friend's dog.
4. You pet a friend's dog, and it starts chasing you.
5. A small, younger child calls you a bad name.
6. A large, older child calls you a bad name.
7. An adult calls you a bad name.
8. Your teacher returns everyone's paper, and you see that you got a low grade.
9. You got a failing grade on your paper.
10. You got an *A* grade on your paper.

Explain to students that this activity will help them practice expressing their feelings. Ask everyone to choose a partner and to decide which child will go first. Read a situation, ask "How do you feel?" and have the person going first in each pair express how she or he would feel, and why.

As appropriate, have the children use this format: "I feel _____ because _____." Continue reading situations and have children alternate responding.

For example, you read, "You pet a friend's dog. How do you feel?" The child says, "I feel happy because I love dogs," "I feel jealous because I want a dog," or any response that shows an acceptable understanding of the situation. Move among the children and coach or prompt as needed.

Give a sticker to each student who expresses feelings. Tell children who do not earn stickers that they will have other opportunities to practice the steps and receive stickers.

Keep your list of situations for the next activity.

Adaptations

1. Concentrate on incidents involving family members.

2. Have children respond to the whole group or to you individually, rather than work alone with a partner.

What If You Don't?

Again use your list of emotion-laden incidents. This time, read a situation and ask the children to tell what might happen if they do not express their feelings, including how the other person involved might feel. Use questions such as the following to guide the children's responses:

1. You get a new toy. (If you don't thank your parents and say that the toy makes you feel happy, how will your parents feel? How will your parents think you feel about the toy? Will your parents get you another toy soon?)

2. You break your new toy. (If you don't tell your parents that breaking the toy makes you feel sad, how will your parents feel? How will your parents think you feel about the toy? Will your parents get you another toy soon?)

3. You pet a friend's dog. (If you don't tell your friend that petting the dog makes you feel happy, how will your friend feel? Will your friend bring the dog around again?)

4. You pet your friend's dog, and it starts chasing you. (If you don't tell your friend that the dog frightens you, how will your friend feel? Will your friend think you're having fun with the dog? Will your friend help you?)

MAINTENANCE

Expressing Feelings Every Day

Materials

Stickers

Observe students daily for opportunities to recognize and compliment those who express their feelings. As appropriate, ask the children to tell you when they have used the skill and to describe what they said and did. Give a sticker to each student who uses the skill.

Expressing Feelings in Literature

Materials

Classroom books and stories such as these:

Blaine, Marge. *The Terrible Thing That Happened at Our House.* New York: Scholastic, 1983.

Bottner, Barbara. *Bootsie Barker Bites.* New York: Putnam Juvenile, 1997.

Keats, Ezra Jack. *A Letter to Amy.* New York: Harper & Row, 1968.

Seuss, Dr. *Thidwick the Big-Hearted Moose.* New York: HarperCollins, 2004.

Udry, Janice May. *Let's Be Enemies.* New York: HarperTrophy, 1988.

Zolotow, Charlotte. *Do You Know What I'll Do?* New York: HarperCollins, 2000.

Select stories that discuss or feature characters expressing feelings. After the children have read or listened to a story, discuss how expressing feelings was important to the characters.

Word Power

Materials

Blackline Master 4 (Badges)

Preparation

Use the blackline master to make badges. Write "Word Power" or draw a picture on each. Attach double-stick tape or safety pins to the backs.

Remind the children that when we express our feelings instead of holding them inside, we help others understand us. We use "word power." Tell them that every time you see them expressing feelings in words, especially when they're upset or want to solve a problem with another person, you'll present a Word Power badge. As necessary, go over the steps of the skill.

Before distributing a badge, tell the child your reason for presenting it. For example, "Jennifer, I'm glad you told Leo why you were upset, instead of arguing or fighting with him." Be alert for students who improve in a particular social skill. A student who has learned not to hit others, sulk, or run away from encounters is an especially suitable recipient.

4 SPEAKING KINDLY AND USING COURTESY WORDS

> ### SKILL STEPS: SPEAKING KINDLY AND USING COURTESY WORDS
>
> 1. Think of what you want to say.
> 2. Think of a way to say it kindly.
> 3. Use a nice voice.

MOTIVATION

Skill Presentation: The Rude Rabbit

Materials

> Four puppets (Will Rabbit, Hank Hawk, Carla Bluejay, Benny Frog); Posters 2, 3

Introduce the four puppets. Tell students that you're going to present a story about these characters called "The Rude Rabbit." Ask the children to listen carefully.

Will Rabbit is rude to Hank Hawk and Carla Bluejay.

Will Rabbit: Boy, am I hungry this morning! I'd better go look for some food. (*Pause.*) There's Hank Hawk, and he's eating something! Great! Hey, Hank! What are you eating?

Hank Hawk: Carrot cake.

Will Rabbit: Yum! Give me some. I'm hungry.

Hank Hawk: I really can't spare any, Will. I have to share this with my brothers and sisters.

Will Rabbit: But I'm hungry! You give me some of that cake right now, or I'm leaving.

Hank Hawk: Then you better leave, Will Rabbit. You are rude!

Ask the children:

- Why does Hank say Will is rude? What does "rude" mean?

Will Rabbit: I'm hungry! Who's going to give me some food? *(Pause.)* Carla! What are you eating? Give me some!

Carla Bluejay: They're sunflower seeds, and I'm taking them to Shelli Squirrel. She's waiting for them.

Will Rabbit: But I'm hungry, and Hank Hawk wouldn't give me any carrot cake. If you don't give me some of those sunflower seeds, I'll leave.

Carla Bluejay: Leave then, Will Rabbit! You won't get any of my sunflower seeds when you're being so rude.

Ask the children:

- Why does Carla also call Will rude? What is wrong with the way Will asks for things?
- Have you ever asked for something the way Will does? What happened?

Benny Frog explains the difference between rude words and polite words.

Will Rabbit: Here I am at the edge of the forest, and I still don't have anything to eat. Why is everyone calling me rude? What does "rude" mean, anyway?

Benny Frog: Why, hello, Will. What's the matter?

Will Rabbit: I'm hungry, and no one will give me anything to eat. They all say I'm rude. What does that mean?

Benny Frog: You are called rude because you aren't kind or polite when you ask for things. You don't use polite words or a kind voice.

Will Rabbit: Oh, whatever do you mean?

Benny Frog: Polite, kind words let others know that you want to be friendly. The words you need to learn first are "please," "thank you," and "may I?"

Ask the children:

- Why does Benny say Will is called rude? (He isn't kind or polite, doesn't use polite words or a kind voice.)
- Why does Benny say Will should use kind words? (So others will know he wants to be friendly.)
- Which kind words does Will need to learn first? (Please, thank you, may I.)

Will learns and practices the steps of the skill.

Will Rabbit: How can I learn to use those words, Benny?

Benny Frog: Just remember that when you want to tell someone how you feel or what you want, you should first think of what you want to say. Then think of a way to say it kindly. Then say it using a nice voice.

Ask the children:

- How does Benny say Will can learn to be kind and polite? (Be sure the steps of the skill are mentioned: think of what you want to say, think of a way to say it kindly, say it using a nice voice.)
- Do you think these steps could help you get along better with people?

Will Rabbit: That doesn't sound too hard.

Benny Frog: It isn't, but it takes practice. There's Carla Bluejay with her sunflower seeds. Try asking her politely for a few. Remember to say "please" and "thank you" and to speak slowly and quietly. If you yell or talk too fast, your friends will keep calling you rude.

Will Rabbit: I'll try it. Thanks, Benny. Hello, Carla.

Carla Bluejay: You stay away from me, you rude rabbit!

Will Rabbit: Carla, I'm sorry I was rude. Benny Frog's been helping me learn to speak kindly and politely.

Carla Bluejay: It's about time you learned that, Will Rabbit!

Will Rabbit: I know. So, Carla, could I please have a few of your sunflower seeds? I'm so hungry!

Carla Bluejay: Well, okay, since you asked so politely, Will. Shelli doesn't need them all.

Will Rabbit: Thank you, Carla. They're delicious!

Carla Bluejay: You're welcome, Will. Glad you like them.

Ask the children:

- How can Will tell that he's learned the skill of speaking kindly and using polite words? (Carla is friendly to him, she gives him food.)

Benny Frog: Good, Will. You spoke quietly and slowly, and you used kind words. Next time, try smiling as you talk. Keep up the good work, and no one will call you rude again.

Will Rabbit: I'll practice until I get it right every time, Benny. That way I'll keep my friends—and I'll get lots of good things to eat!

Ask the children:

- What happened when Will learned to speak kindly and politely to others?
- What steps did Benny teach Will?

Review the skill steps, asking the children to repeat each one:

1. Think of what you want to say.
2. Think of a way to say it kindly.
3. Use a nice voice.

Be sure the children understand the difference between rude and polite ways of speaking, and the different effects of each. Invite them to describe situations in which they were rude or someone was rude to them. Ask them how the situations might have gone if people had been kind and polite.

Display Posters 2 and 3 to prompt discussion of the importance of a friendly facial expression and tone of voice when speaking politely to someone.

PRACTICE

The Rude Rabbit Role Play

Materials

Four puppets (Will Rabbit, Hank Hawk, Carla Bluejay, Benny Frog)

Give the puppets to four children and have them role-play the events of the story: Will Rabbit rudely asks for food from Hank Hawk and Carla Bluejay; they respond angrily. Then Benny Frog explains to Will about speaking kindly and using courtesy words. Will then speaks politely to Hank and Carla; they respond with friendliness. Coach the children as needed. If you prefer not to have children role-play inappropriate behavior, take the role of Will Rabbit yourself.

After the role play, discuss how the skill was presented. Then ask the players to exchange roles and present the scene again. As time permits, allow each child to take a turn with a puppet. When all have participated, have various children role-play speaking kindly and using courtesy words, this time without the puppets. They can use either the story events or another story that you or they devise. Encourage the group to offer the players feedback on the way they perform the skill.

Courtesy Word List

Explain to the children that not only do we need to use a kind voice and manner of speaking, but we also need to use words that others will recognize as polite ones. Ask for the children's help in generating a list of polite words.

Write each suggested word on the chalkboard. Your list might include "Thank you," "Please," "Excuse me," "I'm sorry," "I beg your pardon," "May I?" "You're welcome," and similar courtesy words.

You may wish to have the students generate sentences for each courtesy word. For example: "May I have some crayons?" "Excuse me, but I can't see the chalkboard when you stand there," or "Thank you for helping me."

You might also demonstrate how each word or phrase could first be said rudely, then kindly and politely. Ask various children to practice saying each word or phrase both ways. Be sure they understand the importance of not just saying the words, but saying them in a nice way.

Leave the list displayed, use it in the next activity, and refer to it periodically.

The Courtesy Word Game

Materials

Pictures of common objects, such as foods, pets, toys; list of courtesy words from previous activity; stickers

Have the pictures in a pile, face down. Ask a child to select a picture and say a sentence about the object, using one or more of the courtesy words she or he listed during the previous activity. For example, a child with a picture of an apple might say, "Please give me an apple" or "Thank you for the apple." Prompt and assist as necessary, or ask the children to help each other. Continue until everyone has said at least one sentence using courtesy words.

Give a sticker to each student who uses a courtesy word. Tell students who do not earn stickers that they will have other opportunities to practice the skill and receive stickers.

Courtesy Circle

Materials

Stickers

Have the children sit with you in a circle. Display a simple object, such as a pencil. Direct the child next to you to say, "May I please borrow your pencil?" You reply, "Yes, you may," and give the pencil to the child. The child then says, "Thank you." You return with "You're welcome." Continue until the pencil is passed around the circle and every child has had a chance to use all four courtesy phrases.

Periodically repeat this activity using other courtesy phrases. For example, one child pretends to pass another, saying, "Excuse me," or one child pretends to bump another, saying, "I'm sorry."

Give a sticker to each student who uses a courtesy phrase. Tell students who do not earn stickers that they will have other opportunities to practice the steps and receive stickers.

Adaptation

Concentrate on one or two courtesy phrases at a time, repeating the activity so that eventually all appropriate words are practiced.

Courtesy Partners

Materials

Index cards (optional); stickers

Preparation

Have ready a list of situations or requests calling for courtesy words. If you wish, write or illustrate each on a card. For example:

1. Ask someone to help you pick up the papers you dropped.
2. Ask someone to move aside so you can get by.
3. Ask someone if you can borrow a pencil.
4. Ask someone if you can take a turn riding a bicycle.
5. Ask someone to share the morning snack with you.
6. Ask someone to hold your books while you put on your coat.

Ask the children to pick partners. Orally or on a card, give one child in each pair a situation with a "courtesy direction." The child is to follow the direction, and the partner is to pantomime complying with the request, then the first student is to thank the second. Have the partners change roles so each child gets at least one chance to play both parts. Coach and prompt as necessary.

Give a sticker to each student who performs the skill steps adequately. Tell students who do not earn stickers that they will have other opportunities to practice the steps and receive stickers.

Adaptation

Do as a group activity. Have two children present each situation, or have one child ask you to do something.

MAINTENANCE

Speaking Kindly and Using Courtesy Words Every Day

Materials

> Stickers

Observe students daily for opportunities to recognize and compliment those who speak and behave courteously. As appropriate, ask the children to tell you when they have used the skill and to describe what they said and did. Give a sticker to each student who uses the skill.

Speaking Kindly and Using Courtesy Words in Literature

Materials

> Classroom books and stories such as these:
>
> Meiners, Cherie J. *Be Polite and Kind.* Minneapolis: Free Spirit Publishing, 2003.
>
> Seuss, Dr. *Thidwick the Big-Hearted Moose.* New York: HarperCollins, 2004.
>
> Verdick, Elizabeth. *Words Are Not for Hurting.* Minneapolis: Free Spirit Publishing, 2004.

Select stories that discuss or feature characters speaking or behaving courteously. After the children have read or listened to a story, discuss how speaking kindly and using courtesy words was important to the characters.

Polite Will Rabbit Club

Materials

> Puppet (Will Rabbit); index cards

Preparation

> Use the puppet as the centerpiece of a bulletin board you title "Polite Will Rabbit Club." Leave space to attach cards.

Explain that you've begun a Polite Will Rabbit Club for anyone who speaks courteously to others, as Will Rabbit learned to do in the story. Tell the students that over the next two weeks (or as appropriate to the students' skills and your schedule), each time you see someone speaking courteously to someone else, you will write that person's name on a card and attach it to the board. That person will then be an official member of the Polite Will Rabbit Club.

Continue the activity for as long as you feel necessary to encourage children to speak and behave courteously. You may wish to activate the club once every month or so.

Adaptation

Post various kind, polite, or complimentary words or phrases around or near the puppet. You might use or refer to the list of phrases generated earlier in this skill.

S K I L L

5 SPEAKING ASSERTIVELY

SKILL STEPS: SPEAKING ASSERTIVELY

1. Think about what you want.
2. Think of a way to say it calmly.
3. Say what you want.

MOTIVATION

Skill Presentation: Hank's Crayons

Materials

> Four puppets (Shelli Squirrel, Hank Hawk, Benny Frog, Felicia Fox); Posters 1, 2, 3, 4

Introduce the four puppets. Tell students that you're going to present a story about these characters called "Hank's Crayons." Ask the children to listen carefully.

Hank Hawk is unable to say no when Shelli Squirrel and Benny Frog want to borrow his new crayons.

Shelli Squirrel: Hi, Hank. My, those are nice new crayons you have there!

Hank Hawk: Oh, hello, Shelli. Yes, my mother gave me these crayons. I'm going to use them now on this thank-you card for her.

Shelli Squirrel: I just love to draw with crayons. Can I borrow the blue and yellow ones?

Hank Hawk: Uh, well . . .

Shelli Squirrel: Come on, Hank! I know I broke your other crayons last week, but I'll be careful this time. Don't be selfish!

Hank Hawk: But these are new, and I need . . . Well, okay, I guess.

Shelli Squirrel: Thanks, Hank!

Benny Frog: Hi, there, Hank! I hear you got some great new crayons. Can I borrow a few? I'm making a sign for my lemonade stand.

Hank Hawk: Uh, well . . .

Benny Frog: Give me those crayons, Hank! I need them now!

Hank Hawk: But . . . But . . .

Ask the children:

- Did Hank want to share his new crayons with Shelli and Benny?

- If he didn't want to share, why didn't he say no?

- How do you think Hank felt when he let Shelli and Benny take his crayons?

- Have you ever said yes to your friends when you really meant no? How did you feel?

Felicia Fox tells Hank about straight talk.

Felicia Fox: Hello, Hank. Why do you look so sad?

Hank Hawk: Shelli and Benny took my new crayons! Shelli and Benny are rough, and they'll break my crayons, and I need them for my mother's thank-you card!

Felicia Fox: Well, then, why didn't you say no?

Hank Hawk: I didn't know how. I didn't want them to get mad at me.

Felicia Fox: Sounds like you need to learn Straight Talk, Hank!

Hank Hawk: Straight Talk? What's that?

Felicia Fox: Straight Talk lets you tell your friends nicely that they can't have things you need. When you use Straight Talk, you get what you want and still keep your friends.

Ask the children:

- Why does Hank say he let his friends borrow the crayons? (He didn't know how to say no, he didn't want them to get mad.)
- Why does Felicia say Hank needs to learn Straight Talk? (So he can get what he wants and still keep his friends.)

Hank Hawk: I like to be nice, and I don't want to lose my friends. But I also don't want Shelli and Benny to take my crayons. How can I learn Straight Talk?

Felicia Fox: When you want to tell someone how you feel, first think about what you want.

Hank Hawk: I want them to stop borrowing my crayons.

Felicia Fox: Yes. Then you think of a way to calmly say what you want. Then you say it. You could say, "No, you may not use my crayons now because I need them for my thank-you card."

Ask the children:

- How does Felicia say Hank can use Straight Talk? (Be sure the steps of the skill are mentioned: think about what you want, think of a way to say it calmly, say what you want.)

Felicia explains why Straight Talk isn't mean.

Hank Hawk: But wouldn't that be mean?

Felicia Fox: No. If you use a nice voice, without frowning, then you're just telling them a fact. You could smile a little if it helps you talk politely.

Hank Hawk: But what if they get mad or start begging me for the crayons?

Felicia Fox: Stay calm and explain. You could say, "My mother told me not to let anyone borrow my new crayons" or "I can't let you borrow them because the last time you used my crayons you broke them." If you give a good reason for what you want, people shouldn't be angry with you. You aren't being mean.

Ask the children:

- How does Felicia say Hank can use Straight Talk without being mean? (Use a nice voice, don't frown, give a good reason.)

Hank practices the skill.

Hank Hawk: I like to share sometimes.

Felicia Fox: Sure, it's fun to share. But when you need to keep your things, Straight Talk helps you tell your friends how you feel. I see Benny and Shelli. Try to get your crayons back from them by using Straight Talk. I'll stay here and listen.

Hank Hawk: Benny, I need my crayons back. My mother told me not to let anyone borrow them.

Benny Frog: Well, can I borrow your bike? I'll ride home to get my own crayons.

Hank Hawk: Okay, but I need my bike back by lunchtime. That's when I told my mother I'd be home.

Benny Frog: Okay, Hank, I promise. Thanks a lot.

Hank Hawk: Hi, Shelli. Please give me back my crayons. I need them for my mother's thank-you card.

Shelli Squirrel: Oh, Hank, can't I use them a little longer? Please?

Hank Hawk: No, Shelli. I need them now. Maybe you can borrow them some other time, if you're careful not to break them.

Shelli Squirrel: Well, okay, Hank. I'm sorry I wasn't careful last time. I hope you do give me another chance.

Hank Hawk: Sure, Shelli.

Ask the children:

- What happened when Hank used Straight Talk? (He got his crayons back and kept his friends.)
- How do you think Hank felt when he used Straight Talk?
- Do you think Straight Talk could help you talk to your friends?

Felicia Fox: That was good Straight Talk, Hank. You got your crayons back without losing your friends.

Hank Hawk: I feel a lot better now. I don't have to let everyone take my things. I can just tell them no if I do it nicely. Thanks for the Straight Talk, Felicia!

Felicia Fox: You're welcome!

Ask the children:

- How did Straight Talk help Hank with his friends? (He got what he wanted without losing his friends.)
- What steps did Felicia teach Hank?

Review the skill steps, asking the children to repeat each one:

1. Think about what you want.
2. Think of a way to say it calmly.
3. Say what you want.

You may wish to point out that sometimes it is appropriate to share or cooperate; at other times, however, one has the right to (and should) refuse requests from others. Invite the children to tell about situations in which they needed to be assertive but didn't know how.

Display Posters 1, 2, 3, and 4 to prompt discussion of how facial expressions, tone of voice, and body language make a difference in using Straight Talk. For example, what might happen if you whispered when you're using Straight Talk?

As you present the following activities, recognize that it may take a great deal of practice for students to be able to initiate assertive responses; continue to identify and practice such responses throughout the year.

PRACTICE

Hank's Crayons Role Play

Materials

Four puppets (Shelli Squirrel, Hank Hawk, Benny Frog, Felicia Fox)

Give the puppets to four children and have them role-play the events in the story: Shelli Squirrel and Benny Frog get crayons from Hank Hawk, who doesn't know how to say no. Felicia Fox tells Hank about Straight Talk. Then Hank gets his crayons back by using his new skill. Coach and prompt the children as needed.

After the role play, discuss how the players presented the skill. Then allow each child in the group to take a turn with a puppet.

Next, introduce the differences between assertiveness, aggressiveness, and passivity: call them Straight Talk, Mean Talk, and Weak Talk. Straight Talk statements are spoken calmly and firmly, with no intention to inflict harm and with respect for one's own and others' rights. Mean Talk statements are spoken abusively and don't respect others' rights. Weak Talk statements are spoken timidly, don't express true feelings, and don't respect one's own rights.

To illustrate to children, have them suppose someone has been forbidden by parents to accept candy from others and then is offered candy by a friend. Their response to the situation could be aggressive, passive, or assertive:

Mean Talk: *(In an angry, loud voice.)* No, I won't take that candy—you know I'm not allowed to have it! Why are you always trying to make me do things I'm not supposed to do?

Weak Talk: *(In a timid, weak voice.)* Well, I'm really not supposed to have this. Well, okay, I guess I'll take some.

Straight Talk: *(In a calm, firm voice.)* No, thank you. I'm not allowed to have candy.

As time permits, have children role-play this and other familiar situations that call for assertiveness. Ask them to model (or you do it for them) aggressive and passive responses before they practice responding assertively.

Straight Talk

Materials

Puppets (optional); stickers

With or without puppets, have the children role-play assertive responses to the following situations, or to situations they suggest. Before beginning, remind children of the skill steps and tell them to watch for the steps in the role plays. After each role play, discuss how the skill was performed.

Emphasize the importance of a pleasant or neutral tone of voice and facial expression when making assertive statements. You may wish to have students repeat their statements with aggressive or passive tones of voice and facial expressions, calling attention to the differences. Have the class decide which expression or inflection is most in keeping with Straight Talk. Coach and prompt as needed.

Give a sticker to each student who gives an assertive response. Tell children who do not earn stickers that they will have other opportunities to practice the steps and receive stickers.

Sample situations

1. Some friends are throwing stones at the windows of your school. They ask you to join them. Tell them you won't.

2. It's your turn to play on the jungle gym at recess. A friend tries to take your turn. Tell your friend it's your turn.

3. One of your classmates tells you to call another student a bad name. Tell the classmate you don't want to do that.

4. One of your classmates starts taking your scissors without your permission. Tell your classmate not to take your scissors.

5. You're waiting in line, and a friend tries to cut in front of you. Tell your friend not to cut in.

6. A classmate is trying to take the library book you're looking at. Tell the person not to take it. Ask if the person would like to look at the book when you're finished.

7. A classmate said you did something you did not do. Tell the classmate that you do not like what she said about you.

8. Someone who rides your bus pushes you and takes your school papers every day. Tell him not to do it anymore.

Adaptations

1. Suggest specific dialogue for students and cue them to say it.

2. Describe the situations and ask individual children to tell what they would say.

3. Have children move beyond a single assertive response and improvise added dialogue or additional scenes.

PRACTICE

Which Is Straight Talk?

Materials

Blackline Master 10 (Straight Talk)

Preparation

Use the blackline master to make enough "Straight Talk" handouts for each student.

Distribute the handout and show students the face representing Straight Talk, the face representing Mean Talk, and the face representing Weak Talk. Review, as necessary, the differences between each. Tell students that you will present a situation and then give a response. Students are to decide whether your response is Straight Talk, Mean Talk, or Weak Talk. When they decide, they are to hold up their sheets and point to the appropriate face.

After students vote on each response, pause to discuss their decisions and consider any differences of opinion.

Situation 1: Someone asks to borrow the green paint you're using.

Response 1, Straight Talk: *(Calm, firm, polite.)* I'm using the green paint now, but as soon as I'm finished you can have it.

Situation 2: Someone asks you to go to the store, but you're supposed to go straight home.

Response 2, Weak Talk: *(Soft, unsure.)* Well, I'm supposed to go straight home, but maybe I could go with you for a little while.

Situation 3: Someone is on the swing, and you want a turn.

Response 3, Mean Talk: *(Loud, unfriendly.)* Get off that swing! You've been on it long enough.

Situation 4: You want a friend to help you carry some heavy books.

Response 4, Mean Talk: *(Loud, unfriendly.)* Don't just stand there! Help me carry these books!

Situation 5: A friend tells you to buy candy instead of lunch.

Response 5, Straight Talk: *(Calm, firm, polite.)* No, I can't buy candy. I have to use this money for my lunch.

As time permits, ask the children for different responses to the situations. For example, a Weak Talk response to Situation 1 is "Well, I wanted to use the green paint, but if you need it, well, okay." A Straight Talk response to Situation 2 is "No, I can't go with you. I have to go straight home." A Straight Talk response to Situation 3 is "I'd like to swing too. May I have a turn?" A Straight Talk response to Situation 4 is "These books are heavy. Will you please help me for a minute?" A Mean Talk response to Situation 5 is "No! You are so dumb! I'm buying my lunch with this money!"

Continue to review and discuss the differences in language, tone of voice, and facial expression between assertive, aggressive, and passive responses. Especially emphasize the difference between sounding assertive and sounding mean.

MAINTENANCE

Speaking Assertively Every Day

Materials

Stickers

Observe students daily for opportunities to recognize and compliment those who speak assertively. As appropriate, ask the children to tell you when they have used the skill and to describe what they said and did. Give a sticker to each student who uses the skill.

Speaking Assertively in Literature

Materials

Classroom books and stories such as these:

Bottner, Barbara. *Bootsie Barker Bites.* New York: Putnam Juvenile, 1997.

Lobel, Arnold. *Frog and Toad Are Friends.* New York: Festival 1990.

O'Neill, Alexis. *The Recess Queen.* New York: Scholastic, 2002.

Scarry, Richard. *Richard Scarry's Please and Thank You Book.* New York: Random House, 1978.

Select stories that discuss or feature characters speaking assertively. After the children have read or listened to a story, discuss how speaking assertively was important to the characters.

Straight Talk Box

Materials

Box with slotted lid (such as a tissue box or other suitable container); blank label; tokens (coins, checkers, small pieces of paper or cardboard)

Preparation

Label the box "Straight Talk Box" or draw an appropriate picture.

Show students the Straight Talk Box and explain that it will encourage them to speak assertively. Mention that each day you will listen for how students speak to each other. Every time you hear a student say what he or she wants politely but assertively, you will put a token into the box. You will also add tokens for students who describe to you their use of Straight Talk. At the end of the week, you will choose someone to open the box and count all the tokens.

After the tokens are counted, invite children to describe their experiences using Straight Talk.

Adaptations

1. When you notice a situation calling for assertiveness, cue children to use Straight Talk.

2. Ask children to make a written note of their own or others' assertive statements to put into the box.

3. Set a group goal for number of tokens and reward the class if they reach or exceed it.

UNIT

4

COOPERATING WITH PEERS

Learning to cooperate is vital to children's current and future success with others. The more positive a child's behavior in a group, the more likely that the child will be included in subsequent peer activities.

While working and playing with peers, children get the opportunity to practice and refine their social skills. Children constantly excluded from peer groups are at risk for long-term social incompetence. On the other hand, children who can function harmoniously in groups are permitted a wide range of behaviors; individuality need not be sacrificed to participate with others.

Learning activities tend to be competitive in regular classrooms and individualistic in special classrooms; both situations limit students' opportunities for cooperative interactions and development of peer-related social skills. Competition is not a natural motivator or a prerequisite in preparation for the world of work, and it often leads to antagonistic, hostile interactions. Children who learn to cooperate with others build friendships, learn from each other, and often feel better about themselves, especially if they assume a helping role.

The skills needed for cooperative interactions need to be taught directly and systematically. This is particularly true for students with special needs.

Skills taught in this unit include the following:

- Respecting Others' Property
- Sharing Materials

- Accepting Individual Differences
- Joining a Group Activity
- Mediating Group Rules
- Offering and Giving Help
- Giving and Accepting Criticism

Special Issues

Some of the skills within this section involve sophisticated concepts and may require extra practice. Mediating group rules, for instance, is based on the concept of fairness. Children may need to discuss a variety of fair and unfair situations before they understand that behavior at the expense of others is unfair and should be avoided. A sample situation to discuss might be "Georgia and Paula are playing jacks, but Georgia won't let Paula touch the ball. Is that fair?"

Some children may need to be individually coached in specific behaviors. For example, you may work privately with Nancy on ways to share crayons. Afterward, you may ask her to go to the art table and share crayons with Tom. While she's at the art table, you may find it necessary to prompt her to share.

Depending on your school and community environment, your students may be unaware of the many differences among people. If necessary, use pictures, books, and audiovisual presentations to introduce them to the concepts of, for example, disabilities and various racial and cultural groups. Younger children may need direct instruction about terms such as *same* and *different*. Make certain that students have mastered these concepts before presenting practice and maintenance activities.

Intolerance toward differences is learned. The younger the children in your group, the more likely they are to perceive differences in personality traits or past experiences rather than in race or gender. Older children begin to identify more strongly with their own sex and also may have learned to notice and ostracize people different from themselves.

In the following activities, be particularly careful that students do not perpetuate ethnic or racial stereotypes by using slurs or condescending language.

Taking Part stickers are used as incentives for skill step performance and skill use in practice and maintenance activities throughout this unit. You may wish to distribute copies of Blackline Master 2 (My Taking Part Sticker Collection), which gives students a handy place to store the stickers they earn.

S K I L L

1 RESPECTING OTHERS' PROPERTY

SKILL STEPS:
RESPECTING OTHERS' PROPERTY

1. Ask permission to use someone else's property.
2. Handle it carefully.
3. Return it promptly.

MOTIVATION

Skill Presentation: The Mud Castle

Materials

> Three puppets (Felicia Fox, Shelli Squirrel, Carla Bluejay);
> Posters 1, 2, 3, 4

Introduce the three puppets. Tell students that you're going to present a story about these characters called "The Mud Castle." Ask the children to listen carefully.

Carla Bluejay destroys Felicia Fox's mud castle and takes her pail.

> **Felicia Fox:** Shelli Squirrel, I just love building mud castles!
>
> **Shelli Squirrel:** You're really good at it, too, Felicia. Look at all those rooms and hallways!
>
> **Felicia Fox:** I've been working on this castle all day with my new pail.

Shelli Squirrel: I'm going to get a drink from the river, Felicia. Be right back.

Felicia Fox: Okay, Shelli. *(Pause.)* There's Carla Bluejay, splashing around in the stream. I can't wait to show her my castle. Hey, Carla, come look!

Carla Bluejay: Oh, a mud castle. I just love diving into mud castles and breaking them up with my feathers and claws. Look out!

Felicia Fox: My mud castle! You're ruining it! Stop!

Carla Bluejay: No, no, this is so much fun! Whee!

Felicia Fox: Stop it! Go away! This isn't your castle!

Carla Bluejay: Oh, it's just mud! There—all done! Now I'll just splash around in the water again and wash all the nice mud off! I'll use this pail! *(Leaves.)*

Ask the children:

- What words would you use to describe the way Carla treated Felicia? (Inconsiderate, mean, hurtful, destructive, unkind.)
- How do you think Felicia feels about Carla now?

Shelli Squirrel tells Carla about respecting others' property.

Shelli Squirrel: I'm back, Felicia. Why, what's happened? You look terrible.

Felicia Fox: Oh, Shelli, look at what Carla did to my mud castle! After all my work—I feel terrible!

Shelli Squirrel: I'll help you build a new one, Felicia. We'll do it together and make it even bigger than yours was.

Felicia Fox: You're a good friend. Let's get started—but we'll have to manage without my pail. Carla took it.

Carla Bluejay: What are you two doing?

Shelli Squirrel: We're building a mud castle.

Felicia Fox: Yes, and if you try to ruin this one, we won't ever play with you again.

Carla Bluejay: Oh, I'm tired of kicking mud. I was just doing that before to have fun.

Shelli Squirrel: Well, we're having fun building this. If you want to have fun, then instead of knocking something down, why don't you help us build?

Carla Bluejay: Okay. I'll help.

Shelli Squirrel: You know, wrecking something that belongs to someone else is never fun for that person. Felicia felt really bad.

Carla Bluejay: I was just having fun. I guess I wasn't thinking about Felicia's feelings.

Shelli Squirrel: When you don't respect other people's property, it does hurt their feelings. You can lose friends that way.

Ask the children:

- Why does Shelli say Carla needs to respect other people's property? (So she won't hurt feelings, so she won't lose friends.)

Felicia Fox: That's for sure. I felt terrible when you ruined my castle.

Carla Bluejay: Gee, I'm sorry, Felicia. I really didn't know I was being mean to you. How can I remember not to mess up a mud castle if it isn't mine?

Shelli Squirrel: My mother says that when I want to use something that's not mine, I should ask permission, handle it carefully, and return it promptly. That means return it on time, or when you are supposed to return it.

Ask the children:

- How does Shelli say Carla can remember to respect others' property? (Be sure the steps of the skill are mentioned: ask permission, handle carefully, return promptly.)

Carla Bluejay: Those sound like steps I need to learn. Here's your pail, Felicia. I should have asked if I could use it and then returned it right away. Won't you please keep being my friend?

Felicia Fox: Sure, Carla.

Carla Bluejay: You know, I really like building with you two. This is even more fun than knocking something down!

Felicia Fox: You know, Carla, with a little practice, you could be almost as great a castle builder as I am!

Ask the children:

- How did Felicia feel when Carla ruined her castle?
- What steps did Shelli teach Carla?

Review the skill steps, asking the children to repeat each one:

1. Ask permission to use someone else's property.
2. Handle it carefully.
3. Return it promptly.

Be sure students understand that "promptly" means "on time" or "when the person wants it back." As needed, define "respect" and "property" for children and have them give examples. Help students discriminate between accidental breakage and deliberate destruction. You may wish to discuss and define such terms as "bully," "vandal," and "vandalism."

Encourage students to discern the finer points of respecting property. Picking up someone's fallen coat, for example, does not usually require permission but is a way of showing respect for others' things. You could explain that respect also involves refraining from or avoiding actions that may cause harm to things of unknown ownership. Throwing litter in a vacant lot, for example, may do no visible or appreciable damage, but it is still disrespectful and improper.

Invite the children to tell about situations in which other people didn't respect their property. How did they feel when that happened? Also ask them to mention times when they didn't respect someone else's property. How did that person feel?

Display nonverbal communication Posters 1, 2, 3, and 4 to prompt discussion of the facial expressions and body language that are important for this skill. Focus particularly on the importance of friendly tone of voice and body language when asking for permission to use someone else's property. Display the posters during the remaining activities to prompt or cue children as needed.

PRACTICE

The Mud Castle Role Play

Materials

>   Three puppets (Felicia Fox, Shelli Squirrel, Carla Bluejay)

Give the puppets to three children and ask them to role-play the story's events in a positive way: Felicia Fox builds a mud castle, with Shelli Squirrel helping. Carla Bluejay asks to use Felicia's pail and then is careful with it; Felicia asks to use Shelli's pail while Carla has hers. When Carla returns Felicia's pail, Carla admires the mud castle and begins to help build it. All three characters discuss the skill of respecting others' property. Coach and prompt the children as needed.

>   After the role play, discuss how the skill was portrayed. Then have the players exchange puppets and role-play again. As time permits, allow every child the opportunity to practice with a puppet. When all have participated, have various children role-play respecting others' property, this time without using puppets. They can use either the story's events or a new story they devise. Encourage the class to offer the players feedback on the way they portrayed the skill.

Handling Things with Respect

Materials

>   Stickers

Have students role-play respecting others' property in the following situations, or in others they suggest. Before beginning, remind children of the skill steps and tell them to watch for the steps in the role plays. After each role play, discuss how the skill was performed.

Give a sticker to each student who performs the skill steps adequately. Tell students who do not earn stickers that they will have other opportunities to practice the steps and receive stickers.

Sample situations

1. Roger has a book with beautiful pictures that you want to look at.

2. Tyrone brought a small toy car to school, and you would like to play with it.

3. Ellen brought a game to school, and you'd like to play it with her.

4. You want to take Rachel's new CD home and listen to it tonight.

5. You want to borrow one of Gina's fancy new pencils.

6. You want to look at Byron's art project.

Adaptations

1. Discuss a single situation. Focus on asking permission before using something that belongs to someone else.

2. Have children write responses to the situations and share their ideas with the group.

We Vote for Respect

Describe various situations and ask the children to decide whether they think people are being respectful or disrespectful of others' property. Have students raise their hands to vote. Tally the votes and discuss any differences of opinion. Ask children to explain why they voted as they did.

Sample situations

1. Carrie has gone to recess and left a picture of a jungle she drew for art class on her desk. Her friend Allison thinks the picture would be better if it had more tigers in it. She draws some in herself.

2. Joel has brought a new football he got for his birthday to school. His friends would like to play with it. They ask if they can use it after school.

3. Nick is sick and doesn't come to school one day. Missy wants to use Nick's new crayons to color a picture. She takes Nick's crayons out of his desk, uses them, and puts them back when she's done.

4. Vicky says Mike can borrow one of her CDs if he promises to bring it back the next day. Mike forgets to return the CD until three days later.

5. Kirby lets Tamara borrow his favorite storybook. Tamara takes it home, and her little brother marks up some pages with his crayons.

MAINTENANCE

Respecting Others' Property Every Day

Materials

Stickers; Blackline Master 1 (Individual Social Skills Checklist, optional)

Observe students daily for opportunities to recognize and compliment those who are respectful of others' property. As appropriate, ask the children to tell you when they have used the skill and to describe what they said and did. Give a sticker to each student who uses the skill.

You may wish to use the Individual Social Skills Checklist to record students' progress in this unit's skills.

Respecting Others' Property in Literature

Materials

Classroom books and stories such as these:

Havill, Juanita. *Jamaica's Find*. Boston: Houghton Mifflin, 1993.

Meiners, Cheri. *Respect and Take Care of Things*. Minneapolis: Free Spirit Publishing, 2004.

Seuss, Dr. *The Cat in the Hat*. New York: HarperCollins, 2003.

Seuss, Dr. *Horton Hatches the Egg*. New York: HarperCollins, 2004.

Select stories that discuss or feature characters who respect others' property. After the children have read or listened to a story, discuss how respecting others' property was important to the characters.

Hats Off to Us

Materials

A large hat; index cards

Show students the hat, explaining that it will encourage them to respect others' property. Explain that during the week you will watch for children (and listen to reports about children) whose behavior shows respect for others' property. You will write those students' names on cards, along with a description of their respectful actions, and put the cards in the hat.

At the end of the week, empty the hat and read all the cards. Compliment the students who respected others' property, saying, "Hat's off to you."

2 SHARING MATERIALS

SKILL STEPS: SHARING MATERIALS

1 Think of what you want to do.

2. Think of how you can do it together.

3. Agree on a way.

4. Do it together.

MOTIVATION

Skill Presentation: We Can Share

Materials

Three puppets (Shelli Squirrel, Hank Hawk, Carla Bluejay); Posters 1, 2, 3, 4

Introduce the three puppets. Tell students that you're going to present a story about these characters called "We Can Share." Ask them to listen carefully.

Shelli Squirrel and Hank Hawk don't know how to share.

Shelli Squirrel: Give me that book, Hank! I want it!

Hank Hawk: No, I want it! Give it to me!

Shelli Squirrel: Mine!

Hank Hawk: Mine!

Shelli Squirrel: Oh, no! Look what you did! You made me rip the book in two!

Hank Hawk: I didn't make you do that! It's your fault!

Carla Bluejay: My goodness, what's all the yelling? Have you two seen that nice, new book the librarian left for us to look at? Oh, no! It's ripped in half!

Shelli Squirrel: Hank made me do it!

Hank Hawk: Shelli made me do it!

Carla Bluejay: I think you two better learn about sharing—before any more books are ripped!

Ask the children:

- Why did Shelli and Hank rip the book they both wanted to read? (They couldn't share.)
- How do you think they feel about each other now?
- What does Carla say they'd better learn? (How to share.)

Carla Bluejay tells Shelli and Hank about sharing.

Shelli Squirrel: Sharing? I wanted to read that book by myself!

Hank Hawk: So did I!

Carla Bluejay: Well, sharing means using materials with someone else. It's better to share than to fight and destroy things. You'll feel a lot better if you share. First you think of what you want to do . . .

Hank Hawk: Read that book!

Shelli Squirrel: Read that book!

Carla Bluejay: . . . and then you think of how you could do it together. How could you two have enjoyed that book together?

Hank Hawk: Well, we could have sat together and looked at it. I could have read out loud while Shelli turned the pages.

Shelli Squirrel: Yes, that would have been fun.

Carla Bluejay: Here's another book. Since you agree on a way to read together, how about trying it with this?

Hank Hawk: Let's do that, Shelli.

Shelli Squirrel: Okay, Hank.

Ask the children:

- How does Carla say Hank and Shelli could share? (Be sure the steps of the skill are mentioned: think of what you want to do, think of how you can do it together, agree on a way, do it together.)

Carla Bluejay: You two have learned to share just in time.

Hank Hawk: What do you mean?

Carla Bluejay: Here comes the librarian. You're going to have to share the blame for ripping that book!

Ask the children:

- What happened when Shelli and Hank fought about the book?
- How did the fight make them feel?
- What steps did Carla teach Shelli and Hank?

Review the skill steps, asking students to repeat each one:

1   Think of what you want to do.

2. Think of how you can do it together.

3. Agree on a way.

4. Do it together.

As appropriate, discuss another part of sharing: accommodating others. We can watch what others are doing so we can offer what they need or help out by changing what we're doing. For instance, if we see that a friend needs glue for an art project, we can finish with the glue early and then offer it to the friend. If a friend needs red paint for a project, we could use some other color.

Point out the differences between sharing, borrowing, and taking turns, and help the students list examples of each. Suggest the following criteria for selecting which skill to use:

- Do you really need it?
- When do you need it?
- Does someone else need it, too?
- Should you share, borrow, or take turns?

Invite students to tell about situations in which they wanted to share materials but didn't know how to go about it.

Display nonverbal communication Posters 1, 2, 3, and 4 to prompt discussion of the facial expressions and body language that are usually part of these skill steps. Emphasize the need for a friendly voice and appropriate body language when coming to an agreement about sharing something. Display the posters during the remaining activities to prompt or cue children as needed.

PRACTICE

We Can Share Role Play

Materials

Three puppets (Shelli Squirrel, Hank Hawk, Carla Bluejay)

Give the puppets to three children and ask them to role-play the story's events in a positive way: Carla Bluejay explains about sharing to Shelli Squirrel and Hank Hawk, who agree on a way to share the book they both want to read. Coach or prompt the children as needed.

After the role play, discuss the way the skill was presented. Then have the players exchange puppets and role-play again. As time permits, allow each child an opportunity to practice with a puppet. When all have participated, ask various children to role-play sharing, this time without using a puppet. They might use the story events or devise another situation. Ask the group to offer the players feedback on the way they presented the skill.

What Can We Do with This?

Materials

Several puzzles and other classroom items children can share; stickers

Tell students that in this activity they will practice sharing classroom materials. Present a familiar classroom activity, such as a puzzle, and have students give several examples of ways it might be shared by two or more children. For example, they might decide that each child would be given all the pieces for one section of the puzzle or that they could work together to decide on the placement of each piece.

After the discussion, organize students in small groups, give each group a puzzle, and have them try one of the proposed sharing methods.

Continue with other classroom materials and activities. For example:

- Using sports equipment
- Writing a letter to a sick classmate
- Feeding the animals
- Passing out a snack
- Delivering a note to the office

Give a sticker to each student who performs the skill steps adequately. Tell students who do not earn stickers that they will have other opportunities to practice the steps and receive stickers.

MAINTENANCE

Sharing Materials Every Day

Materials

Stickers

Observe students daily for opportunities to recognize and compliment those who share. As appropriate, ask the children to tell you when they have used the skill and to describe what they said and did. Give a sticker to each student who uses the skill.

Sharing Materials in Literature

Materials

Classroom books and stories such as these:

Crary, Elizabeth. *I Want It* (2nd edition). Seattle: Parenting Press, 1996.

Crary, Elizabeth. *I Want to Play* (2nd edition). Seattle: Parenting Press, 1996.

Keats, Ezra Jack. *Peter's Chair*. New York: Viking Juvenile, 1998.

Meiners, Cheri. *Share and Take Turns*. Minneapolis: Free Spirit Publishing, 2003.

Meiners, Cheri. *Talk and Work It Out*. Minneapolis: Free Spirit Publishing, 2005.

Select stories that discuss or feature characters sharing. After the children have read or listened to a story, discuss how sharing was important to the characters.

The Sharing Board

Preparation

Title a bulletin board the "Sharing Board." Have available a list of classroom activities for which pairs of children can share materials. For example:

- Washing tables using one bucket of soapy water
- Giving water to classroom pets using one water bottle
- Stapling using one stapler
- Sharpening pencils using one pencil sharpener
- Picking up litter using one trash can
- Alphabetizing books using one shelf
- Painting at an easel using one easel

Show students the Sharing Board, which will encourage them to share. Discuss your list of activities and materials. Encourage everyone to think of one way to share in each of the activities. Explain that you will be selecting several pairs of students each day to perform these tasks, watching to see how well the two students share materials. Tell the students that when two of them complete an activity by sharing, you will put their names on the Sharing Board.

Keep the Sharing Board active until each student has had several opportunities to share.

3 ACCEPTING INDIVIDUAL DIFFERENCES

> ## SKILL STEPS:
> ## ACCEPTING INDIVIDUAL DIFFERENCES
>
> 1. Think about the ways people are like you.
>
> 2. Think of the good things about people.
>
> 3. Treat people as you want to be treated.

MOTIVATION

Skill Presentation: Benny Plays, Too

Materials

> Four puppets (Hank Hawk, Benny Frog, Shelli Squirrel, Carla Bluejay); Posters 1, 2, 3, 4

Introduce the four puppets. Tell students that you're going to present a story about these characters called "Benny Plays, Too." Ask the children to listen carefully.

Benny Frog is left out of a softball game.

> **Hank Hawk:** Good morning, Benny. Oh, dear, it's too nice a morning to look so blue. What's wrong?
>
> **Benny Frog:** Hank, frogs just can't run!
>
> **Hank Hawk:** Why, I know that, Benny! Frogs are best at croaking and hopping.

Benny Frog: Right. Well, Shelli Squirrel and Carla Bluejay seem to think I could run if I just tried. They won't let me play softball with them because I don't run.

Hank Hawk: Hmmm. It sounds as if they don't know how much fun it is to be friends with animals different from them. Come with me, Benny. Let's talk to them.

Ask the children:

- How is Benny different from Shelli Squirrel and Carla Bluejay? (He doesn't run.)

- How does Benny feel about Shelli and Carla's not letting him play softball because he's not a runner? (Hurt, sad.)

- What does Hank say Shelli and Carla don't know? (It's fun to be friends with others who are different.)

Hank shows that Benny isn't better or worse than Shelli and Carla, just different.

Shelli Squirrel: Hi, Hank. Want to join our game?

Hank Hawk: Sure, Shelli. And Benny wants to play, too.

Shelli Squirrel: Oh, no, Hank. Benny's slow. He only hops! With him, we'd play all day and never get anywhere!

Carla Bluejay: That's right, Hank. Lazy frogs can't play softball!

Benny Frog: (*Crying.*) You two are the meanest animals I have ever met. I'm going home. (*Leaves.*)

Shelli Squirrel: You know, Hank, we really don't want to be mean to Benny. But he keeps nagging to join our game. Wouldn't it be silly to play softball with a lazy frog?

Hank Hawk: Benny isn't lazy! Frogs are different from birds and squirrels—not better or worse, just different. They can't run, but they are great at croaking and hopping. This would be a boring forest if we all did exactly the same things.

Ask the children:

- How does Benny feel about being called lazy?
- Do you think Benny is lazy? Why or why not?
- Why does Hank say life would be boring if everyone did the same things?

Hank Tells Carla and Shelli about accepting differences.

Carla Bluejay: Oh, Hank, Benny's too different from us to be fun to play with.

Hank Hawk: How do you know? Have you ever tried playing with him?

Carla Bluejay: Well . . . no. He's too different.

Hank Hawk: Carla and Shelli, you need to learn about accepting animals who are different from you. If you don't learn that, you'll miss out on lots of fun and friendships.

Shelli Squirrel: How do we "accept" Benny?

Hank Hawk: When someone seems different from you, think about the ways they are like you. How is Benny like you?

Shelli Squirrel: Well, he enjoys games and school and ice cream. He lives with his family, like we do.

Carla Bluejay: He talks and sings songs and tells jokes like we do.

Hank Hawk: Right! Now how about thinking of the good things about Benny?

Shelli Squirrel: He's good at croaking and hopping, as you said.

Carla Bluejay: He shares. He has a nice laugh. He's a good sport.

Hank Hawk: Now all you need to do is treat Benny as you would want to be treated. Would you like to be kept from playing a game because you weren't a fast runner?

Ask the children:

- Why does Hank say Shelli and Carla need to learn about accepting differences? (So they won't miss out on fun and friendships.)
- How does Hank say they can learn to accept Benny? (Be sure the steps of the skill are mentioned: think about the ways people are like you, think of the good things about people, treat people as you want to be treated.)

Hank Shows Shelli and Carla how to include Benny.

Shelli Squirrel: But you have to be fast to play softball.

Hank Hawk: Only if you're stuck with one set of rules. How about changing the rules so Benny could play?

Carla Bluejay: Why should we do that?

Hank Hawk: If you change the rules, you'll keep Benny as a friend. You'll also have a lot more fun than if you play the same way all the time.

Shelli Squirrel: Hmmm. What if we set up the bases so Benny could hop to them, instead of run?

Hank Hawk: Great idea!

Ask the children:

- Why does Hank say Shelli and Carla should change the rules to include Benny? (To keep Benny as a friend, to have more fun.)

Carla Bluejay: That might work. I've heard he's a pretty good batter and not too bad at pitching.

Shelli Squirrel: Let's go talk to Benny, Carla. I'll tell you the truth, I was feeling bad about the way we treated him.

Carla Bluejay: So was I. I wasn't feeling very much like playing. Now I do again— these new rules will be fun!

Shelli Squirrel: Thanks, Hank. Do you still want to play with us?

Hank Hawk: Sure, now that we'll all be together.

Ask the children:

- How does Benny feel when he isn't included in the softball game?
- How do Carla and Shelli feel when they decide to change the rules and invite Benny to play?
- What steps did Hank teach Carla and Shelli?

Review the skill steps, asking the children to repeat each one:

1. Think about the ways people are like you.
2. Think of the good things about people.
3. Treat people as you want to be treated.

In a discussion geared to your students' abilities, help the children understand that everyone is different from others in some ways but we all have many characteristics and feelings in common. Explain that differences among people are sometimes obvious, sometimes not. Obvious, noticeable differences include physical traits such as eye color, skin color, height, weight, gender, race and ethnicity, certain disabilities, native language, and some aspects of social and economic status. Less obvious differences include talents, personality traits, religion, life experiences, and likes and dislikes. Emphasize that these differences are neither good nor bad. Many occur naturally; others are personal preferences. All such differences should be accepted and valued.

Invite the children to talk about situations in which they or someone else was not accepted by others because of differences.

Display nonverbal communication Posters 1, 2, 3, and 4 to prompt discussion of the facial expressions and body language that are usually part of these skill steps. Emphasize the fact that communicating in a friendly and polite way is an important part of accepting those who are different. Display the posters during the remaining activities to prompt or cue children as needed.

PRACTICE

Benny Plays, Too Role Play

Materials

Four puppets (Hank Hawk, Benny Frog, Shelli Squirrel, Carla Bluejay)

Give the puppets to four children and ask them to role-play the events in the story: Benny Frog tells Hank Hawk about being excluded from Carla Bluejay and Shelli Squirrel's game; Benny shows hurt and sadness. Hank tells Carla and Shelli about accepting differences. Carla and Shelli apologize to Benny and invite him to play. Coach and prompt as needed.

After the role play, discuss how the skill was presented. Then ask the players to exchange puppets and role-play again. As time permits, allow each child to practice with a puppet. When all have participated, have various children role-play accepting individual differences, this time without using puppets. They can use either the story or another situation you or they devise. Encourage the group to offer the players feedback on the way they performed the skill.

Let Me Accept Everyone

Materials

Stickers

Have students role-play accepting differences in the following situations, or in others they suggest. Before beginning, remind children of the skill steps and tell them to watch for the steps in the role plays.

Ask the players to present in words the steps calling for them to think. (For example, in the first suggested situation they might say, "I know Gregory has trouble reading those cards. I'm not going to act impatient when he reads slowly. He and I both like math better than reading.") Also ask them to show how they could adapt to or help the student with the difference. Assist the children as needed.

After each role play, discuss how the skill was performed. Give a sticker to each student who performs the skill steps adequately. Tell students who do not earn stickers that they will have other opportunities to practice the steps and receive stickers.

Sample situations

1. Gregory wears glasses and has trouble reading game cards with small print. How can you show this doesn't matter to you?

2. Cory comes to school in dirty, torn clothes. How can you show this doesn't matter to you?

3. Marianne has many allergies and can't eat the food at your party. How can you help her have a good time?

4. Cynthia was born with one arm. She wants to play basketball with you and your friends. How can you help her join your game?

5. Bail speaks very little English. He wants to sit with you at lunch. How can you show you welcome him?

6. Ramira wears unusual clothes from her native country. She asks you to go to the library with her. How can you show her you'd like to go?

7. Mai has just come to this country. The teacher asks you to show her around school. How can you help Mai feel welcome?

8. Alexander uses a wheelchair. He's in your gym class. What can you do to help him participate in the class?

Adaptations

1. Take the part of the student with differences and have children role-play the skill with you.

2. Ask children to write responses to the situations and share their ideas with the group.

3. Record students' ideas about accepting individual differences and present them in a language experience chart or class storybook.

What About You?

Materials

Two duplicate sets of number cards

Arrange your group in a circle. Say that you are going to play a game to help them practice accepting individual differences. Distribute one set of number cards to half the group and the matching set to the other half. Explain the game: You'll call out a number. The two students who have that number will move to the middle of the circle. Each will tell one way they are like each other and one way they are different. They are to state each difference as a fact, without judgment—for example, "I am like you because we both have brown eyes. I am different from you because I wear glasses." Continue until all have participated. If time permits, repeat the exercise, redistributing the numeral card sets so students have different partners.

Adaptations

1. Ask children to state invisible or more subtle differences such as family size, birth order, or cultural traditions.

2. Vary the game by changing the number of students who meet in the center to compare. Four students may be able to tell how they are similar to or different from one, two, or three of the other children.

3. Ask children in larger groups to state how their partners are like and different from them.

What about Them?

Preparation

Arrange with another teacher to bring both classes into a common room to explore personal similarities and differences with the goal of practicing acceptance. Preferably, work with a class of a different age from yours so that the children are more likely to be strangers. Ask your colleague to prepare his or her class for the activity.

Explain to your class that they are going to meet some other children and will see what they have in common. Before you go, suggest some specific questions they can use to explore similarities and differences (for example, "How old are you?" "Where do you live?" "What's your favorite subject?" "Have you always gone to this school?" "Do you have any brothers or sisters?"). Tell students that they are to respond to each of the other person's answers with their own answers to the questions. You might take time to role-play the conversations.

Join the two classes and ask each of your students to choose someone to get to know. (You may want to use two sets of number cards, as in the preceding activity, or some other method of random selection.) Give each of the pairs a few minutes to find out about each other. When time is up, ask your students to name some of the similarities and differences they learned. If appropriate, ask the children from the other class to contribute to the reports.

Adaptations

1. Follow up this activity by discussing how your students felt about the information they learned. Were they surprised by any of their similarities to the other children? Were they surprised by any of their differences?

2. Permit students to write simple statements or to draw a picture depicting something they learned about another child.

3. Make arrangements for just a few of your students at a time to talk with students from another class.

Nicely Noted

Materials

Blackline Master 4 (Badges); stickers

Preparation

Use the blackline master to make a badge for each student, writing "I'm Unique!" or drawing a picture on each. Attach double-stick tape or safety pins to the backs.

Assemble the children in a circle. Have them take turns coming to the center. For each child, point out one neutral or positive difference between her or him and the others. Examples include an article of clothing, hair or eye color, street lived on, sibling's name, special talent or ability such as being a good singer, notable experience, or personality trait.

After noting a child's special difference, have the others mention one or two things they like about the child. Prompt as necessary, focusing on helping children appreciate each other. If children should remark about some sensitive characteristic, make the point that what's important about people is what they do, not how they look or where they're from. Then give the child a badge to wear. Continue until each child has had a turn.

Give a sticker to each child who shows appreciation for a classmate. Tell students who do not earn stickers that they will have other opportunities to practice the steps and receive stickers.

Adaptation

Ask children to think about friends outside the class who have distinct differences from them, such as disabilities, ethnicity, race, or language. Discuss how the friendships are enriched by these differences. For example, learning about a friend's family customs can help us understand our friend better and perhaps help us feel more comfortable with our friend's family.

MAINTENANCE

Accepting Individual Differences Every Day

Materials

Stickers

Observe students daily for opportunities to recognize and compliment those who show acceptance of differences. As appropriate, ask the children to tell you when they have used the skill and to describe what they said and did. Give a sticker to each student who uses the skill.

Accepting Individual Differences in Literature

Materials

Classroom books and stories such as these:

Henkes, Kevin. *Chester's Way.* New York: HarperTrophy, 1997.

Seuss, Dr. *Horton Hears a Who Pop-up.* New York: Robin Corey Books, 2008.

Seuss, Dr. *The Sneetches and Other Stories.* London: Picture Lions, 2003.

Zolotow, Charlotte. *The Hating Book.* New York: HarperTrophy, 1989.

Select stories that discuss or feature characters accepting individual differences. After the children have read or listened to a story, discuss how accepting individual differences was important to the characters.

We Are the Class

Preparation

Select a brief academic or play task calling for cooperation that students can do in a small group (for example, arranging picture cards in categories, building a tower out of interlocking bricks or logs, drawing a group picture). Plan to assign two to four children per group, putting together students with obvious or subtle differences. For example, you can group children with differences in race, gender, disabilities, ethnicity, language, or social group; children who don't typically interact with each other; or children with distinct abilities, likes and dislikes, learning styles.

Assemble students in their groups and assign tasks. Depending on your students' familiarity with cooperative learning groups, help them understand how they are to interact by giving specific rules for cooperation. Visit each group to help children cooperate and work together.

Following the small-group work, discuss with the class what they accomplished and how they helped each other. Praise students for working or playing well together. Emphasize that they have been successful if they were able to complete or work on the task harmoniously with everyone participating.

Organize your students into such groups regularly, giving each child the opportunity to work with everyone else in the class.

Agreeing to Be Different

Preparation

Prepare a bulletin board called "Agreeing to Be Different." Attach a photograph of each student: Take them yourself, use school pictures, or ask children to bring a photo from home. Beneath each photograph, put a statement about the child that notes some distinct, positive trait; characteristic; or life experience. Write every student's name on a slip of paper and put all the slips in a pile or container.

Ask each student to draw a name from the container and to say something positive about that classmate. Coach or prompt as necessary. Write each statement on a piece of paper and post it below your statement. Each day, have children draw another name and make another positive statement about a classmate that you can post. Continue until everyone has said something positive about everyone else.

4 JOINING A GROUP ACTIVITY

> ### SKILL STEPS: JOINING A GROUP ACTIVITY
>
> 1. Go up to a person in the group.
> 2. Make eye contact and smile.
> 3. Ask politely if you may join.
> 4. Check that the person has understood you.

MOTIVATION

Skill Presentation: Felicia Asks to Join

Materials

Four puppets (Will Rabbit, Shelli Squirrel, Hank Hawk, Felicia Fox); Posters 1, 2, 3, 4

Felicia Fox doesn't know how to join an activity.

Will Rabbit: Hi, Shelli. Hello, Hank. That's a nice playhouse you're building.

Shelli Squirrel: Thanks, Will. We nearly lost it a minute ago!

Will Rabbit: What do you mean?

Shelli Squirrel: Felicia Fox came along and pushed into us so hard she nearly knocked down the walls!

Will Rabbit: Why did Felicia do that? Was she mad at you?

Hank Hawk: I don't think so. We couldn't figure out what she wanted.

Will Rabbit: There's Felicia now. I'll ask her. *(Pause.)* Hi, Felicia. Isn't that a fine playhouse that Shelli and Hank are building?

Felicia Fox: I . . . I . . .

Will Rabbit: What's wrong, Felicia? Why did you try to push the playhouse down?

Felicia Fox: I didn't! I wanted to help build it!

Will Rabbit: Help build it? Then why didn't you?

Felicia Fox: I didn't know how to tell Shelli and Hank what I wanted. All I could do was hug their wonderful playhouse—and I nearly knocked it down! Then I just ran away. I feel awful.

Ask the children:

- What did Felicia Fox mean when she hugged the playhouse? (She wanted to help build it.)
- Why do you think Shelli and Hank couldn't understand what Felicia wanted?
- How does Felicia feel about not being understood?
- Have you ever wanted to join an activity but didn't know what to do or say?

Will tells Felicia how to join an activity.

Will Rabbit: Don't feel awful, Felicia. All you need is to learn how to join.

Felicia Fox: How to join?

Will Rabbit: Yes. When you see friends doing something you'd like to do, you can go up to one of them.

Felicia Fox: Shelli or Hank?

Will Rabbit: Yes. Look in that person's eyes and smile. That's to show you're friendly.

Felicia Fox: I guess hugging their playhouse didn't seem very friendly!

Will Rabbit: Probably not. Next, ask the person politely if you may join the activity, then check to be sure the person has understood what you want. Usually, the person will be friendly to you.

Ask the children:

- What does Will say Felicia needs to learn? (How to join an activity.)
- How could she join her friends' activity? (Be sure the steps of the skill are mentioned: go up to the person, make eye contact and smile, politely ask to join, check to be sure the person has understood.)

Felicia practices the skill.

    Felicia Fox: How do I ask politely?

    Will Rabbit: You might say, "May I please help you build this beautiful playhouse?"

    Felicia Fox: Do you think they'd let me?

    Will Rabbit: I think so, if they understand that you're friendly and want to join them. How about trying it with Shelli and Hank?

    Felicia Fox: Okay. If I don't try, I'd feel bad all day. *(Pause.)* Hank, I'd love to help build your playhouse. Could I join you?

    Hank Hawk: Sure, Felicia. We'd like the help.

    Shelli Squirrel: When you pushed the playhouse before, we thought you must not like it.

    Felicia Fox: I wasn't pushing. I was hugging. But Will's been telling me how to be more clear about what I want. And what I really want is to work with you two on that playhouse!

Ask the children:

- How does Felicia know she's used the skill correctly? (Hank and Shelli say she can join them, they are friendly to her.)

    Will Rabbit: Your playhouse will be built in a jiffy with all this help! Say, Shelli, could I please join you, too?

    Shelli Squirrel: The more the merrier, Will!

Ask the children:

- What was Felicia Fox's problem? (She didn't know how to ask to join an activity.)
- What steps did Will teach her?

Review the skill steps, asking the children to repeat each one:

1. Go up to a person in the group.
2. Make eye contact and smile.
3. Ask politely if you may join.
4. Check that the person has understood you.

Invite the children to tell about situations in which they've wanted to join an activity but didn't know what to do or say. You may wish to recall for the children the skill of Straight Talk and explain that asking to join requires them to be assertive. Also mention that when they are in a group and someone asks to join them, they should answer the person politely. Emphasize the importance of allowing others to join in because we all like to be treated nicely when we want to join an activity.

Display nonverbal communication Posters 1, 2, 3, and 4 to prompt discussion of the facial expressions and body language that are usually part of these skill steps. Review the importance of these techniques as they were used in previous skills and apply them to the specific situation of joining a group activity. Display the posters during the remaining activities to prompt or cue children as needed.

PRACTICE

Felicia Asks to Join Role Play

Materials

Four puppets (Will Rabbit, Shelli Squirrel, Hank Hawk, Felicia Fox)

Give the puppets to four children and ask them to role-play the events in the story: Shelli Squirrel and Hank Hawk work on their playhouse. Felicia Fox runs up and hugs the playhouse, nearly knocking it down. Will Rabbit tells Felicia how to join a group activity. Felicia uses the skill to join Shelli and Hank, then Will uses the skill and joins, too. Coach and prompt as necessary.

After the role play, discuss how the skill was portrayed. Then ask the players to exchange puppets and role-play again. As time permits, allow each child a chance to practice with a puppet. Then ask various children to role-play joining a group activity, this time without using puppets. They might use the story events or devise another situation. Ask the group to offer feedback on the way the players portrayed the skill.

In Circles We Go

Materials

CD or cassette player; CD or cassette of familiar music; stickers

Explain that you are going to play a game that will help the children practice asking to join an activity. Divide the class into two groups. Have one group form a tight circle; the other group should form a loose circle around them. Have the two groups face each other. Explain that when you start the music, the groups are to walk, staying in their circles, one group clockwise, the other counterclockwise. At a point, you will stop the music and call out an activity, such as "Walk tiptoe." Each child in the inside circle is then to ask the person facing if he or she can join in that activity ("Can I tiptoe with you?"). The partner in the outside circle is to agree politely ("Yes, I would like to tiptoe with you").

Begin the music and have the children walk. Stop the music and say, for example, "Walk tiptoe." Monitor the children's responses, coaching as needed. Then allow the partners to tiptoe together briefly until you signal them back to the circle. Begin the music again and repeat, specifying other easy motor activities, such as "Gallop," "Skip," "Pretend to be an airplane," or "Run in place."

After several rounds, have the groups change places so all students practice both asking to join and responding.

Give a sticker to each student who performs the skill steps adequately. Tell students who do not earn stickers that they will have other opportunities to practice the steps and receive stickers.

Adaptations

1. Use the same activity each time you stop the music.

2. After playing this game several times, vary it to allow students to practice asking someone else to join an activity. When you stop the music and specify an activity, one child is to ask the other, "Will you [take a walk with me]?" The partner is to respond, "Yes, I would like to [take a walk with you]."

Can I Join You?

Materials

Stickers

Have students role-play joining a group activity in the following situations, or in others they suggest. Before beginning, remind children of the skill steps and tell them to watch for the steps in the role plays. After each role play, discuss how the skill was performed.

Give a sticker to each student who performs the skill steps adequately. Tell students who do not earn stickers that they will have other opportunities to practice the steps and receive stickers.

Sample situations

1. You want to join some friends who are going to the playground.

2. You want to join some classmates who are painting a mural.

3. You want to join your cousins who are going on a picnic.

4. You want to join some friends who are walking to a school assembly.

5. You want to join some friends who are playing basketball.

Adaptation

Have children role-play with you.

MAINTENANCE

Joining a Group Activity Every Day

Materials

Stickers

Observe students daily for opportunities to recognize and compliment those who join group activities. As appropriate, ask the children to tell you when they have used the skill and to describe what they said and did. Give a sticker to each student who uses the skill.

Joining a Group Activity in Literature

Materials

Classroom books and stories such as these:

Cosgrove, Stephen. *Wheedle on the Needle* (revised edition). *Los Angeles:* Price Stern Sloan, 2002.

Crary, Elizabeth. *I Can't Wait* (2nd edition). Seattle: Parenting Press, 1996.

Crary, Elizabeth. *I Want to Play* (2nd edition). Seattle: Parenting Press, 1996.

Hoban, Russell. *Best Friends for Frances*. New York: HarperTrophy, 1976.

Meiners, Cheri. *Join In and Play*. Minneapolis: Free Spirit Publishing, 2004.

Udry, Janice May. *Let's Be Enemies*. New York: HarperTrophy, 1988.

Select stories that discuss or feature characters joining group activities. After the children have read or listened to a story, discuss how joining activities was important to the characters.

If You Ask

Preparation

Have available various toys and games that your students enjoy.

Tell the children that they can join many activities if they ask. Explain that you have some favorite activities available and that over the next weeks, students will take turns asking to join.

Select several students to begin using a toy or game, designating one child to say yes to the student who asks to join. Ask another child to come up and ask to join. If appropriate for your children, have them use their own words to ask; otherwise, supply a sentence.

After a student has asked to join and been accepted, allow several minutes for the child to play with the group. Then repeat until each child has asked to join.

Follow this procedure at least once a week for the rest of the year.

Join Your Friends

Materials

Index cards; two containers

Preparation

Title a bulletin board "I Joined My Friends!" On index cards, write or draw various familiar classroom activities, such as "housekeeping center," "attribute blocks," "number bingo game," or "computer." Also on cards, write the names of a few groups of two or three students. Place the activity cards in one container and the group name cards in another.

Each day, ask a student to draw an activity card and a group name card. Tell the children named on the card to initiate the chosen activity during free time and to accept into their group the student who asks to join. Instruct the student who drew the cards to practice the skill. That student's name will then be added to the bulletin board.

After children have practiced the skill, add them to groups, replacing children who will ask to join other activities. Repeat until all names are on the bulletin board and all children have practiced asking to join.

For reinforcement, ask children to tell the class the statement they used when they ask to join.

S K I L L
5 MEDIATING GROUP RULES

SKILL STEPS: MEDIATING GROUP RULES
1. Think about whether the rules are fair.
2. Think about how the rules might be changed.
3. Offer new rules.
4. Ask what others think.
5. Make sure everyone agrees.
6. Use the new rules.

MOTIVATION

Skill Presentation: Felicia Changes the Rules

Materials

> Two puppets (Felicia Fox, Hank Hawk); Posters 1, 2, 3, 4

Introduce the two puppets. Tell students that you're going to present a story about these characters called "Felicia Changes the Rules." Ask the children to listen carefully.

Felicia Fox's basketball team can't agree on rules.

> **Felicia Fox:** Ooh, I am so mad! I am mad!
>
> **Hank Hawk:** I can see that, Felicia! What happened? I thought you and your basketball team had a game today.
>
> **Felicia Fox:** We did. It ended early. It always ends early!
>
> **Hank Hawk:** Why? Did someone have to leave?

Felicia Fox: We all had to leave! No one on that whole team can follow rules!

Hank Hawk: What do you mean?

Felicia Fox: No one will play by the rules. Everyone always wants to change things their way.

Hank Hawk: Their way?

Ask the children:

- Why is Felicia angry? (Basketball team won't follow rules, members want to change rules.)

- Do you think it's ever fair to change the rules of a game?

Hank tells Felicia about agreeing on rules.

Felicia Fox: Will Rabbit and Benny Frog want extra points for high jumps, since no one else can jump like they can. Carla Bluejay wants to be able to fly to the basket. Shelli Squirrel wants extra points for speed, since she runs so fast. Have you ever heard of anything so silly?

Hank Hawk: What about you, Felicia? What do you think of the rules?

Felicia Fox: I think they're fine as they are. Of course, I think anyone who can make a basket one-handed should get extra points. I'm great at that!

Hank Hawk: Hmmm. I think your team needs to learn how to agree on rules.

Ask the children:

- What kind of changes do the team members want to make?

- What does Hank say they need to learn? (How to agree on rules.)

Felicia Fox: I started the team! I think I should make the rules!

Hank Hawk: But everyone on your team wants to make the rules. You'll never get to play.

Felicia Fox: You're right. How on earth will we ever agree?

Hank Hawk: First of all, you all need to think about whether the rules are fair. If they aren't fair, the second step is thinking about changing the rules.

Felicia Fox: Rules are rules.

Hank Hawk: You can change rules as long as everyone in the game agrees. You can have any rules you want.

Felicia Fox: I suppose. What new rules would make everyone happy?

Hank Hawk: It sounds to me as if everyone on the team wants extra points for the thing they do best. Will and Benny jump, Carla flies, Shelli runs fast, and you throw the ball with one hand.

Felicia Fox: Gee, I never thought of it that way. We are different in the kinds of things we can do.

Hank Hawk: Everyone is. That's why sometimes you have to change the rules so the game will be fair to everyone. Why don't you gather your team together and offer new rules? That's the third step in agreeing.

Ask the children:

- When does Hank say rules can be changed? (When everyone agrees.)
- What does Hank say is the first step in agreeing on rules? (Think about whether rules are fair.)
- What's the second step? (Think about how rules could be changed.)
- What's the third step? (Offer new rules.)

  Felicia Fox: What if no one likes my rules?

  Hank Hawk: They will if the rules seem fair. After you offer them, ask what the others think. Make sure everyone agrees.

Ask the children:

- What does Hank say are the next two steps in agreeing? (Ask what others think, make sure everyone agrees.)

> **Felicia Fox:** I'll try it, Hank. Maybe we can agree on some changes.
>
> **Hank Hawk:** I hope so, Felicia. I know how much you like to play basketball. And wait—I forgot the last step.
>
> **Felicia Fox:** What's that?
>
> **Hank Hawk:** After everyone agrees, you use the new rules. You play ball!

Ask the children:

- Why couldn't Felicia Fox's basketball team play together? (They couldn't agree on rules.)
- What steps did Hank teach Felicia?

Review the skill steps, asking the children to repeat each one:

1. Think about whether the rules are fair.
2. Think about how the rules might be changed.
3. Offer new rules.
4. Ask what others think.
5. Make sure everyone agrees.
6. Use the new rules.

In your discussion, emphasize that the characters in the story wanted rules that reflected the differences among the players and that changing the rules, even of a popular game like basketball, is possible. Reinforce the idea that any set of rules, whether standard or changed, needs to be agreed on by the players. Talk about the bad feelings caused by unfair rules and the good feelings created by rule changes with which everyone agrees.

Invite the children to tell about situations in which they wanted to change rules but didn't know how to go about it.

As your students practice this rather difficult skill, monitor them to be sure they understand and can apply the concepts. At various times, discuss with students their personal definitions of "fair" and "unfair." As appropriate, help them define the terms "negotiate" and "compromise." Review the skill steps as needed.

Display nonverbal communication Posters 1, 2, 3, and 4 to prompt discussion of the facial expressions and body language that are usually part of these skill steps. Focus especially on the need for friendly communication when negotiating or compromising on rules. Display the posters during the remaining activities to prompt or cue children as needed.

PRACTICE

Felicia Changes the Rules Role Play

Materials

Two puppets (Felicia Fox, Hank Hawk)

Give the puppets to two children and ask them to role-play the events in the story: Felicia Fox tells Hank Hawk about the problems her team members are having with the rules of basketball. Hank tells Felicia the steps for agreeing on rules. Felicia promises to use the skill with her team. Coach and prompt the children as necessary.

After the role play, discuss how the skill was presented. Then have the players exchange puppets and role-play again. As time permits, allow every child an opportunity to practice with a puppet. Then ask various children to role-play mediating group rules, this time without using the puppets. They might use the story events or devise another situation. Ask the group to offer feedback on the way the skill is presented.

Adaptation

Play the role of Hank Hawk yourself so you can reiterate the skill steps for the children.

Deciding Together

Materials

Stickers

Have students role-play mediating group rules in the following situations, or in others they suggest. Before beginning, remind children of the skill steps and tell them to watch for the steps in the role plays. After each role play, discuss how the skill was performed.

Give a sticker to each student who performs the skill steps adequately. Tell students who do not earn stickers that they will have other opportunities to practice the steps and receive stickers.

Sample situations

1. Jared and Marty are playing with marbles. They don't know the rules. How could they make up their own?

2. Heather and Melody are playing hopscotch. Ashley, who has just moved to the neighborhood, knows a different way to play. The three girls decide to make up a new set of rules. How can they do this?

3. Dustin wants to join his brother Matt and sister Jenny, who are playing Scrabble, but Dustin needs spelling help. How could the three of them make up new rules so they could play together?

4. Joe uses a wheelchair. His class is playing Red Rover. How could they change the rules so Joe can play and everyone will be safe?

5. David and Lynne are swinging hand over hand on the monkey bars, racing from one end to the other. Autumn wants to join them, but she's too short to reach the bars. How could they change the rules so Autumn can race, too?

Make Your Own Rules

Materials

Game pieces and materials such as dice, checkers, timers, spinners, cards, game boards, play money; stickers

Give the game materials to a group of students and tell them to make up a game. Instruct them to agree on an objective, a name, and a set of rules, using the skill steps. Give them a specified time limit and tell them that when time is up, you will come back to watch them play the game. When you do, check to see that everyone understands and agrees on the rules. Assist students as needed.

Repeat the activity until all children have participated, varying the materials.

Give a sticker to each student who mediates rules and to each student who agrees to use new rules. Tell students who do not earn stickers that they will have other opportunities to practice the skill steps and receive stickers.

MAINTENANCE

Mediating Group Rules Every Day

Materials

Stickers

Observe students daily for opportunities to recognize and compliment those who mediate group rules. As appropriate, ask the children to tell you when they have used the skill and to describe what they said and did. Give a sticker to each student who uses the skill.

Mediating Group Rules in Literature

Materials

Classroom books and stories such as these:

Crary, Elizabeth. *I Can't Wait* (2nd edition*)*. Seattle: Parenting Press, 1996.

Crary, Elizabeth. *I Want It* (2nd edition). Seattle: Parenting Press, 1996.

Crary, Elizabeth. *I Want to Play* (2nd edition). Seattle: Parenting Press, 1996.

Meiners, Cheri. *Join In and Play*. Minneapolis: Free Spirit Publishing, 2004.

Meiners, Cheri. *Know and Follow Rules*. Minneapolis: Free Spirit Publishing, 2005.

Meiners, Cheri. *Talk and Work It Out*. Minneapolis: Free Spirit Publishing, 2005.

Select stories that discuss or feature characters mediating group rules. After the children read or listen to a story, discuss how agreeing on group rules was important to the characters.

We Changed the Rules

Preparation

Label one side of a bulletin board "We Changed the Rules" and the other "We Agreed." Leave room for students' names.

Explain that the new bulletin board is for encouraging students to agree on changes in some game rules. Say that every time you see students propose new ways to play a game or do an activity, and other students agreeing to play by the new rules, you'll add names to the appropriate side of the board. (Games might include Go Fish, Concentration, or Tic-Tac-Toe; activities might include distributing or cleaning up gym or art supplies, forming small groups, or lining up.)

Encourage students to report to you instances of successful mediation that occur when you are not able to watch. Discuss these incidents and add the appropriate names to the board.

Each week, recognize the children whose names are on the board. Ask them to talk about the way they used the skill.

Adaptation

Initiate and monitor rule-changing sessions.

6 OFFERING AND GIVING HELP

SKILL STEPS: OFFERING AND GIVING HELP

1. Think about what people are doing.

2. Think about what you could do to help.

3. Ask if you can help.

MOTIVATION

Skill Presentation: Hank Learns to Help

Materials

> Five puppets (Carla Bluejay, Hank Hawk, Benny Frog, Shelli Squirrel, Will Rabbit); Posters 1, 2, 3, 4

Introduce the five puppets. Tell students that you're going to present a story about these characters called "Hank Learns to Help." Ask the children to listen carefully.

Hank Hawk is in a hurry and can't help.

Carla Bluejay: Hank! Hank!

Hank Hawk: Hi, Carla! Can't talk now. I'm in a hurry!

Carla Bluejay: Oh, Hank, please stop for a minute and help me tie this vine around this big box. It's very important.

Hank Hawk: No, I can't stop. I have to keep moving.

Benny Frog: Oh, Hank, please stop and help me blow up these balloons. It's very important.

Hank Hawk: No, I can't stop. I'm in a hurry.

Shelli Squirrel: Hank, please help me carry these cupcakes. It's very important.

Hank Hawk: No, no. I'm late!

Ask the children:

- What do Carla, Benny, and Shelli want Hank to do? (Help them.)

- Why doesn't he help? (He's in a hurry.)

Hank finds out he should have stopped to help.

Will Rabbit: *(Sadly.)* Hello, Hank.

Hank Hawk: Will, I'm finally here for our checkers game! Sorry I'm late, but don't be sad! It's a wonderful day!

Will Rabbit: It was supposed to be a wonderful day—but it isn't. Today is my birthday, and my friends said they would come over for a party. Shelli Squirrel was bringing cupcakes, Benny Frog was bringing balloons, and Carla Bluejay said she'd wrap my gift with vines to bring over. But no one's here!

Hank Hawk: What? Do you mean Carla, Shelli, and Benny were all on their way here for a birthday party?

Will Rabbit: I thought they were. But I guess they didn't want to come.

Hank Hawk: Oh, they wanted to come all right. As I was hurrying over, each of them asked me for help, but I wanted to keep going. If I had stopped to help them wrap your present, blow up your balloons, and carry your cupcakes, we would all be having a great time right now. I feel terrible. Why didn't I stop to help?

Ask the children:

- Why does Hank feel terrible? (He didn't stop to help, he didn't help with Will's party.)
- Have you ever decided not to help someone? How did you feel?

Will tells Hank how to offer help.

Will Rabbit: My grandmother says that to help someone, you should first think about what they're doing. Then you should think about what you could do to help. Then it's time to ask if you can help. When you help, my grandmother says, the work is easier and you show you're a good friend.

Hank Hawk: Oh, yes. I just didn't think. Let's both go back and help them now. It's not too late to have a great party.

Will Rabbit: You know, I think helping each other out is the best gift that friends can give. Let's go.

Ask the children:

- Why didn't Hank help Carla, Shelli, and Benny?
- How did Hank feel when he found out why they needed his help?
- According to Will, what are the advantages of helping others? (Work is easier, it shows friendship.)
- What steps did Will teach Hank?

Review the skill steps, asking the children to repeat each one:

1. Think about what people are doing.
2. Think about what you could do to help.
3. Ask if you can help.

Display nonverbal communication Posters 1, 2, 3, and 4 and relate them to the specific skill of helping someone else, particularly Step 3. Use the posters to prompt or cue children as needed.

Invite the children to tell about situations in which they wanted to help but didn't know how or times when they failed to help.

As students practice the skill, prompt discussion of what the person being helped might be feeling.

PRACTICE

Will Learns to Help Role Play

Materials

> Five puppets (Carla Bluejay, Hank Hawk, Benny Frog, Shelli Squirrel, Will Rabbit)

Give the puppets to five children and have them role-play: Hank Hawk stops to help Carla Bluejay with her package, Benny Frog with his balloons, and Shelli Squirrel with her cupcakes. Then Hank and Will Rabbit talk about the steps of the skill. Coach and prompt the children as needed.

After the role play, discuss how the skill was portrayed. Then ask the players to exchange puppets and role-play the scene again. As time permits, give every child the opportunity to practice with a puppet. When all have participated, have various children role-play helping, without using the puppets. They might use the story events or devise another situation. Encourage the group to offer the players feedback on the way they presented the skill.

The Lost Glove

Materials

> Two puppets (Shelli Squirrel, Benny Frog)

Introduce the puppets. Tell the children that you're going to use these characters to demonstrate the skill of offering and giving help. Then present "The Lost Glove":

Shelli Squirrel: Oh, dear. Oh, dear!

> **Benny Frog:** What's the matter, Shelli? Why are you so upset?

Shelli Squirrel: I lost one of my new gloves. My mother will be very angry with me if I don't find it.

Benny Frog: That's too bad. I'm going to play ball with Will Rabbit. I guess you can't come with me. Hope you find your glove. *(Leaves.)*

Shelli Squirrel: I would have liked to play with Will and Benny. But I've got to find my glove!

Discuss Shelli Squirrel's problem and what students think should be done. Help them see that searching for the glove is an important priority for Shelli. Ask for suggestions on how the glove might be found. Elicit the response that Benny Frog could have helped Shelli look for it.

Now present "The Lost Glove Is Found":

Shelli Squirrel: Oh, dear. Oh, dear!

Benny Frog: What's the matter, Shelli? Why are you so upset?

Shelli Squirrel: I lost one of my new gloves. My mother will be very angry with me if I don't find it.

Benny Frog: That's too bad. Can I help you look for it? I was on my way to play ball with Will Rabbit, but I can do that later.

Shelli Squirrel: Thanks, Benny. That's really nice of you.

Benny Frog: I'll look over here.

Shelli Squirrel: I'll look over here.

Benny Frog: What about by this . . . Here it is! I found it!

Shelli Squirrel: Oh, thank you, Benny! You are such a good friend!

Benny Frog: You're welcome. Come with me to Will's. We can all play ball.

Discuss the differences between the two scenes and the emotions each involved. Prompt the children to say that helping others makes both the helper and the person being helped feel better.

Adaptation

Help the children develop follow-up scenes that show the skill being used in situations involving the students themselves.

How Would You Help?

Materials

Stickers

Preparation

Have available a list of situations in which people need help. For example:

1. You see a friend struggling with a heavy load of books.
2. You see a friend who can't detach a bicycle chain.
3. You see a parent standing in the school hall, looking confused.
4. You see your brother crying because he can't find a toy.
5. You see a friend come in soaking wet from the rain.

Present each situation and ask students how they might respond. If no one mentions it, suggest that it's important to ask if the person needs help. Explain that sometimes people don't want help. For example, a person who's fallen may not be hurt, a person may want to be independent, a person may not know you. Emphasize that finding out if the person needs help should come before actually helping.

After your discussion, ask various children to role-play the situations. Ask that they verbalize the steps calling for thinking ("I'm thinking that my friend has too many books to carry. I'm thinking I could take some of those books"). After each role play, discuss how the skill was presented. Coach and prompt as needed.

Give a sticker to each student who performs the skill steps adequately. Tell students who do not earn stickers that they will have other opportunities to practice the steps and receive stickers.

Adaptations

1. Discuss and role-play a single situation.
2. Ask children to give, draw, or write responses to the situations and share their ideas with the group.
3. Record students' ideas about helping and present them to the class as a language experience chart or class storybook.

MAINTENANCE

Offering and Giving Help Every Day

Materials

Stickers

Observe students daily for opportunities to recognize and compliment those who help others. As appropriate, ask the children to tell you when they have used the skill and to describe what they said and did. Give a sticker to each student who uses the skill.

Offering and Giving Help in Literature

Materials

Classroom books and stories such as these:

Bridwell, Norman. *Clifford's Pals*. New York: Cartwheel, 2005.

Crary, Elizabeth. *I Want It* (2nd edition). Seattle: Parenting Press, 1996.

Freeman, Don. *A Pocket for Corduroy*. New York: Penguin, 1980.

Galdone, Paul. *The Little Red Hen*. Boston: Clarion Books, 2006.

Select stories that discuss or feature characters helping others. After the children have read or listened to a story, discuss how helping was important to the characters.

Classy Helpers

Materials

Blackline Master 4 (Badges)

Preparation

Use the blackline master to make badges, writing "Classy Helper" or drawing a picture on each. Attach double-stick tape or safety pins to the backs. Title a bulletin board "Classy Helpers."

Tell children that you'll be watching all week to see who is a Classy Helper. That means someone who offers to help even when not asked and gives help only when a person really needs help. At the end of the week, select a child to be the Classy Helper of the week. Put the child's name on the bulletin board, ask her

or him to tell about helping, and present a badge. Continue the
activity as long as it seems to encourage students to use the skill.

Helping Hand

Materials

Blackline Master 11 (Helping Hand)

Preparation

Post the Helping Hand in a prominent place.

Show children the Helping Hand and tell them that every time
one class member helps another, you will enter the helper's name
on the hand. When everyone's name has been added, you'll
arrange for a class reward (such as a popcorn party).

As you enter names, give public recognition to the helper. You
might also ask either the child who offered assistance or the child
who received it to describe what happened.

SKILL

7 GIVING AND ACCEPTING CRITICISM

MOTIVATION

Skill Presentation: Felicia and Hank Learn about Criticism

Materials

Three puppets (Hank Hawk, Felicia Fox, Benny Frog); Posters
1, 2, 3, 4

Introduce the three puppets. Tell students that you're going to
present a story about these characters called "Felicia and Hank
Learn about Criticism." Ask the children to listen carefully.

Hank Hawk doesn't know how to give criticism, and Felicia Fox doesn't know how to accept criticism.

Hank Hawk: I'm glad it's art day. I love painting, especially with these watercolors.

Felicia Fox: Yes, they're fun to stir. Whee!

Hank Hawk: *(Angrily.)* Stop stirring so hard, Felicia! You're splashing them on the table! Here, look at me. Stir them like this.

Felicia Fox: I know how to stir paint. Leave me alone.

Hank Hawk: No, you don't know how to stir paint! The teacher told us to be careful. Haven't you learned anything?

Felicia Fox: Smart aleck! I'm ready to paint! *(Pause.)* Uh-oh.

Hank Hawk: You splashed us both! Your brush is too wet! Look at the way I put paint on my brush. Watch me!

Felicia Fox: I know how to paint. I'm just as good a painter as you are. *(Pause.)* Uh-oh, I knocked the paint on the floor. Don't slip . . .

Hank Hawk: Ouch! You idiot! You're a terrible painter!

Felicia Fox: And you're rude. I never want to paint with you again!

Ask the children:

- Why are Hank and Felicia arguing? (Felicia isn't following directions but won't listen to Hank, Hank is rude to her.)

- How could they stop arguing and spend more time painting? (As needed, suggest that both need to be polite and helpful.)

Benny Frog tells Hank and Felicia about giving and accepting criticism.

Benny Frog: What's all the noise, you two?

Hank Hawk: Felicia won't do things the right way. She's a terrible painting partner!

Felicia Fox: Hank thinks he knows everything. He's mean!

Benny Frog: I think we have two problems here. Hank doesn't know how to tell someone they've done something wrong. Felicia doesn't know how to listen when someone tells her the right thing to do.

Ask the children:

- What two problems does Benny say Hank and Felicia have? (Hank doesn't know how to give criticism, Felicia doesn't know how to accept criticism.)

Hank Hawk: I told her she was wrong. She didn't listen.

Felicia Fox: Why should I listen to someone so rude?

Benny Frog: You'll both be happier working together if you just follow a few steps my dad taught me. If you don't, you'll probably have to stop painting for the day.

Ask the children:

- Why does Benny say they should follow the steps his father taught him? (They'll be happier working together, they'll get to continue painting.)

Hank Hawk: What are the steps for me, Benny?

Benny Frog: When you want to tell someone about something they've done wrong, use a nice voice, use kind words, and help the person do the right thing.

Felicia Fox: Yes, Hank, he's right! If you'd been nice, I might have listened to you.

Hank Hawk: Okay, okay. What about Felicia's steps?

Benny Frog: Felicia, when someone tells you about something you're doing wrong, you need to listen politely and think about what the person is saying. Then let the person show you her or his way. After that, thank the person.

Felicia Fox: Hmmm. I guess if I'd followed those steps, I wouldn't have gotten so mad. I get messier when I'm mad.

Benny Frog: We get a lot more done and get along with our friends better when we're nice to each other.

Hank Hawk: Want to try being partners again, Felicia?

Felicia Fox: Sure, Hank. We've lost a lot of time arguing. I'd much rather paint!

Ask the children:

- Why do Felicia and Hank decide that it is good to give and accept criticism politely? (They won't get mad, can get more done, will get along better with friends.)

- What steps did Benny teach Hank? What steps did he teach Felicia?

Review the two sets of skill steps, asking the children to repeat each one:

When telling someone about something they have done wrong:

1. Use a nice voice.

2. Use kind words.

3. Help the person do the right thing.

When someone tells you about something you have done wrong:

1. Listen politely.

2. Think about what the person is saying.

3. Let the person show you their way.

4. Thank the person for helping you.

In your discussion, help the children understand that we work together best when we know the right ways to give and receive criticism. Make sure the students understand what is meant by "criticism" (telling someone when they are doing something wrong) and the difference between giving and receiving criticism. As appropriate, help children to differentiate between helpful and harmful criticism. Explain that not every suggestion offered by others is right or helpful; when in doubt, they should check with an authority. As students develop some competence in this area, they should also understand that they have the right to reject someone's criticism and refuse someone's correction, but they should do so politely.

Invite the children to tell about situations in which they needed to give criticism to someone but didn't know how to do it nicely. Ask them also about times in which they didn't accept criticism politely.

Display nonverbal communication Posters 1, 2, 3, and 4 to prompt discussion of the facial expressions and body language that are usually part of these skill steps. Emphasize the importance of using a friendly voice and body language when giving criticism and when responding to criticism from others. Display the posters during the remaining activities to prompt or cue children as needed.

PRACTICE

Felicia and Hank Learn about Criticism Role Play

Materials

Three puppets (Hank Hawk, Felicia Fox, Benny Frog)

Give the puppets to three children and ask them to role-play the events in the story: Painting partners Felicia Fox and Hank Hawk are mad at each other. Benny Frog tells them about giving and accepting criticism nicely, so they can have fun painting again. Then Hank offers Felicia some polite criticism, and Felicia listens to Hank politely and thanks him for his help. Coach and prompt the children as needed.

After the role play, discuss how the skill was portrayed. Then ask the players to exchange puppets and role-play again. As time permits, allow every child an opportunity to practice with the puppets. When all have participated, have various children role-play giving and accepting criticism, this time without using puppets. They can use the events of the story or some other scenario you or they devise. Ask the class to offer feedback on the way the players present the skill.

Adaptations

1. Keep the role plays brief and the language simple. If children don't understand the concept of criticism, emphasize the correct way to tell someone how to do things and how to accept criticism.

2. Encourage children to enact more extensive scenes and to suggest their own appropriate responses to giving and receiving criticism.

What Would You Say?

Materials

Stickers

Have students role-play giving and accepting criticism in the situations listed below, or in situations they suggest. Before beginning, remind children of the two sets of skill steps, and tell them to watch for both in the role plays. After each role play, discuss how the skill was performed.

1. During your kickball game, Brandon kicks the ball and then runs in the wrong direction. Tell Brandon he's running in the wrong direction. Show him the right way to run.

2. Stephen wants to run a computer program, but he keeps pressing the wrong keys. Tell him he's pressing the wrong keys. Show him the right way to run the program.

3. You and Elise are putting a puzzle together. Elise keeps putting a piece in the wrong place. Tell her she's putting the piece in the wrong place. Show her the right place to put it.

4. You and Mia are doing your number work together. Mia is counting incorrectly. Tell Mia she's counting wrong. Show her the right way to count.

Give a sticker to each student who performs the skill steps adequately. Tell students who do not earn stickers that they will have other opportunities to practice the steps and receive stickers.

Adaptations

1. Discuss one situation only.

2. Act out a scenario yourself and have the children role-play giving you criticism.

3. Have children give, draw, or write responses to the situations and share their ideas with the group.

4. Record students' ideas about giving and accepting criticism, and present them in a language experience chart or class storybook.

Here's What I Say

Materials

Stickers

Tell children that they will practice giving and accepting criticism by playing a game. Ask them to pick partners, designating one child Partner 1 and the other Partner 2. Explain the game: You will call out a direction for movement (suggestions follow) for either Partners 1 or Partners 2. Those children are to deliberately do the movement incorrectly. Their partners are to give criticism following the skill steps; the children who performed incorrectly are to accept criticism following the skill steps.

Continue, alternating partners, until each child gets the opportunity to perform both roles. Assist children as needed.

Give a sticker to each student who performs the skill steps adequately. Tell students who do not earn stickers that they will have other opportunities to practice the steps and receive stickers.

Sample situations

1. Touch the top of your head and stand on your left foot.
2. Cover your left eye with your right hand.
3. Touch both knees, then hop on one foot.
4. Raise your right hand and scratch your left ear.
5. Stand behind your chair and tap your foot.
6. Cross your arms behind your back.
7. Lie on your back and pretend you are making angels in the snow.

Adaptations

1. Keep the directions simple. Only use multiple activities in one set of instructions if most children are successful.
2. Ask children to make up their own directions. They can create more complicated directions by adding qualifiers such as "right," "left," "backward," and "sideways."

MAINTENANCE

Giving and Accepting Criticism Every Day

Materials

> Stickers

Observe students daily for opportunities to recognize and compliment those who give and accept criticism appropriately. As applicable, ask the children to tell you when they have used the skill and to describe what they said and did. Give a sticker to each student who uses the skill.

Giving and Accepting Criticism in Literature

Materials

> Classroom books and stories such as these:
>
> DePaola, Tomie. *Oliver Button Is a Sissy.* San Diego: Harcourt Brace Jovanovich, 1979.
>
> Lobel, Arnold. *Days with Frog and Toad.* New York: HarperTrophy, 1984.
>
> Meiners, Cheri. *Talk and Work It Out.* Minneapolis: Free Spirit Publishing, 2005.
>
> Parish, Peggy. *Amelia Bedelia Helps Out.* New York: HarperTrophy, 2005.

Select stories that discuss or feature characters criticizing each other. After the children have read or listened to a story, discuss how giving and accepting criticism was important to the characters.

Show Me How, Show Me Now

Review the skills of giving and accepting criticism. Tell students that they are to practice these skills each time they work in small groups on cooperative learning activities. During such activities, encourage and compliment children as they practice the skills. Each week, post the names of students who performed the skills correctly.

Vary the composition of your groups and continue the activity as long as needed.

5   PLAYING WITH PEERS

Although the ability to play is generally taken for granted, many children do not play well. Some lack the athletic prowess to play competitively, while others have perceptual/cognitive limitations that interfere with understanding how to play. Some children do not know how to respond appropriately to playmates and play situations.

Play provides an extremely important arena for the development of children's social skills. Children with inadequate play skills are likely to be rejected or ignored by their peers, thereby restricting the opportunities for acquiring new behaviors and for trying out and refining existing skills.

Skills taught is this unit include the following:

- Taking Turns
- Putting Materials Away
- Playing Group Games
- Helping Others Participate
- Following Game Rules
- Winning and Losing

Special Issues

The purpose of this unit is not only to teach play-related social skills, such as winning and losing behavior, but also to emphasize that children's play skills can be developed and improved. Regardless of their natural abilities, most children, with some individual coaching, can progress enough to be accepted by their peers. As children improve in their abilities to play games, no matter how small the gains, their self-esteem is enhanced. Similarly, these activities advance the notion that children need to be tolerant of their less-skilled peers and to encourage and help them.

Beyond the development of motor skills, the social skills in this unit encourage children to find particular play strengths. The child who is only fair at kickball may be one of the best players in the class at board games. If that child is helped to feel good about her or his skill at board games and can get other children to join in board games, then the lack of proficiency in kickball ceases to be important. As the following activities suggest, adults can help foster children's self-esteem by publicly recognizing individuals for their progress, their particular strengths, and their efforts to assist peers.

> *Taking Part stickers are used as incentives for skill step performance and skill use in practice and maintenance activities throughout this unit. You may wish to distribute copies of Blackline Master 2 (My Taking Part Sticker Collection), which gives students a handy place to store the stickers they earn.*

S K I L L

1 TAKING TURNS

SKILL STEPS: TAKING TURNS

1. Find out when it is your turn.
2. Wait for your turn.
3. Play when it is your turn.

MOTIVATION

Skill Presentation: Hooray for Felicia Fox

Materials

> Three puppets (Will Rabbit, Hank Hawk, Felicia Fox); Posters 1, 2, 3, 4

Introduce the three puppets. Tell students that you're going to present a story about these characters called "Hooray for Felicia Fox." Ask them to listen carefully.

Felicia Fox doesn't know how to take turns.

> **Will Rabbit:** Uh-oh, Hank, look. Here comes Felicia Fox to play kickball with us.
>
> **Hank Hawk:** Oh, no. It's no fun playing when she's here.
>
> **Felicia Fox:** Hi, Will! Hi, Hank! I just love to play kickball! Here I go!
>
> **Will Rabbit:** Felicia, you kicked the ball away from me just as I was swinging my foot back!

Felicia Fox: Oh, yes, isn't kickball fun?

Will Rabbit: It isn't when you're around, Felicia. I'm going home.

Felicia Fox: Why? It's lots of fun playing kickball, isn't it, Hank?

Hank Hawk: No, Felicia. It isn't fun when you play. I'm going, too.

Felicia Fox: Wait! Don't go! I thought we were all having fun together.

Hank Hawk: We don't have as much fun when you're here. Whenever you see someone pitching, you run up and grab the ball. You run the bases with us, and you always want to kick. You don't take turns.

Ask the children:

- Why don't Hank and Will like to play kickball with Felicia? (She doesn't take turns.)
- How do they feel about Felicia's not taking turns? (Bad, angry, no fun to play with.)

Will and Hank tell Felicia about taking turns.

Felicia Fox: Okay, I'll take turns. What is "taking turns"?

Will Rabbit: Taking turns is a way for everyone to get to play. We all like to be the kicker, but the game is no fun if everyone kicks and no one throws or catches.

Hank Hawk: Before we start playing, we decide when everyone will kick. We take turns. When we take turns, we find out when it is our turn, wait for our turn, and play when it's our turn. That's fair, and we all feel good about it.

Ask the children:

- What does Will say "taking turns" means? (Everyone gets to play.)

- How do we take turns? (Be sure the steps of the skill are mentioned: find out when it is your turn, wait for your turn, play when it is your turn.)
- Why do we take turns? (To be fair, to feel good about playing together.)

Felicia agrees to take turns.

> **Felicia Fox:** But nobody told me when it's my turn to kick. Does that mean I don't get to play?
>
> **Hank Hawk:** No, you can play. But when you first come here, you need to ask for your turn. Then we'll tell you who kicks before you, and you can kick after they do.
>
> **Felicia Fox:** But what do I do when someone else is kicking the ball?
>
> **Will Rabbit:** We take turns throwing, catching, and playing the bases. When you're not kicking the ball, you can take a turn at third base.
>
> **Hank Hawk:** If you promise to wait your turn to kick, Felicia, I'll stay here and play.
>
> **Felicia Fox:** But when will my turn be?
>
> **Hank Hawk:** We already agreed that Will would kick after me. You can go after Will.
>
> **Felicia Fox:** Okay. I don't want everyone to go home. I'll play third base and wait for my turn to kick.
>
> **Will Rabbit:** Fair enough, Felicia Fox! Hooray for you!

Ask the children:

- How do Hank and Will feel about Felicia when she starts kicking the ball without waiting her turn?
- How does deciding to take turns help Felicia? (She gets to kick the ball some of the time, she gets to play with Hank and Will because they like playing with her when she waits for her turn.)
- What steps did Hank and Will teach Felicia?

Review the skill steps, asking the children to repeat each one:

1. Find out when it is your turn.

2. Wait for your turn.

3. Play when it is your turn.

Point out the differences between sharing, borrowing, and taking turns, and help the students list examples of each. Review the skills of joining a group activity and sharing materials. Questions that children can ask themselves about taking turns include the following:

- Will everyone get a chance to play?
- Do I know when it is my turn?
- Did I play when it was my turn?

Invite the children to tell about situations in which they played with someone who didn't take turns. How did they feel? Also ask them to tell about times when they didn't take turns. How did others feel?

If appropriate, discuss ways students might help make everyone's turn about the same length. For instance, children playing on the swings may decide that each person will get only five pushes; children taking turns on a bicycle might each circle the playground twice.

Display nonverbal communication Posters 1, 2, 3, and 4. Review the importance of friendly communication in group activities. Link these techniques to the skill of taking turns by emphasizing the need for a pleasant tone of voice and friendly body language when asking to take a turn or when responding to someone's asking for a turn during an activity. Display the posters during the following activities, using them to coach or prompt children as needed.

PRACTICE

Hooray for Felicia Fox Role Play

Materials

Three puppets (Will Rabbit, Hank Hawk, Felicia Fox)

Give the puppets to three children and ask them to role-play the events in the following story, in which Will Rabbit and Hank

Hawk tell Felicia Fox about taking turns. Then the three play kick-ball together peaceably. Coach and cue the children as needed.

After the role play, discuss how the skill was portrayed. Then ask the players to exchange puppets and role-play again. As time permits, allow every child an opportunity to practice with a puppet. When all have participated, have various children role-play taking turns, this time without using puppets. They might use the story events or devise another situation. Encourage the class to offer the players feedback on the way they performed the skill.

Whose Turn Is It?

Materials

Stickers

Have students role-play taking turns in the following situations, or in others they suggest. Before beginning, remind children of the skill steps and tell them to watch for the steps in the role plays. After each role play, discuss how the skill was performed.

Give a sticker to each student who performs the skill steps adequately. Tell students who do not earn stickers that they will have other opportunities to practice the steps and receive stickers.

Sample situations

1. You, Mickey, Noah, and Sondra all want to play checkers.
2. You and Sylvia both want to ride a bicycle.
3. You, Dwayne, and Ingrid all want to use the black marker for your picture.
4. During recess, you and Corinne both want to use the one swing.
5. You and James both want to play a song on the piano.

Adaptation

Record students' ideas about taking turns and present them in a language experience chart or class storybook.

Wall Builders

Materials

Building blocks and other materials students can take turns using (puzzle pieces, crayons, math manipulatives); stickers

Explain that you are going to help students practice taking turns. Select a student to work with you as you demonstrate building a wall with blocks. Put down a block, then hand the student a block to put beside yours. Continue taking turns placing the blocks as you talk about the skill: Two people are taking turns and cooperating as they use the same set of materials.

You might say something like "I'll start by putting a block on this side. Now you take one and place it on that side. Let's keep watching to make sure our wall is straight. It's your turn again. Good job! Now it's my turn."

Now select two students to take turns dismantling the wall, block by block. As they demonstrate, have other students talk about taking turns, as you did for the building sequence. Give many students a chance to say that the two demonstrators are taking turns, cooperating, and working together.

Repeat the demonstration several times using other activities, such as putting together a puzzle, coloring, or working with math manipulatives. Keep the demonstrations brief and frequent, focusing on the verbal component.

Give a sticker to each student who takes turns. Tell students who do not earn stickers that they will have other opportunities to practice the steps and receive stickers.

Adaptations

1. Start with a simple activity, such as putting beads in a container.
2. Move to more challenging activities, such as making a cut-paper collage, constructing a straw-and-paper kite, or illustrating a mural.

MAINTENANCE

Taking Turns Every Day

Materials

Stickers; Blackline Master 1 (Individual Social Skills Checklist, optional)

Observe students daily for opportunities to recognize and compliment those who take turns. As appropriate, ask the children to tell you when they have used the skill and to describe what they said and did. Give a sticker to each student who uses the skill.

You may wish to use the Individual Social Skills Checklist to record students' progress in this unit's skills.

Taking Turns in Literature

Materials

Classroom books and stories such as these:

Crary, Elizabeth. *I Can't Wait* (2nd edition). Seattle: Parenting Press, 1996.

Crary, Elizabeth. *I Want to Play* (2nd edition). Seattle: Parenting Press, 1996.

Meiners, Cheri. *Share and Take Turns*. Minneapolis: Free Spirit Publishing, 2004.

O'Neil, Alexis. *The Recess Queen*. Scholastic, 2002.

Owens, Terrell and Parker, Courtney. *Little T Learns to Share*. Dallas: BenBella Books, 2006.

Udry, Janice May. *What Mary Jo Shared*. New York: Scholastic, 1991.

Select stories that discuss or feature characters taking turns. After the children have read or listened to a story, discuss how taking turns was important to the characters.

The Taking Turns Wall

Materials

Connecting toy bricks or building blocks; name cards

Discuss with students various classroom activities for which they need to take turns. These might include indoor or outdoor games; responsibility as class messenger, monitor, or line leader; cooperative learning activities; teacher's assistant. Encourage the children to talk about the importance of taking turns in each activity and, if appropriate, the consequences of not taking turns. Explain that you will be observing students as they participate in these activities to see how well they take turns.

Show students the connecting bricks or blocks. Say that when class members take turns during an activity, you will write their names on cards, tape the cards to bricks, and attach one brick per student to make a "Taking Turns Wall."

As you add bricks to make the wall, you might also write students' names on slips of paper and attach them to a "Taking Turns" bulletin board. Continue the activity until each student has had several opportunities to take turns and the bricks have formed a good-sized wall.

You may wish to begin by using only recreational activities, then progress to cooperative academic activities. You may also wish to leave the wall intact and have students take turns in all your classroom helper jobs throughout the year.

2 PUTTING MATERIALS AWAY

SKILL STEPS: PUTTING MATERIALS AWAY

1. Check what needs to be put away.

2. Check where it goes.

3. Put it away neatly.

MOTIVATION

Skill Presentation: Shelli's Kite

Materials

Two puppets (Carla Bluejay, Shelli Squirrel)

Introduce the two puppets. Tell students that you're going to present a story about these characters called "Shelli's Kite." Ask them to listen carefully.

Shelli Squirrel can't find her kite.

Carla Bluejay: My goodness, Shelli, what are you looking for? You're throwing all our kites out of that box!

Shelli Squirrel: I can't find my kite! My beautiful kite that I shaped like a squirrel and painted like a rainbow!

Carla Bluejay: Everyone's coming today to fly kites, aren't they? We have a good breeze, and we all finished our kites yesterday.

Shelli Squirrel: Yes, and I worked so hard on my kite! Oh, Carla, please help me find it!

Carla Bluejay: I'll help you look. *(Pause.)* No, Shelli, it's not here.

Shelli Squirrel: I feel terrible! I was so excited about flying my beautiful kite today!

Ask the children:

- Why is Shelli Squirrel upset? (She can't find her kite.)
- Why do you think she can't find her kite?

Shelli Squirrel shows she doesn't know how to put away materials.

Carla Bluejay: You know, Shelli, I think we can't find your kite because you didn't put it back in the box yesterday. Do you remember putting it away?

Shelli Squirrel: No. I don't remember if I did or not. But somebody would have put it away if I didn't.

Carla Bluejay: I noticed that you forgot to put your kite away several times this week. Every day, someone had to remind you to put your kite in the box. Are you sure you don't remember what you did with it yesterday?

Shelli Squirrel: I just can't remember. Oh, dear, do you think someone threw it away by mistake?

Carla Bluejay: I hope not. *(Pause.)* Here it is, Shelli! I found it behind this stack of books.

Shelli Squirrel: Oh, yes, now I remember! I took my kite with me when I went to our reading corner to read a story. I must have left it there. I wonder why no one put it away for me.

Ask the children:

- Why couldn't Shelli find her kite? (She didn't put it away.)
- Do you ever depend on other people to put your things away, as Shelli did? Is that a good idea? Was it a good idea for Shelli?

Carla tells Shelli how to put away materials.

Carla Bluejay: Shelli, would you like to know how to put away your things?

Shelli Squirrel: I sure would, Carla. Then I'd never lose anything again.

Carla Bluejay: I can't promise that, Shelli. But as you can see, you can't always count on someone else to take care of your things. You need to take charge yourself.

Shelli Squirrel: You're right, Carla. How do I do that?

Carla Bluejay: It's really not hard. When you finish with something, first check what needs to be put away. Next, check where it goes. Then put it away neatly. That way, you'll always know where your things are.

Shelli Squirrel: I'll practice until I remember, Carla. I love this kite too much to lose it! And here comes everyone! It's time to have fun in the wind!

Ask the children:

- What happened because Shelli didn't put away her kite? (She couldn't find her kite.)
- How did this make Shelli feel? (She felt bad because she wanted to fly kites with her friends.)
- What steps did Carla teach Shelli?

Review the skill steps, asking the children to repeat each one:

1. Check what needs to be put away.
2. Check where it goes.
3. Put it away neatly.

Invite the children to tell about times they forgot to put their things away. What happened? How did they feel? Why is it a mistake to depend on other people to find what we lose and to put away what we forget?

To reinforce the value of this skill, you may wish to list and post several consequences children have encountered when they forgot to put away materials. As needed, point out the aesthetic advantages of a neat, organized environment. Also mention that we feel better when we take charge of our own things.

PRACTICE

Shelli's Kite Role Play

Materials

> Two puppets (Carla Bluejay, Shelli Squirrel)

Give the puppets to two children and ask them to role-play the events in the story: Shelli Squirrel looks for her kite; Carla Bluejay helps her find it. Then Carla tells Shelli how to put away materials and explains why the skill is important.

After the role play, discuss how the skill was presented. Then ask the players to exchange puppets and role-play again. As time permits, allow each child an opportunity to practice with a puppet. When all have participated, have various children role-play putting away materials, this time without using the puppets. They might use the story events or devise another situation. Encourage the class to offer feedback on the way the skill is presented.

Materials Monitors

Material

> Blackline Master 4 (Badges); stickers

Preparation

> Use the blackline master to make badges, writing "Materials Monitor" or drawing a picture on each. Attach double-stick tape or safety pins to the backs.

For each area in your classroom with materials to be kept in order, assign one or two children to be the week's Materials Monitor; distribute badges. Monitors are to inspect their assigned area and tell you about any materials that are not properly put away. You'll ask other children to put away the materials. Emphasize that everyone is to be responsible for keeping the classroom neat and sharing housekeeping tasks. Compliment students for following through, even if they were reminded.

Explain that although no one always remembers to put everything away perfectly, a good goal is to have things generally well cared for. You may stipulate conditions. For example, promise a class reward (such as a popcorn party) at the end of the week if no more than two items are left out each day.

Give a sticker to each student who follows the skill steps adequately. Tell students who do not earn stickers that they will have other opportunities to practice the steps and receive stickers.

Adaptations

1. Discuss with students what needs to be put away and what doesn't. Discuss what might happen if items aren't put away: how an item might get underfoot, what might happen next time they want the item, where the item might end up if not put away.

2. Have the children role-play or discuss other activities in which things need to be put away, such as making a sandwich, playing a game, or painting. Have the children show how each item used should be cleaned and put away.

MAINTENANCE

Putting Away Materials Every Day

Materials

Stickers

Observe students daily for opportunities to recognize and compliment those who put away materials. As appropriate, ask the children to tell you when they have used the skill and to describe what they did. Give a sticker to each student who uses the skill.

Putting Away Materials in Literature

Materials

Classroom books and stories such as these:

Meiners, Cheri. *Respect and Take Care of Things.* Free Spirit Publishing, 2004.

Seuss, Dr. *The Cat in the Hat.* New York: HarperCollins, 2003.

Seuss. Dr. *The Cat in the Hat Comes Back.* New York: Random House Books for Young Readers, 2006.

Seuss, Dr. *Wacky Wednesday.* New York: Random House Books for Young Readers, 1974.

Select stories that discuss or feature characters cleaning up or putting away materials. After the children have read or listened to a story, discuss how putting away materials was important to the characters.

Neat Like Me

Take the children to various classroom locations where materials need to be put away. At each place, discuss the materials and demonstrate how they are to be stored or cleaned up. Ask various children to practice removing and replacing materials. Solicit suggestions on how various materials might be cared for, emphasizing that there are many different ways of keeping things in order.

You may wish to assign individuals or groups to be responsible for each area in the classroom; allow the children to decide how the materials should be put away. If practical, color-code shelves with their materials. Continue this activity throughout the year.

Matching Materials

Materials

Colored labels

Preparation

As appropriate, increase the organization of your room to encourage children to put away materials. For example, place a colored label on each cupboard or shelf. Place the same color label on the materials kept there. You might categorize materials further by adding a shape to each color code. For example, if math materials have blue labels, number recognition games might have blue triangles, set-to-numeral correspondence activities might have blue squares, and computation exercises might have blue circles.

Discuss your organization with the class and tell them that the labels on the materials and the labels on the shelves should always match. Demonstrate how to put away materials using this system of matching. Ask that each student use the system after finishing with any materials. At the end of each day or week, discuss your organizational system and review the skill steps.

Adaptations

1. Have the children assist you in creating the organizational system they will follow.

2. Monitor children throughout the day rather than waiting until the end of the day or week to improve organization.

3 PLAYING GROUP GAMES

MOTIVATION

Skill Presentation: Carla Learns to Play

Materials

Four puppets (Will Rabbit, Carla Bluejay, Felicia Fox, Benny Frog)

Introduce the four puppets. Tell students that you're going to present a story about these characters called "Carla Learns to Play." Ask the children to listen carefully.

Carla Bluejay doesn't know how to play group games.

Will Rabbit: Hi, Carla. Why are you sitting here all by yourself with your "Groovy Gorilla" game all set up?

Carla Bluejay: Hi, Will. Oh, I'm hoping someone will come play with me.

Will Rabbit: I just passed Felicia and Benny playing "The Haunted Forest." They didn't look like they'd be looking for another game today. They were having lots of fun already.

Carla Bluejay: Yes. I don't know why, but they call me "the games goof-up." They never come to play with me.

Will Rabbit: You seem sad, Carla. Let's go ask Felicia and Benny why they leave you out of games.

Carla Bluejay: All right. *(Pause.)* Felicia, Benny, why won't you come play with me?

Felicia Fox: Not now, Carla. I'm right in the middle of my turn.

Carla Bluejay: That looks like fun. Let me spin the spinner. Oops!

Benny Frog: You knocked our pieces off the board! Carla, you're the "games goof-up." We don't want to play with you.

Carla Bluejay: Why do you call me that?

Will Rabbit: Yes, why do you, Benny? You've made Carla feel bad.

Benny Frog: Carla never plays games right.

Ask the children:

- Why does Carla Bluejay feel bad? (Benny and Felicia don't ask her to play, they call her the "games goof-up.")

- Why do you think Benny says that Carla never plays games right?

- Has anyone ever told you that you don't know how to play a game right? Have you ever been left out of games? How did you feel?

Will tells Carla about playing group games.

Felicia Fox: We started calling her the "games goof-up" after the "Berry Pickers" game last week. She moved her piece so hard that she tipped over the board.

Carla Bluejay: I didn't mean to do that.

Benny Frog: You never mean to. But you always wreck our games because you don't play right.

Carla Bluejay: I want to play right. What should I do, Will?

Will Rabbit: It sounds like you need to remember a few simple steps about playing games, Carla. First of all, you should always ask if you can play. If your friends say you can play, then learn the game rules and follow them carefully. And always take turns.

Carla Bluejay: I'll remember. I don't want to be the "games goof-up" anymore.

Will Rabbit: Can Carla join your game if she remembers the steps for playing games?

Felicia Fox: I suppose so.

Benny Frog: Sure, Carla. I'm sorry we were mean.

Ask the children:

- Why did Felicia and Benny call Carla names and refuse to play with her? (She didn't know how to play group games.)
- What steps did Will teach her?

Review the skill steps, asking students to repeat each one:

1. Ask permission to play.
2. Learn the game rules.
3. Follow the rules carefully.
4. Take your turn.

In your discussion, emphasize that asking if you can join others is a prerequisite for playing with them. Also point out that there are several ways to find out the rules for a game, including reading or listening to the directions, watching a demonstration of the rules, or observing others playing the game.

Invite the children to tell about times when they had trouble playing a game. How were they treated? How did they feel? What might they have done?

PRACTICE

Carla Learns to Play Role Play

Materials

Four puppets (Will Rabbit, Carla Bluejay, Felicia Fox, Benny Frog)

Give the puppets to four children and ask them to role-play the events of the story: Felicia Fox and Benny Frog tell Carla Bluejay she can't play their board game; Carla is hurt. Will Rabbit explains to Carla about playing group games. Carla follows the skill steps and joins the game. Coach and prompt the children as needed.

After the role play, discuss how the skill was presented. Then ask the players to exchange puppets and role-play again. As time permits, allow every child an opportunity to practice with a puppet. When all have participated, have various children role-play the skill, this time without using puppets. They might use the story events or devise another scenario. Encourage the class to offer the players feedback on the way they presented the skill.

Asking for Fun

Materials

Familiar games; stickers

Ask the children to stand or sit in a circle. Inside the circle, assemble a small group to practice playing a group game. Assign the game they'll play and explain to the class that you will model the skill first. Have the students in the small group begin playing. Announcing the skill steps you are following, first ask if you can play the game with them. Mention the rules you've observed, asking the other players if you've presented them accurately. Then play the game, following the rules carefully and taking your turn.

Now call on a student from the circle to take your place modeling the skill. Remind the student to review the rules, ask to join, follow the rules carefully, and take turns. Choose another child from the circle to replace your student model, and so on. Continue, changing games as necessary, until all students have practiced the skill. Cue the children and monitor the games as needed.

Give a sticker to each student who performs the skill steps adequately. Tell children who do not earn stickers that they will have other opportunities to practice the steps and receive stickers.

Adaptation

After you've modeled the skill, have children form several small groups and take turns practicing the skill in a variety of familiar games. You may want to designate one student in each group as a recorder who uses a check sheet to see that the players follow the steps.

MAINTENANCE

Playing Group Games Every Day

Materials

Stickers

Observe students daily for opportunities to recognize and compliment those who show good social skills during group games. As appropriate, ask the children to tell you when they have used the skill and to describe what they said and did. Give a sticker to each student who uses the skill.

Playing Group Games in Literature

Materials

Classroom books and stories such as these:

Crary, Elizabeth. *I Can't Wait* (2nd edition). Seattle: Parenting Press, 1996.

Crary, Elizabeth. *I Want It* (2nd edition). Seattle: Parenting Press, 1996.

Crary, Elizabeth. *I Want to Play* (2nd edition). Seattle: Parenting Press, 1996.

Meiners, Cheri. *Join In and Play*. Minneapolis: Free Spirit Publishing, 2004.

Naylor, Phyllis Reynolds. *King of the Playground*. New York: Aladdin, 1994.

Select stories that discuss or feature characters playing group games. After the children have read or listened to a story, discuss how using social skills during group games was important to the characters.

Great Game Players

Preparation

Title a bulletin board "Great Game Players."

Show students the bulletin board and explain that you hope to encourage good social skills in group games. Say that you'll be observing students to see how well they have learned the skill steps. Each time you observe someone asking permission to play, learning the rules, following the rules, and taking turns, you'll place he or his name on your bulletin hoard. Also ask students to tell you when classmates follow the skill steps, so you can place more names on the board.

Tell the children that when everyone's name appears once on the board, you'll reward the class with a special game privilege, such as extra time to play a favorite game. Emphasize to the children that their goal is a group one: The whole class will be rewarded when everyone's name appears on the board. Encourage children to work together and assist each other while practicing the skill steps. Cue children and monitor the games as needed, continuing the activity for as long as seems useful.

S K I L L

4 HELPING OTHERS PARTICIPATE

SKILL STEPS:
HELPING OTHERS PARTICIPATE

1. Ask if the person wants to join.

2. Explain the rules.

3. Check to see if the person understands.

4. Demonstrate the game.

5. Let the person practice.

6. Say something nice about how the person is playing.

MOTIVATION

Skill Presentation: Room for Hank Hawk

Materials

> Three puppets (Benny Frog, Hank Hawk, Will Rabbit); Posters 1, 2, 3, 4

Introduce the three puppets. Tell students that you're going to present a story about these characters called "Room for Hank Hawk." Ask them to listen carefully.

Will Rabbit won't let Hank Hawk join his games.

> **Benny Frog:** Hello, Hank. Why are you sitting by yourself? I just saw Will Rabbit and his friends playing a great game of Freeze Tag.

Hank Hawk: Yes, Will and his friends play fun games every day. I always hear them laughing. But Will says there's no room for me.

Benny Frog: No room? What does he mean?

Hank Hawk: I don't know. I'm not very good at games, but if he'd let me play, maybe I'd get better. I sure wish I could play now.

Benny Frog: Go talk to Will, Hank. You two need to be better friends.

Hank Hawk: Okay. Thanks.

Ask the children:

- Why do you think Will won't let Hank play?
- How do you think Benny feels about this?

Benny tells Will about helping others participate.

Benny Frog: Hi, Will. Is your game over?

Will Rabbit: Hi, Benny. I'd sure like to play Freeze Tag again, but all my friends had to go home.

Benny Frog: I just talked to Hank Hawk, Will. He'd love to play Freeze Tag with you.

Will Rabbit: Oh, no, I can't play with Hank. He doesn't know how to play, he runs in the wrong direction, and he's always spoiling our games. It's much better if he just sits and watches.

Benny Frog: But you really want to keep playing, don't you?

Will Rabbit: I sure do.

Benny Frog: Well, I can't play with you now, but Hank is ready and willing. Maybe he doesn't play well because no one's ever helped him. If you helped him play, you'd have more fun. You'd improve your own game by teaching Hank. And you'd also be a better friend to Hank than you are when you say there's no room for him.

Ask the children:

- Why does Benny say Will should help Hank play? (To have more fun, to improve his own game, to be a better friend.)

Will Rabbit: You could be right. But how do I help him?

Benny Frog: First, ask Hank if he'd like to play. If he says yes—and I think he will— explain the rules and check to see that he understands them. Maybe no one's ever told him the rules for Freeze Tag.

Will Rabbit: Hmmm. What else do I need to do?

Benny Frog: Demonstrate the game for Hank. Show him how you play. Let him practice and say something nice about how he's playing.

Ask the children:

- How does Benny say Will could help Hank play? (Be sure the steps of the skill are mentioned: ask if the person wants to join, explain the rules, check to see if the person understands, demonstrate, let the person practice, say something nice about how the person is playing.)

Will Rabbit: I suppose I could do that. Then if Hank shows he really can play, I'll get another game!

Benny Frog: Right. And another friend. There's Hank now, and he's feeling bad because you won't play with him.

Will Rabbit: Hi, Hank. Would you like to play Freeze Tag with me? I'll show you how.

Hank Hawk: Me, Will? I thought there was no room for me.

Will Rabbit: Benny showed me how to make room for you, Hank! Let's go!

Ask the children:

- Why does Benny say that it would be a good idea for Will to ask Hank to play with him? (He will get to keep playing tag, he will be a better friend to Hank because he will make Hank feel better.)

- What steps did Benny teach Will?

Review the skill steps, asking the children to repeat each one:

1. Ask if the person wants to join.

2. Explain the rules.

3. Check to see if the person understands.

4. Demonstrate the game.

5. Let the person practice.

6. Say something nice about how the person is playing.

In your discussion, emphasize that most people can learn to play better if they're coached and helped to play. Be sure children understand that helping others play leads to more fun, better playing for all, and closer friendships. As necessary, discuss terms such as "coach," "encourage," "guide," "demonstrate," "suggest," and "direct." Point out the differences between guiding and encouraging versus bossing and showing off.

Invite the children to tell about times when they wanted to play but no one would help them. How did they feel? Also ask about times when they excluded others from play. How did the other person feel?

Display nonverbal communication Posters 1, 2, 3, and 4 to prompt discussion of the facial expressions and body language that are usually part of these skill steps. Emphasize the importance of friendly communication when inviting someone to join a game, explaining the rules, and saying something nice about how the person is playing. Display the posters during the remaining activities to prompt or cue children as needed.

PRACTICE

Room for Hank Hawk Role Play

Materials

Three puppets (Hank Hawk, Benny Frog, Will Rabbit)

Give the puppets to three children and encourage them to role-play: Benny Frog tells Will Rabbit how to help Hank Hawk participate in Freeze Tag. Will then uses the skill steps to help Hank play. Coach and prompt the children as needed.

After the role play, discuss how the skill was presented. Then ask the players to exchange puppets and role-play again. As time permits, allow every child an opportunity to practice with a puppet. When all have participated, have various children role-play helping others participate, this time without using puppets. They might use the story events or devise another situation. Encourage the class to offer the players feedback on the way they portrayed the skill.

Me and My Shadow

Materials

Stickers

Arrange students in pairs and ask partners to face each other. Tell them they will practice helping others participate by "shadowing" their partner as you call out various activities. As needed so that both partners do the activity correctly, children are to ask if their partner wants to join, explain the activity, check to see if the partner understands, demonstrate, allow practice, and compliment each other.

Give a sticker to each student who performs the skill steps adequately. Tell students who do not earn stickers that they will have other opportunities to practice the steps and receive stickers.

Suggested activities

1. Hop on both feet three times.
2. Hold both ankles and take two steps.
3. Clasp your hands behind your knees.
4. Touch your right knee with your left hand.
5. Put your right hand on your ear and touch your right elbow.

Hey, Coach!

Materials

Stickers

Pair students, designating one person as coach and one as learner. Assign each pair a motor activity such as jumping rope, running a race, tossing bean bags, playing hopscotch, or playing kickball. Tell children they are to practice the skill steps of helping others participate by coaching each other on how to perform the assigned activity. Demonstrate the skill steps with a student assistant by explaining rules, checking for understanding, demonstrating, allowing practice, and praising. Mention that in other circumstances, they would first ask the person if he or she wants to join the activity. Emphasize the importance of being kind and positive with partners.

After a designated time period, have partners switch roles. Compliment students who coach well and those who accept coaching well.

Give a sticker to each student who performs the skill steps adequately. Tell students who do not earn stickers that they will have other opportunities to practice the steps and receive stickers.

Adaptation

Have more physically competent students coach first.

MAINTENANCE

Helping Others Participate Every Day

Materials

Stickers

Observe students daily for opportunities to recognize and compliment those who help others participate. As appropriate, ask the children to tell you when they have used the skill and to describe what they said and did. Give a sticker to each student who uses the skill.

Helping Others Participate in Literature

Materials

Classroom books and stories such as these:

Crary, Elizabeth. *I Can't Wait* (2nd edition). Seattle: Parenting Press, 1996.

Crary, Elizabeth. *I Want to Play* (2nd edition). Seattle: Parenting Press, 1996.

Meiners, Cheri. *Join In and Play*. Minneapolis: Free Spirit Publishing, 2004.

Meiners, Cheri. *Share and Take Turns*. Minneapolis: Free Spirit Publishing, 2004.

Select stories that discuss or feature characters helping others participate in games. After the children have read or listened to a story, discuss how helping others participate was important for the characters.

Great Coaches

Materials

Blackline Master 4 (Badges)

Preparation

Use the blackline master to make badges, writing "Great Coach" or drawing a picture on each. Attach double-stick tape or safety pins to the backs.

Introduce the badges as a special reward for children who help others in games. Tell the class that you will watch to see who helps others participate in a game or activity. When you see a student following the skill steps, you will announce a Great Coach and give that student a badge.

Continue the activity as long as it encourages children to use the skill.

FOLLOWING GAME RULES

SKILL STEPS: FOLLOWING GAME RULES

1. Learn the rules.

2. Watch others play.

3. Ask to join when you know the rules.

4. Take turns during the game.

5. Try hard when it is your turn.

MOTIVATION

Skill Presentation: Will's Hopscotch

Materials

> Four puppets (Will Rabbit, Shelli Squirrel, Hank Hawk, Felicia Fox)

Introduce the four puppets. Tell students that you're going to present a story about these characters called "Will's Hopscotch." Ask the children to listen carefully.

Will Rabbit doesn't know how to follow rules.

> **Will Rabbit:** Oh, boy, there are Shelli, Felicia, and Hank playing hopscotch! I love hopscotch!
>
> **Shelli Squirrel:** Oh, no! Here comes Will Rabbit!
>
> **Hank Hawk:** What's the matter? Don't you like playing with him?

Felicia Fox: You'll see!

Will Rabbit: Hi, everyone! Hopscotch! Can I play?

Shelli Squirrel: You can, Will, but you have to be last and wait your turn.

Will Rabbit: Oh, no, I want my turn now. You've all had a chance to play—I haven't. I'm throwing my stone.

Hank Hawk: You have to start in the first block, Will, not the third one.

Will Rabbit: I want to start in this one. You're all ahead of me. I want to catch up.

Felicia Fox: That's not the way to do it. You can't start wherever you want to.

Hank Hawk: You're jumping with both feet! That's not the way to play hopscotch! Only one foot goes in each block.

Shelli Squirrel: Let us show you how to play.

Will Rabbit: No, I know what I'm doing. This is really fun. I'm going to hop through the blocks again.

Felicia Fox: You're out! You stepped on a line. It's my turn.

Will Rabbit: Oh, no, I get another turn. Look out!

Shelli Squirrel: Ouch! You knocked us all down!

Hank Hawk: Not only that, he's taken two more turns!

Will Rabbit: I won! I won!

Shelli Squirrel: We're going to play somewhere else. Don't you come with us, Will. You don't know how to play by the rules.

Ask the children:

- Why don't Shelli, Felicia, and Hank want to play with Will? (He doesn't follow rules.)
- How does Will make his friends feel? (Angry, unhappy.)

Will's friends tell him about following rules.

Will Rabbit: Oh, go ahead. I don't care. I like to play by myself. (*Pause.*) Oh, yes, it's great to play alone! I don't have to take turns, I can start on any block, and I'm never out. *(Pause.)* Hmmm. Am I having any fun? *(Pause.)* Nope, I'm really not having much fun. I wonder if my friends would let me join their new game. I'm tired of playing alone.

Hank Hawk: Oh, no, you don't, Will! You're not barging into this game!

Will Rabbit: I'm really sorry I ruined your last game, Hank. Can you please teach me how to have fun playing hopscotch? I'm tired of playing alone.

Felicia Fox: The first thing you need to do, Will, is learn the rules of this game. Then you need to watch us play.

Shelli Squirrel: Yes, and then you can ask to join us when you know the rules.

Will Rabbit: Okay. I'll do all that. I really want to play with you.

Hank Hawk: Then when you play with us, you need to take turns and try hard when it's your turn.

Ask the children:

- Why does Will decide he doesn't want to play by himself? (He's lonely, it's no fun.)
- How do his friends tell Will to have fun at hopscotch? (Be sure the steps of the skill are mentioned: learn rules, watch others play, ask to join, take turns, try hard.)

Will Rabbit: I'll try hard. I promise. It's no fun playing hopscotch alone.

Hank Hawk: And it's no fun trying to play where you can't find us, Will! I'm glad you're going to follow the rules at last.

Ask the children:

- How did Will's friends feel when he didn't follow the rules of the game? (They were angry with Will and didn't want to play with him anymore.)
- What steps did Will's friends teach him?

Review the skill steps, asking children to repeat each one:

1. Learn the rules.
2. Watch others play.
3. Ask to join when you know the rules.
4. Take turns during the game.
5. Try hard when it is your turn.

As needed, help children define and understand terms such as "follow the rules" and "play fair." Invite students to tell about times when they haven't followed rules and times when others haven't followed rules. How does not following rules make people feel? What would happen if no one followed game rules?

PRACTICE

Will's Hopscotch Role Play

Materials

Four puppets (Will Rabbit, Shelli Squirrel, Hank Hawk, Felicia Fox)

Give the puppets to four children and ask them to role-play the events in the story: Shelli Squirrel, Felicia Fox, and Hank Hawk leave Will Rabbit to play hopscotch alone, telling him he doesn't know how to follow rules. Will feels lonely playing alone and asks his friends to help him follow rules. The friends teach Will the skill, Will follows the steps, and the four play hopscotch together.

After the role play, discuss how the skill was presented. Then ask the players to exchange puppets and role-play again. As time permits, allow every child the opportunity to practice with a puppet. When everyone has participated, have various children role-play following game rules, this time without using puppets. They might use the story events or devise another scenario. Encourage the class to offer feedback on the way the skill is performed.

Follow the Rules

Materials

Stickers

Explain that students are going to play games that will be fun only if everyone follows the rules. Select a familiar game, such as "Little Carla Saucer," "Hide the Eraser," "Hot and Cold," or "Doggie, Doggie, Your Bone Is Gone." Have students follow the rules and play. If any child has trouble playing, prompt the child to follow the skill steps. Monitor the children as needed, complimenting them for following rules.

Continue the activity, changing games if you like, until every child has had a chance to practice and to be praised for following rules.

Give a sticker to each child who follows the rules. Tell students who do not earn stickers that they will have other opportunities to practice the steps and receive stickers.

Follow the Path

Materials

Stickers

Preparation

With chalk or masking tape, create an irregular path along the floor. Have available a list of signals in response to which children will perform certain actions. For example, when you ring a bell, the children will sit; when you clap your hands, the children will raise their right hands; when you turn out the lights, the children will hop on their left feet; when you tap a stick, the children will stand still; when you whistle, the children will put their hands on their hips.

Explain that you are going to play a game and that it is important to follow the rules. Line up the children on the path, single file. Tell them they are to march along the path until you give a signal. At the signal, they are to perform a certain action. Go over your list of signals and actions; let students practice.

Begin the game, continuing as long as children follow the rules. If anyone has trouble, assist the child in following the skill steps. You may wish to stop occasionally to review the signals and practice the actions.

Give a sticker to each child who follows the rules. Tell students who do not earn stickers that they will have other opportunities to practice the steps and receive stickers.

Adaptation

Increase or reduce the number of signals and the relative difficulty of the actions.

I Know the Rules

Materials

Familiar games; stickers

Tell the children that they are going to play some games with their friends. Assign children to small groups and ask each group to select one of the games you've provided.

Before they begin, one child in each group is to review the game rules with the other children. As they play, circulate among them, encouraging everyone to play by the rules and to assist each other as needed.

After each group has completed its game, have them switch games. Again have a child in each group review the rules. Continue as time permits.

You might allow children to change rules to vary the games, make them easier to play, or account for fluctuating numbers of players or pieces of equipment. Explain that this procedure is fine as long as everyone gets to help make decisions about the changes and as long as the final changes are agreed on by all the players. As appropriate, remind children of the Mediating Group Rules skill from Unit 4.

Give a sticker to each child who follows the rules. Tell students who do not earn stickers that they will have other opportunities to practice the steps and receive stickers.

MAINTENANCE

Following Game Rules Every Day

Materials

Stickers

Observe students daily for opportunities to recognize and compliment those who follow game rules. As appropriate, ask the children to tell you when they have used the skill and to describe what they said and did. Give a sticker to each student who uses the skill.

Following Game Rules in Literature

Materials

Classroom books and stories such as these:

Crary, Elizabeth. *I Can't Wait* (2nd edition). Seattle: Parenting Press, 1996.

Crary, Elizabeth. *I Want to Play* (2nd edition). Seattle: Parenting Press, 1996.

Meiners, Cheri. *Join In and Play*. Free Spirit Publishing, 2004.

Meiners, Cheri. *Know and Follow Rules*. Minneapolis: Free Spirit Publishing, 2005.

O'Neill, Alexis. *The Recess Queen*. New York: Scholastic, 2002.

Select stories that discuss or feature characters following game rules. After the children have read or listened to a story, discuss how following rules was important to the characters.

Super Player

Materials

Blackline Master 4 (Badges)

Preparation

Use the blackline master to make badges, writing "Super Player" or drawing a picture on each. Attach double-stick tape or safety pins to the backs.

Explain that each day, you are going to watch for a Super Player, someone who always plays by the rules and is especially good at cooperating with friends. That person will be awarded a Super Player badge.

As you award a badge, recognize and compliment the Super Player. Look especially for children who may be less skilled at games but who try hard to follow rules.

SKILL

6 WINNING AND LOSING

SKILL STEPS: WINNING AND LOSING

When you win a game:

1. Say "Thank you!" when congratulated.
2. Smile.
3. Shake hands.
4. Say something nice to the other player.

When you lose a game:

1. Say "Congratulations!" to the winner.
2. Smile.
3. Shake hands.

MOTIVATION

Skill Presentation: Hank Hawk Helps

Materials

> Three puppets (Shelli Squirrel, Felicia Fox, Hank Hawk); Posters 1, 2, 3, 4

Introduce the three puppets. Tell students that you're going to present a story about these characters called "Hank Hawk Helps." Ask the children to listen carefully.

Shelli Squirrel doesn't know how to be a good winner, and Felicia Fox doesn't know how to be a good loser.

Shelli Squirrel: I won! I won! You're just a dumb fox, Felicia! Running so fast up the road and then going to sleep waiting for me! Well, I won this race! I passed you, and I beat you!

Felicia Fox: I didn't lose, you cheated!

Shelli Squirrel: I did not cheat! You're just mad because you lost. Dumb fox!

Felicia Fox: Sneaky squirrel! Cheater!

Shelli Squirrel: Liar!

Hank Hawk: Stop, you two! I was taking a nap, and you woke me up with your yelling. What's going on?

Shelli Squirrel: My, everyone's sleeping today! You and this dumb fox!

Felicia Fox: Shelli, stop it!

Hank Hawk: Someone tell me what happened.

Shelli Squirrel: We were running a race and Felicia fell asleep before she crossed the finish line. I passed her, and I won, but she called me a cheater!

Felicia Fox: Shelli called me a "dumb fox"! She's been so mean!

Hank Hawk: It sounds like you both need to learn how to be good winners and losers.

Ask the children:

- Why are Shelli and Felicia arguing?
- What do you think it means to be a "good winner" and a "good loser"?

Hank tells Shelli and Felicia about good winning and good losing.

Shelli Squirrel: A good winner?

Felicia Fox: A good loser?

Hank Hawk: Shelli, when you won the race, what did you want Felicia to say to you?

Shelli Squirrel: I wanted her to congratulate me for winning. I wanted her to smile, shake my hand, and tell me I ran a good race.

Hank Hawk: And Felicia, when you lost, what did you want Shelli to say to you?

Felicia Fox: I just didn't want her to tease me. She should have said something nice, like, "You really got off to a quick start."

Hank Hawk: All good thoughts! Why don't you say those things to each other now?

Shelli Squirrel: I'm sorry you lost, Felicia. You are a good runner.

Felicia Fox: Congratulations on winning. I guess I shouldn't have gone to sleep if I'd really wanted to win. You won fair and square.

Hank Hawk: Great, Shelli and Felicia. Now you're friends again. No race is worth losing a friend.

Ask the children:

- How did Shelli and Felicia make each other feel after the race? (They made each other feel upset and angry by calling each other names and being bad sports.)
- What does it mean to be a good winner?

Review the skill steps, asking the children to repeat each one.

When you win a game:

1. Say "Thank you!" when congratulated.
2. Smile.
3. Shake hands.
4. Say something nice to the other player.

When you lose a game:

1. Say "Congratulations!" to the winner.
2. Smile.
3. Shake hands.

As appropriate, discuss with children the difference between "luck" and "skill" in winning games. Explore the feeling some people have that those who win games are only lucky and don't need to be congratulated.

Invite the children to tell about times when they've played with poor losers or poor winners. How did they feel?

Display nonverbal communication Posters 1, 2, 3, and 4 to prompt discussion of the facial expressions and body language that are usually part of these skill steps. Emphasize the need for friendly, sincere communication after a game (when giving or receiving congratulations), whether a person lost or won. Display the posters during the remaining activities to prompt or cue children as needed.

PRACTICE

Hank Hawk Helps Role Play

Materials

Three puppets (Shelli Squirrel, Felicia Fox, Hank Hawk)

Give the puppets to three children and ask them to role-play the events in the story: Shelli and Felicia are mad at each other as Hank enters. Hank tells them about good winning and losing. Shelli and Felicia practice their new skills. Coach and prompt the children as needed.

After the role play, discuss how the skills were portrayed. Then ask the players to exchange puppets and role-play again. As time permits, allow every child an opportunity to practice with a puppet. When all have participated, have various children role-play winning and losing, this time without using puppets. They might use the story events or devise another scenario. Encourage the class to offer feedback on the way the skills are portrayed.

I Win! I Lose!

Materials

Blackline Master 12 (I Win / I Lose); stickers

Preparation

Use the blackline master to make "I Win" and "I Lose" cards. Have available a list of easy, familiar games and activities students can practice with (tic-tac-toe, a brief race, a spelling bee, hangman, tug of war).

As needed, review the skill steps for good losing and good winning. Explain that the children are going to practice these skills by pretending to win and lose at some games. Place the tags face down and have each child pick one. Ask students with "I Lose" tags to select a partner from those with "I Win" tags.

Assign a familiar game and have the partners role-play winning and losing, following the skill steps. Afterward, have students exchange roles. Recognize and compliment those who win and lose with appropriate behavior.

Give a sticker to each student who performs the skill steps adequately. Tell students who do not earn stickers that they will have other opportunities to practice the steps and receive stickers.

Adaptations

1. Choose games that involve simple motor skills and no luck factors. Focus on one or two of the winning and losing responses.

2. Assign games that involve some luck. Encourage children to add additional appropriate actions or comments when they win or lose.

Matching Winners and Losers

Materials

Familiar children's card games for two players; stickers

Tell the children that they will practice their skills of winning and losing by playing cards. Have everyone pick a partner and play one of the games. As children win and lose, coach them as necessary to use the skill steps.

Continue until both children in each pair have had a chance to win and lose.

Give a sticker to each student who performs the skill steps adequately. Tell students who do not earn stickers that they will have other opportunities to practice the steps and receive stickers.

Adaptation

After children play familiar card games, combine skill practice with academic practice by having them play at matching number and number–word cards, letters and beginning-sound pictures, science questions and answers, or any other set of matching items.

MAINTENANCE

Winning and Losing Every Day

Materials

Stickers

Observe students daily for opportunities to recognize and compliment appropriate winning and losing behavior. As applicable, ask the children to tell you when they have used the skills and to describe what they said and did. Give a sticker to each student who uses the skills.

Winning and Losing in Literature

Materials

Classroom books and stories such as these:

Brown, Laurie. *How to Be a Friend: A Guide to Making Friends and Keeping Them.* New York: Little, Brown Books for Young Readers, 2001.

Crary, Elizabeth. *I Want to Play* (2nd edition). Seattle: Parenting Press, 1996.

Jordan, Deloris. *Salt in His Shoes: Michael Jordan in Pursuit of a Dream.* New York: Aladdin, 2003.

Meiners, Cheri. *Join In and Play.* Minneapolis: Free Spirit Publishing, 2004.

Select stories that discuss or feature characters winning and losing. After the children have read or listened to a story, discuss how winning and losing behavior was important to the characters.

Winner's Circle

Materials

Five or six feet of yarn or string; tagboard; stickers

Preparation

Tie the ends of the yarn together and glue the yarn to the tagboard in a large circle. Over the top of the circle, write "Winner's Circle." Display in a prominent place.

Tell the children that they will try to fill the Winner's Circle by showing good winning and losing skills. Every time you see or hear of someone being a good loser or a good winner, you will write the student's name on a sticker and put the sticker in the Winner's Circle. Point out that all students who have learned this skill are winners, whether or not they actually win a game.

Continue this activity for as long as it seems useful, prompting children as needed and complimenting those who make the Winner's Circle. Once each week or so, assemble the group, review the growing number of stickers in the Winner's Circle, and go over the skill steps.

U N I T

6 RESPONDING TO AGGRESSION AND CONFLICT

Some of the most important social skills assist children in responding to minor and more serious acts of aggression. All children confront aggression occasionally; for some, conflict is at least as frequent as cooperation and friendliness. Young children model behavior they have seen in others, testing what is suitable for fulfilling their needs. When they start school, they may either encounter aggression among peers for the first time or have come prepared to be aggressive to others as a way of getting what they want.

In this unit, children will discuss and practice the steps for the following skills:

- Ignoring Aggression
- Getting Away from Aggression
- Asking for Help
- Responding Defensively
- Negotiating Conflicts

When children respond to aggression with either counter-aggression or passivity, they are likely to escalate the aggression or otherwise exacerbate the problem. Still, many continue to make the same inadequate responses. If, for instance, Phillip cries each time Jason teases him, his crying may well incite Jason to increase his teasing. Phillip, however, isn't aware of how he is reinforcing Jason, nor does he know what alternative actions might get Jason to stop.

The activities in this unit encourage children to think about what they really want when conflict occurs and what they ought to do or say to help themselves achieve that end. In the example above, Phillip might ignore Jason, walk away, ask for help, or defend himself. He might also negotiate an end to the conflict. Children have the opportunity to practice each of these alternatives here. With guidance and reinforcement, Phillip could learn constructive ways to respond to Jason's behavior.

Special Issues

It is extremely important that teachers establish conditions that encourage students to respond to conflict in desired ways. Frequent and public acknowledgement of nonaggressive, constructive, and appropriately assertive responses to aggression can reduce such aggression.

The immediate emotional release one gets from aggressive alternatives often makes these behaviors inherently reinforcing. Additionally, children do not easily associate subsequent negative or counterproductive consequences with their aggressive actions. Therefore, teachers are advised to provide powerful reinforcing contingencies when children display appropriate alternatives to aggression. It is hoped that, eventually, the frequent performance of the desired behaviors will permit the child to come under the control of natural contingencies of reinforcement and cause the behavior to become internalized and maintained without external rewards.

Although the emphasis in this unit is on nonaggressive alternatives to aggression and conflict, teachers and parents should be aware of psychological and physical safety issues. Many times, children are unable to handle these problems by themselves, especially if they are being victimized by school bullies. Under these circumstances, there may be need for adult intervention to ensure that the child is given the opportunity to develop within a mentally healthy and physically safe environment.

Without question, the least desired alternative under these conditions is to encourage children to respond to their victimization with counteraggression.

A related issue is to help students understand their responsibility when they observe others being bullied. To say or do nothing often encourages bullying behavior. During these lessons, teachers should help children learn appropriate ways to comfort friends or classmates who have been bullied and, when necessary, seek help.

> *Taking Part stickers are used as incentives for skill step performance and skill use in practice and maintenance activities throughout this unit. You may wish to distribute copies of Blackline Master 2 (My Taking Part Sticker Collection), which gives students a handy place to store the stickers they earn.*

SKILL

1 IGNORING AGGRESSION

SKILL STEPS: IGNORING AGGRESSION

1. Don't look at the person.

2. Don't talk to the person. Think about other things.

3. Think about good things that will happen if you don't look at the person or say anything to the person.

MOTIVATION

Skill Presentation: The Apple Pie Plan

Materials

> Three puppets (Felicia Fox, Will Rabbit, Shelli Squirrel)

Introduce the three puppets. Tell students that you're going to present a story about these characters called "The Apple Pie Plan." Ask them to listen carefully.

Shelli Squirrel doesn't know how to ignore Felicia Fox when she teases.

> **Felicia Fox:** Runt, runt, runt! Shelli Squirrel is a little runt! (*Leaves.*)

> **Will Rabbit:** Felicia, where are you running? Shelli, what happened? You look like you've been in a fight. You haven't been fighting with Felicia again, have you?

Shelli Squirrel: I couldn't help it! She called me "runt." Just because I'm small, Felicia calls me names. I have to fight to stop her teasing.

Ask the children:

- Why does Shelli fight Felicia? (Felicia teases her.)
- Do you think Shelli has to fight to stop the teasing? What else could she do?

Will tells Shelli how she can ignore Felicia.

Will Rabbit: You don't have to fight, Shelli. The more you fight Felicia, the more she's going to tease you. What you need to do is ignore her.

Shelli Squirrel: Ignore her? What does that mean?

Will Rabbit: That means not looking at Felicia and not saying anything to her when she calls you names. You ignore her and think about good things that will happen to you if you ignore her and don't get in trouble.

Ask the children:

- What does Will say Shelli should do when Felicia teases? (Ignore her.)
- What does it mean to ignore someone who bothers you? (Be sure the skill steps are mentioned: don't look at the person, don't talk to the person, think about good things that will happen if you ignore her or him.)

Shelli Squirrel: What other things should I think about?

Will Rabbit: Well, how about apple pie? If you don't get in a fight with Felicia Fox, you can stay for lunch and get apple pie.

Shelli Squirrel: Apple pie? Apple pie is my favorite dessert in the world. You always get the apple pie for me in the lunch line, Will, because I can't reach it.

Will Rabbit: Right. Well, now let's start the Apple Pie Plan to get Felicia to stop teasing you.

Shelli Squirrel: I like anything to do with apple pie!

Will Rabbit: When Felicia teases you, you need to tell yourself that you don't want to get into trouble by fighting. Instead of fighting, think, "If I don't fight, I will stay for lunch and get apple pie."

Ask the children:

• Why does Will tell Shelli to think about apple pie when Felicia teases her?

• What good thing could happen to you if you ignored someone's teasing? What could you think about when someone teases you?

Shelli uses the Apple Pie Plan to ignore Felicia's teasing.

Shelli Squirrel: Apple pie, apple pie. *(Pause.)* Oh, no, here comes that Felicia again!

Felicia Fox: Hello, runt! Did you grow any since our last fight?

Will Rabbit: *(Whispering to Shelli.)* Don't look at her or talk to her, Shelli. Think that you'll get apple pie if you don't get in trouble.

Shelli Squirrel: *(To herself.)* Apple pie, apple pie. How I love apple pie.

Felicia Fox: What's the matter, runt? Afraid to fight a big fox like me?

Shelli Squirrel: *(To herself.)* I'm going to have apple pie for dessert today. Yum!

Will Rabbit: See? Felicia's going away to talk to someone else. No fight today!

Shelli Squirrel: No fight. It's hard to listen to Felicia's teasing, but I do love thinking about apple pie. Thanks, Will, you're a true friend.

Will Rabbit: You're welcome, Shelli, and you know what? I'll bet that after Felicia sees you're going to ignore her teasing, she'll give it up. Maybe she'll become a true friend, too.

Ask the children:

- What happened when Shelli ignored Felicia's teasing instead of fighting with her? (Felicia got bored and stopped teasing Shelli.)
- What steps did Will teach Shelli?

Review the skill steps, asking the children to repeat each one:

1. Don't look at the person.
2. Don't talk to the person. Think about other things.
3. Think about good things that will happen if you don't look at the person or say anything to the person.

Help students understand that ignoring involves both avoiding contact with the person bothering us and using self-talk (for example, thinking about some reward such as apple pie) to help ignore the person. Be sure to emphasize that ignoring is to be used when someone is doing something unkind. Students shouldn't ignore others simply because they don't like someone or to make someone feel bad. Also explain that some behavior may be too severe or dangerous to ignore, such as physical attacks.

Invite children to tell about times when they ignored someone who was bothering them and times when they didn't. Discuss the consequences of both courses of action.

PRACTICE

The Apple Pie Plan Role Play

Materials

Three puppets (Felicia Fox, Will Rabbit, Shelli Squirrel)

Give the puppets to three children and ask them to role-play the events in the story: Will Rabbit tells Shelli Squirrel about ignoring Felicia Fox's teasing and using the Apple Pie Plan. When Felicia begins teasing, Shelli tries out the plan, with Will's coaching. Felicia leaves when her teasing is ignored. Prompt the children as necessary. Avoid having children role-play inappropriate behavior by playing the part of Felicia Fox yourself.

After the role play, discuss how the skill was presented. Then ask the players to exchange puppets and role-play again. As time permits, allow every child an opportunity to practice with a puppet. When all have participated, have various children role-play ignoring aggression, this time without using puppets. They might use the story events or devise another situation. Encourage the class to offer the players feedback on the way they presented the skill.

Ignoring with Shelli, Will, and Felicia

Materials

Three puppets (Shelli Squirrel, Will Rabbit, Felicia Fox); stickers

As necessary, review the events of the story. Say that students will have a chance to play Shelli and Will as they ignore Felicia's teasing. (Give two children the Shelli Squirrel and Will Rabbit puppets; you hold the Felicia Fox puppet.)

Explain the activity: Shelli and Will pretend to be walking together. As they walk by Felicia, have Felicia tease Shelli and Will. For example, as Felicia you'll say, "Hello, Shelli Squirrel Runt," "Where are you going, you long-eared rabbit?" and "Are you both running home to your mommies, little runts?" Will and Shelli are to help each other ignore the teasing by going over the skill steps (don't look at her, don't talk to her, think about something else).

After the role play, have the class discuss whether the characters managed to ignore the teasing. Then choose two more children and repeat the activity.

The emphasis in this activity is on the performance of the skill steps, not the teasing remarks. If some children respond to the teasing, prompt them to ignore it and have them repeat the role play.

Give a sticker to each child who follows the skill steps adequately. Tell students who do not earn stickers that they will have other opportunities to practice the steps and receive stickers.

See No Evil, Hear No Evil

Materials

Blackline Masters 13a, 13b (Friendly Face / Unfriendly Face)

Preparation

Use the blackline masters to make a friendly mask and an unfriendly mask.

Have the children form a line facing you. Show them the masks. Explain that you'll use the masks to cover your face as you make friendly and unfriendly statements. When students see the friendly mask and hear a friendly statement, they are to take one step toward you. When they see the unfriendly mask and hear an unfriendly statement, they are to turn their backs and take a step away from you.

Continue until children have responded to several friendly and several unfriendly statements.

Friendly statements

1. I like you.

2. You have a nice smile.

3. I like to play with you.

4. You are a good worker.

5. You're fun to talk to.

Unfriendly statements

1. I don't like you.

2. That's an ugly picture you drew.

3. Who would want to play with you?

4. You are no fun to talk to.

5. You are funny looking.

Adaptations

1. Offer physical and verbal prompting throughout the activity.

2. Allow children to use the masks and present friendly and unfriendly statements that you give them or that they create. Monitor as needed.

MAINTENANCE

Ignoring Aggression Every Day

Materials

> Stickers; Blackline Master 1 (Individual Social Skills Checklist, optional)

Observe students daily for opportunities to recognize and compliment those who ignore aggressive behavior. As appropriate, ask the children to tell you when they have used the skill and to describe what they said and did. Give a sticker to each student who uses the skill.

You may wish to use the Individual Social Skills Checklist to record students' progress in this unit's skill.

Ignoring Aggression in Literature

Materials

> Classroom books and stories such as these:
>
> Burnett, Karen. *Simon's Hook.* Felton, CA: GR Publishing, 1999.
>
> Crary, Elizabeth. *I Want It* (2nd edition). Seattle: Parenting Press, 1996.
>
> Crary, Elizabeth, *My Name Is Not Dummy* (2nd edition). Seattle: Parenting Press, 1996.
>
> Ludwig, Trudy. *Just Kidding.* Berkeley, CA: Tricycle Press, 2006.

Select stories that discuss or feature characters who ignore aggressive behavior. After the children have read or listened to a story, discuss how ignoring aggression was important to the characters.

Ignoring Chain

Materials

> Interlocking plastic pieces, or paper to make loops

Preparation

> Make a sign saying "Ignoring Chain" and post it near a cupboard door that has a handle (or on a bulletin board). Have available the plastic pieces or paper loops.

Explain that ignoring teasing is a sign of strength and that students will be practicing ignoring, which will show that they are strong as a chain. Fasten a plastic piece or a paper loop to the cupboard door handle (or bulletin board) and announce that any time you see or hear about someone ignoring teasing, you will add a link to the chain.

As you add a link, praise the child for ignoring and have that student help you attach the link to the chain. At the end of each week, call attention to the length of the chain. Encourage students to report to you if they have used this skill or if they see anyone using it outside school.

SKILL

2 GETTING AWAY FROM AGGRESSION

SKILL STEPS:
GETTING AWAY FROM AGGRESSION

1. Don't look at the person.
2. Don't talk to the person.
3. Walk away from the person.
4. Go to a safe place.

MOTIVATION

Skill Presentation: Will's Quick Getaway

Materials

> Three puppets (Will Rabbit, Hank Hawk, Carla Bluejay)

Introduce the three puppets. Tell the children that you're going to present a story about these characters called "Will's Quick Getaway." Ask them to listen carefully.

Hank Hawk takes Will Rabbit's berries.

Will Rabbit: Oh, what nice berries I've collected for my supper!

Hank Hawk: Hello, there, Will. Are those berries you've got? How about giving me one?

Will Rabbit: Okay.

Hank Hawk: Yum, that was good. Give me another one.

Will Rabbit: Well, okay, but these are for my supper. You can get some for yourself if you look through those bushes over there. *(Pause.)* Hey, you just ate another of mine!

Hank Hawk: That's right, Will. I'm still hungry. Don't tell me to go get my own, because I don't feel like it.

Will Rabbit: I picked these for my supper. I can't give you all my food.

Hank Hawk: Why not? I'm hungry. Give me another berry.

Will Rabbit: Well, just one more.

Hank Hawk: Another one! I want another berry!

Will Rabbit: No! No more.

Hank Hawk: Do you want to fight, Will? I'm a better fighter than you are, you know.

Ask the children:

- How is Hank Hawk treating Will Rabbit? (Meanly, unkindly, threateningly.)
- What do you think Will should do when Hank says he'll fight him?

Will gets away from Hank quickly.

Carla Bluejay: Here's another berry, Hank. Catch.

Hank Hawk: Got it! Hey, where are you going? Come back! I want another berry!

Will Rabbit: *(Panting.)* I got away, I got away.

Carla Bluejay: Will, you're out of breath. What happened?

Will Rabbit: I had to run to get away from Hank Hawk. He was eating all my berries, and he said he'd fight me if I didn't keep giving him more.

Carla Bluejay: You were smart to run away, Will. Sometimes, when someone makes you feel bad or angry—and ignoring doesn't help—you can just walk away. But other times you need to get away quickly.

Will Rabbit: How can I tell what to do?

Ask the children:

- When do you think it's a good idea to walk away from someone?

- When do you think it's a good idea to get away quickly?

Carla Bluejay tells Will about getting away from a bad situation.

Carla Bluejay: If someone is just bothering you, you can try ignoring the person. If that doesn't work, then getting away is sometimes the best thing to do. Don't look at the person or talk to the person. Walk away and go to a safe place.

Will Rabbit: But Hank said he'd fight me.

Carla Bluejay: Yes. When someone tries to take your things or hurt you, you need to leave right away. You can run instead of walk to get away from someone who could hurt you.

In your discussion, you might point out that there are times when walking away isn't possible, such as during class. At such times, children could use other skills, such as telling an adult.

Ask the children:

- When does Carla say it's right to ignore a person? (When the person is bothering you.)

- When does she say you should get away from a person? (When ignoring doesn't work.)

- When does she say you should leave a person as quickly as you can? (When the person tries to take your things or hurt you.)

- How does Carla say Will could get away from someone who made him feel bad or angry? (Be sure the skill steps are mentioned: don't look at the person, don't talk to the person, walk away, go to a safe place.)

Will Rabbit: I'm glad to know that getting away is the right thing to do sometimes. Thanks, Carla.

Carla Bluejay: You're welcome, Will. Are you still hungry? I know where to find the juiciest berries you've ever tasted!

Ask the children:

- What might have happened if Will hadn't gotten away from Hank Hawk? (He might have gotten hurt in a fight or been forced to give away all his berries.)
- What steps did Carla teach Will?

Review the skill steps, asking the children to repeat each one:

1. Don't look at the person.
2. Don't talk to the person.
3. Walk away from the person.
4. Go to a safe place.

Particularly if the children in your group need adult supervision at all times, emphasize that walking away to a safe place can mean walking to a trusted adult.

Invite children to tell about times when they had to leave a threatening situation or wished they could leave. As appropriate, help students list various ways of getting away, such as running home, walking to the nearest neighbor, going from a deserted location to a populated place, taking an alternative route to avoid danger.

Because the idea of leaving a situation unresolved may be new to children, repeat this discussion as necessary.

You might also post the following sentence: "If someone is making you feel frightened, angry, or bad—walk away!"

PRACTICE

Will's Fast Getaway Role Play

Materials

Three puppets (Will Rabbit, Hank Hawk, Carla Bluejay)

Give the puppets to three children and ask them to role-play the events in the story. Hank Hawk pesters Will Rabbit for berries. Hank threatens to fight Will. Will gets away and meets Carla

Bluejay. Then Will and Carla discuss leaving a threatening situation. Avoid having children role-play inappropriate behavior by taking the part of Hank Hawk yourself. Coach and prompt the children as necessary.

After the role play, discuss how the skill was performed. Then ask the players to exchange puppets and role-play again. As time permits, allow every child an opportunity to practice with a puppet. When all have participated, have various children role-play getting away from aggression, this time without using puppets. They might use the story events or devise another situation. Encourage the class to offer the players feedback on the way they presented the skill.

Walking Away Game

Assemble the students in a circle or a line facing you. Tell them that this game will help them practice walking away when someone makes them feel bad or angry. Explain that you will describe various situations. If a situation seems unfriendly (meaning verbally or physically threatening), they are to turn around and walk several steps away from you. If the situation seems friendly or nonthreatening, they are to walk several steps toward you.

Sample situations

1. Someone you know asks you to play.

2. Someone you know tears up your paper.

3. Someone you know helps you up when you fall.

4. Someone you know stomps in a puddle to splash you.

5. Someone you know calls you a bad name and tells you to come closer.

6. Someone you know threatens to fight you.

7. Someone you know brings you flowers.

As appropriate, discuss any situations that do not elicit unanimous responses from the children. Emphasize the importance of understanding others' intentions. A child who is allergic to flowers, for example, might decide to walk away from someone who presents them. Explain that some situations can't be clearly identified as friendly or unfriendly and that some unfriendly situations call for reactions other than walking away.

As needed, repeat this activity several times, using a variety of situations. You may want to repeat it at intervals throughout the year and after subsequent lessons on asking for help and responding defensively.

Adaptation

Conduct this activity in small groups or with individuals.

We Walk Away

Materials

Stickers

Ask students to pick partners. Explain that you will present an uncomfortable or threatening situation for one partner to initiate. The other partner is to respond by following the steps and leaving the situation, avoiding all argument, physical contact, and altercation.

Before beginning, discuss that it is sometimes (but not always) appropriate to leave without showing anger. It is almost always appropriate to leave without showing aggression.

Continue the activity, having partners change roles. If you prefer not to have students role-play inappropriate behavior, do the activity as a group and take the role of the initiator yourself.

Give a sticker to each student who performs the skill steps adequately. Tell students who do not earn stickers that they will have other opportunities to practice the steps and receive stickers.

Sample situations

1. A student playing does not want another student to join.
2. A student is accidentally bumped by another and wants to fight.
3. A student calls another student "Baby."
4. A student makes fun of another student's art project.
5. A student threatens to take another student's homework.

Adaptations

1. Supply children with a specific response to a situation or ask them to choose from two options that you provide.

2. Ask children to pick appropriate responses from a posted list and then defend their choice to the group.

MAINTENANCE

Getting Away from Aggression Every Day

Materials

Stickers

Observe students daily for opportunities to recognize and compliment those who walk away from aggressive or counterproductive situations. As appropriate, ask the children to tell you when they have used the skill and to describe what they did. Give a sticker to each student who uses the skill.

Getting Away from Aggression in Literature

Materials

Classroom books and stories such as these:

Cosgrove, Stephen. *Hucklebug/Rev.* Los Angeles: Price Stern Sloan, 2001.

Crary, Elizabeth. *I Want It* (2nd edition). Seattle: Parenting Press, 1996.

Crary, Elizabeth. *My Name Is Not Dummy* (2nd edition). Seattle: Parenting Press, 1996.

Keats, Ezra Jack. *Goggles.* New York: Puffin, 1998.

McCain, Becky. *Nobody Knew What to Do: A Story about Bullying.* Morton Grove, IL: Albert Whitman, 2001.

Select stories that discuss or feature characters choosing to get away from unpleasant or threatening situations. After the children have read or listened to a story, discuss how getting away was important to the characters.

Walk!

Materials

Green construction paper

Preparation

   Title a bulletin board "Walk!" With the green paper, make small circles.

Show children the bulletin board, explaining that it will remind them to walk away from bad situations, such as fighting, arguing, name-calling, or destroying property. Announce that you will watch for anyone who walks away from a situation to avoid getting hurt or in trouble. Each time you see or hear of a student using the skill, you will add a green circle to the board, because in traffic, green means "go."

   As needed, cue students by pointing to the board or by saying, "Green means go!" Before adding a circle, praise the student who used the skill.

3 ASKING FOR HELP

SKILL STEPS: ASKING FOR HELP

1. Go to a safe place.
2. Find a trusted adult.
3. Explain your feelings.
4. Ask for help.

MOTIVATION

Skill Presentation: Carla Asks for Help

Materials

> Three puppets (Carla Bluejay, Shelli Squirrel, Hank Hawk)

Introduce the three puppets. Tell students that you're going to present a story about these characters called "Carla Asks for Help." Ask them to listen carefully.

Shelli Squirrel keeps stealing Carla Bluejay's food.

Carla Bluejay: I've found so many nice seeds and nuts to store for the winter! Now I'll just fly back to my hole . . . Oh, no! Where is all the food I gathered yesterday? It's gone! I'll bet Shelli Squirrel stole it again! What should I do?

Ask the children:

- What do you think Carla should do to stop Shelli from stealing her food?

Carla tries talking to Shelli, but it doesn't work.

Carla Bluejay: I'm going to talk to Shelli. Maybe I can get her to stop taking my food. *(Pause.)* Shelli?

Shelli Squirrel: Oh, hi, Carla. Nice day, isn't it?

Carla Bluejay: Shelli, I know you've been taking my food. I can't let you do that because then I won't have anything to eat this winter. You have to find your own food.

Shelli Squirrel: Okay, Carla. I'll leave your food alone and find my own. *(Pause, then whispering.)* I don't like to look for food. It's a lot easier to take Carla's!

Carla Bluejay: Okay, I've got more seeds. Now I'll put them in this hole . . . Oh, no! That Shelli Squirrel stole my food again! Asking her to stop didn't work. I'll have to think of something else.

Ask the children:

- What do you think Carla should do?

Carla moves to another tree, but Shelli finds her.

Carla Bluejay: I know what I'll do. I'll move to another tree so Shelli can't find me. *(Pause.)* Here's a nice one! Now I'll go get food.

Shelli Squirrel: Hmmm, I see Carla moved to another tree. Yum, I'll just climb up and take these seeds and nuts.

Carla Bluejay: Back to my new tree. *(Pause.)* I can't believe it! Shelli found me! I can't stop her from taking my food! I'll be hungry all winter! Oh, what should I do?

Ask the children:

- What do you think Carla should do?

Carla asks Hank Hawk for help.

Carla Bluejay: I just don't know what to do. Maybe if I go to Hank Hawk, he'll help me. *(Pause.)* Hank, can you help me? Shelli Squirrel keeps taking my food, and I can't stop her. I've tried talking to her and moving to another tree, but nothing worked.

Hank Hawk: I'm glad you came to me for help, Carla. I'm older than you, and I've had more experience. As my Uncle Oscar always says, "Sometimes we just can't solve our problems by ourselves. Sometimes we have to ask for help." He told me what to do when someone makes us angry or afraid and we can't get the person to go away or stop.

Carla Bluejay: That sounds like something I need to remember. What are the steps?

Hank Hawk: Uncle Oscar says we should first go to a safe place and then find someone older we trust. Then we should explain our feelings and ask for help. You did all those things without Uncle Oscar's telling you, Carla.

Ask the children:

- When does Hank say we should ask for help? (When we've tried to solve our problem by ourselves but couldn't, when we can't get away from someone or make them stop what they're doing.)

- What steps did Hank learn from his Uncle Oscar? (Be sure all the skill steps are mentioned: go to a safe place, find a trusted person who's older, explain your feelings, ask for help.)

Hank helps Carla.

Carla Bluejay: So I did the right thing? I wasn't sure if I should ask for help or not.

Hank Hawk: You did the right thing. First you tried to solve your problem yourself. Then you came to me for help. Now, let's see. I think that both of us should go tell Shelli to give you back your food. Then we'll go to her hole every morning and follow her to be sure she gathers her own food.

Carla Bluejay: She won't like that! She's lazy! It's easier to take my food.

Hank Hawk: I know. But we need to make Shelli understand that it's wrong to take someone else's food. Once she gets used to gathering her own food, she might feel proud about taking care of herself.

Carla Bluejay: Yes, it's a good feeling to gather your own food. And it's good to know I can ask for help when I can't solve a problem myself!

Ask the children:

- When does Hank say Carla should ask for help with a problem? (When she can't solve it herself.)
- What steps did Hank teach Carla?

Review the skill steps, asking the children to repeat each one:

1. Go to a safe place.
2. Find a trusted adult.
3. Explain your feelings.
4. Ask for help.

Invite the children to tell about times when they asked for help solving a problem. What happened? How did they feel?

Emphasize that asking for help is not the ideal first solution to all problems and that, if possible, we should try to help ourselves before asking others. Explain that when aggression is clearly beyond a child's control and other reasonable alternatives have been exhausted, seeking help is an important skill to have.

If appropriate, provide or solicit a list of situations in which asking for help is only one of many possible solutions. For example, if someone cuts ahead of you in line, you might ask the person to take turns, leave the line and join another, ignore the person and stay where you are, or ask an adult for help.

PRACTICE

Carla Asks for Help Role Play

Materials

> Three puppets (Carla Bluejay, Shelli Squirrel, Hank Hawk)

Give the puppets to three children and ask them to role-play the events in the story. Shelli Squirrel steals Carla Bluejay's food. Carla tries to get Shelli to stop by talking to Shelli and moving to another tree, both without success. Carla then asks Hank Hawk for help. Hank praises Carla for asking for help and tells her the skill steps Uncle Oscar taught him. Avoid having children role-play aggressive behavior by taking the role of Shelli Squirrel yourself. Prompt and coach the children as needed.

> After the role play, discuss how the skill was presented. Then have the players exchange puppets and role-play again. As time permits, allow every child an opportunity to practice with a puppet.

> When all have participated, have various children role-play asking for help, this time without using the puppets. They might use the story events or devise another situation. Encourage the class to offer the players feedback on the way they presented the skill.

Here's My Sign

Materials

> Blackline Master 14 (Help Me / I Can Handle It); craft sticks or tongue depressors, two for each child

Preparation

> Use the blackline master to make "Help Me" and "I Can Handle It" signs for each student. Cut out the signs and glue them to sticks. If you wish, color the signs.

Distribute the signs. Tell students that you'll read various situations. After each, students are to think about what they would do. When they decide, they are to hold up their Help Me sign if they think they should get help or their I Can Handle It sign if they think they could help themselves. Mention that the class won't be comparing or commenting on choices.

In the next activity, students will hear these situations again and get a chance to role-play their choice. As necessary, remind children to think carefully before they hold up a sign.

Sample situations

1. Someone bigger is pushing you on the playground.
2. Someone older is threatening to hurt you.
3. An adult you don't know tells you to get in a car.
4. Someone takes your money away from you.
5. Someone has been taking your lunch every day.

Carla Asks Hank

Materials

Stickers

Remind the children that in the story, Carla Bluejay decided to ask Hank Hawk for help after she was unable to stop Shelli Squirrel from taking her food. Ask students to pick partners. One partner is to play Carla Bluejay, the other Hank Hawk. Explain that you will read the situations from the previous activity. This time, instead of voting on whether they'd solve the problem themselves or ask for help, students will role-play their choices.

If the child playing Carla Bluejay decides to solve the problem independently, Carla is to tell Hank Hawk what she did to solve it. If Carla decides to ask for help, she is to explain her feelings to Hank and ask for his help. The child playing Hank is to praise Carla either for solving her problem or for asking for help. If Carla asks for help, Hank is to go over Uncle Oscar's skill steps. Supervise and monitor the children as needed.

Present each situation twice, so children can exchange roles. If you wish, before students decide whether they would ask for help, discuss how situations could be either friendly or unfriendly, depending on circumstances.

Give a sticker to each student who either solves a problem independently or performs the skill steps adequately. Tell students who do not earn stickers that they will have other opportunities to practice the steps and receive stickers.

Adaptations

1. Add situations of verbal or physical aggression your children have encountered.

2. Ask students to discuss their solutions to these problems as if they were giving help to someone else.

MAINTENANCE

Asking for Help Every Day

Materials

Stickers

Observe students daily for opportunities to recognize and compliment those who appropriately ask for help with the aggressive behavior of others. As applicable, ask the children to tell you when they have used the skill and to describe what they said and did. Give a sticker to each student who uses the skill.

Asking for Help in Literature

Materials

Classroom books and stories such as these:

Crary, Elizabeth. *I Can't Wait* (2nd edition). Seattle: Parenting Press, 1996.

Crary, Elizabeth. *I Want It* (2nd edition). Seattle: Parenting Press, 1996.

Crary, Elizabeth. *My Name Is Not Dummy* (2nd edition). Seattle: Parenting Press, 1996.

McCain, Becky. *Nobody Knew What to Do: A Story about Bullying*. Morton Grove, IL: Albert Whitman, 2001.

Thomas, Pat. *Stop Picking On Me*. Hauppauge, NY: Barrons Educational Series, 2000.

Select stories that discuss or feature characters seeking help with the aggressive behavior of others. After the children have read or listened to a story, discuss how asking for help was important to the characters.

The Help Me Tower

Materials

Items with which to build a tower (rings, blocks, plastic cups, tissue boxes) or paper shapes for a bulletin board tower

Preparation

Make and post a sign, "Help Me Tower."

Tell children that the Help Me Tower will be built to encourage them to ask for help in difficult situations. Say that each time you see or hear of someone using the skill steps to ask for help, you will add to the tower.

Tell children to keep in mind that it is important to ask for help only if we really need help, not when we can handle a situation ourselves. Say that you hope the tower will grow slowly but steadily.

Before you add to the tower, commend the student who has used the skill.

S K I L L

4 RESPONDING DEFENSIVELY

SKILL STEPS: RESPONDING DEFENSIVELY

1. Try to stay away from the person.
2. Try to run away.
3. Yell for help.

MOTIVATION

Skill Presentation: Benny Frog Defends Himself

Materials

> Two puppets (Shelli Squirrel, Benny Frog)

Introduce the two puppets. Tell the children that you're going to present a story about these characters called "Benny Frog Defends Himself." Ask them to listen carefully.

Benny Frog is scared by a snake.

Shelli Squirrel: Benny, you look scared and out of breath. What happened?

Benny Frog: I . . . I . . . I almost got swallowed by a snake!

Shelli Squirrel: A snake?

Benny Frog: Yeah, and you saved me, Shelli!

Shelli Squirrel: I saved you? But I wasn't even there!

Benny Frog: I know. But I remembered what you told me one day about defending myself when I think someone will hurt me.

Ask the children:

- What do you think "defending yourself" means?

Shelli Squirrel and Benny Frog tell about defending themselves.

Shelli Squirrel: Oh, yeah. That was the time I defended myself against those children who were throwing stones at me.

Benny Frog: You'd been out looking for nuts.

Shelli Squirrel: Yeah, and when I was looking around the tree, the children kept throwing stones at me, forcing me to run away.

Benny Frog: That's like what happened to me. I was sitting on a lily pad when all of a sudden a snake grabbed me! I hopped onto the shore, but that snake was too quick and grabbed me again!

Ask the children:

- What did Benny and Shelli do first when they were afraid of being hurt? (Tried to get away.)

Shelli Squirrel: When the children kept hurting me, I was very afraid. I tried to ignore them and ran around the tree, but I knew I was in danger.

Benny Frog: I begged the snake to let me go, but it wouldn't. I tried to think fast and clearly, just like you told me.

Shelli Squirrel: Yes. I remembered that my father said if ever I was afraid of someone, I should get home as fast as I could. And he said I should also yell for help.

Benny Frog: Right. As I pulled away from the snake, I croaked as loudly as I could. I made a terrible racket!

Shelli Squirrel: Good thinking. I'm not loud, but I am quick. I surprised the children by running quickly up the tree and hopping through three trees. The children left, and I went home as fast as my legs could carry me.

Ask the children:

- What did Shelli and Benny do after they tried to get away but couldn't? (Made a racket, yelled, croaked loudly, ran quickly.)

Benny Frog: My croaking scared the snake! It slithered away, and I hopped away faster than I've ever hopped before!

Shelli Squirrel: Oh, Benny, I'm so glad I helped you protect yourself! My father says the first thing to remember is to stay away from anyone who wants to harm you. But if you get in trouble—and you and I were really in trouble—you need to try to get away, and you need to yell for help.

Benny Frog: Yes, and if you're really afraid, it's all right to yell and kick and make a terrible racket!

Shelli Squirrel: Right! The most terrible racket!

Ask the children:

- Why did Shelli Squirrel and Benny Frog need to defend themselves? (They were in real danger, they felt afraid.)
- What steps did they follow to defend themselves?

Review the skill steps, asking the children to repeat each one:

1. Try to stay away from the person.
2. Try to run away.
3. Yell for help.

Invite the children to tell about times when they defended themselves against someone they thought would hurt them. Did they protect themselves, or did they fight back? If they fought back, what happened?

> *Note: If any child begins to tell about an incident of physical abuse by an adult, talk with the child about it*

when class is done to determine whether the incident should be reported.

PRACTICE

Benny Frog Defends Himself Role Play

The major focus of this activity is on teaching children the importance of protecting themselves in dangerous situations by acting defensively rather than fighting back. Because most children in hostile situations have difficulty distinguishing between defending themselves and being aggressive, the safest course is to emphasize getting away. Children need to learn how to recognize and avoid potentially harmful situations, whether they occur with peers or with adults. They also need to try escaping from potential harm.

Materials

Two puppets (Shelli Squirrel, Benny Frog)

Give the puppets to two children and ask them to role-play the events in the story: Shelli Squirrel and Benny Frog exchange stories of how they defended themselves against the children and the snake by using the skill steps.

After the role play, discuss how the skill was presented. Then have the players exchange puppets and role-play again. As time permits, allow every child an opportunity to practice with a puppet. When all have participated, have various children role-play responding defensively, this time without using the puppets. They might use the story events or devise another situation. Encourage the class to offer feedback on the way the skill is presented.

Defend Myself! It's Okay!

Materials

Blackline Master 15 (Defend Myself / It's Okay); craft sticks or tongue depressors, two for each child

Preparation

    Use the blackline master to make "Defend Myself" and "It's Okay" signs for each student. Cut out the signs and glue them to sticks. If you wish, color the signs.

Distribute the signs. Tell students that you'll read various situations. After each, students are to think about whether they would consider the situation nonthreatening or whether they should defend themselves. When they decide, they are to hold up either their "Defend Myself" or their "It's Okay" sign.

    Remind students that defending themselves is important if they feel threatened or if the situation seems dangerous.

    As appropriate, discuss each situation with students, asking them to explain why they voted as they did. Mention that in the next activity, the children will role-play these situations.

Sample situations

1. An adult offers you candy if you will go for a ride.

2. You see some kids arguing on the playground.

3. Your friend asks you to come swimming with her.

4. Some kids start teasing you and calling you names.

5. Your friend tries to push you toward a snarling dog on a chain.

6. Some kids try to get you to fight another student.

Adaptations

1. Instead of the signs, use plain red and green paper, explaining that red means "stop" or "danger" and green means "go" or "safe," just as with traffic signals.

2. Use situations that reflect actual experiences the children have had.

Play Alone

Materials

    Stickers

Read the situations from the previous activity and ask various children to role-play their responses. Select more capable students to role-play first. Discuss each situation after responses are presented. Emphasize that we usually have choices about what to do and often there are several good choices. Have students think of other ways to respond to the situations; have them role-play each alternative. Prompt and coach as needed.

Next, ask students to tell about their own experiences in similar situations and encourage them to role-play their real-life responses. Distribute stickers to all students who participate. Mention that you will continue to pass out stickers to anyone who shares real-life experiences of responding defensively.

As appropriate, review the difference between aggression and self-defense to remind students that protecting ourselves or escaping is almost always preferable to inflicting injury or harm.

MAINTENANCE

Responding Defensively Every Day

Materials

Stickers

Observe students daily for opportunities to recognize and compliment those who respond defensively in threatening situations. As appropriate, ask the children to tell you when they have used the skill and to describe what they said and did. Give a sticker to each student who uses the skill appropriately.

Defending Yourself in Literature

Materials

Classroom books and stories such as these:

Keats, Ezra Jack. *Goggles.* New York: Puffin, 1998.

McCain, Becky. *Nobody Knew What to Do: A Story about Bullying.* Morton Grove, IL: Albert Whitman, 2001.

Meiners, Cheri. *Talk and Work It Out.* Minneapolis: Free Spirit Publishing, 2005.

Thomas, Pat. *Stop Picking on Me.* Hauppauge, NY: Barrons Educational Series, 2000.

Select stories that discuss or feature characters defending themselves in threatening situations. After the children have read or listened to a story, discuss how defending themselves was important to the characters.

Ignoring/Getting Away/Asking/Defending File

Materials

Manila folder; stickers of various kinds

Preparation

Title a manila folder the "Ignoring/Getting Away/Asking/Defending File" and decorate it. Write each student's name on a piece of paper, leaving room for stickers, and staple the page to the inside of the folder.

Show the folder to the students and tell them the file is for keeping a record of times they've used the four skills studied so far in this unit: Ignoring, Getting Away, Asking for Help, and Defending Yourself. Take time to review each skill and the circumstances calling for each. Tell students that when you see or hear about someone choosing an appropriate way to deal with a difficult or dangerous situation, you will place a sticker of the student's choice next to that person's name. Mention that defending oneself is the skill they should use only when they feel afraid because of what someone else is doing.

As you add to the file, commend children who tell you about appropriately ignoring, getting away, and asking for help. You might ask students to name the skill they used. When a child describes acting in self-defense, discuss whether any alternative responses might have worked. If you can ascertain that the child used self-defense appropriately, label and compliment the child's decision.

Periodically share the file with the group. Review the four skills as needed, discussing when each is appropriate.

5 NEGOTIATING CONFLICTS

SKILL STEPS: NEGOTIATING CONFLICTS

1. Talk about the problem.
2. Say what you want to do.
3. Listen to what the other person wants to do.
4. Agree on a plan.
5. Follow your plan.

MOTIVATION

Skill Presentation: A Raft Problem

Materials

Three puppets (Hank Hawk, Felicia Fox, Will Rabbit); Posters 1, 2, 3, 4

Introduce the three puppets. Tell students that you're going to present a story about these characters called "A Raft Problem." Ask them to listen carefully.

Hank Hawk and Felicia Fox argue.

Hank Hawk: It's my turn to use the raft, Felicia!

Felicia Fox: Your turn? It is not! I've only had it for a few minutes!

Hank Hawk: A few minutes? You've had it forever!

Felicia Fox: I have not! I've barely gotten it into the water!

Hank Hawk: I want that raft back now! Give it to me!

Felicia Fox: Stop pulling on this raft, Hank! We're both going to fall in! *(They both fall in.)* The water's cold!

Hank Hawk: My feathers are wet! Why didn't you give me the raft when I asked for it?

Will Rabbit: What's all the racket? Why are you both in the water instead of on the raft? You hate getting wet.

Ask the children:

- What problem are Felicia and Hank having?
- How do they feel about the problem? How could they solve their problem?

Will Rabbit suggests that Felicia and Hank make a plan.

Felicia Fox: Hank wouldn't let me take my turn! He grabbed the raft back.

Hank Hawk: You were taking too long!

Will Rabbit: I don't think either one of you is having any fun with the raft. What you need is a plan to use it without fighting over it.

Hank Hawk: A plan?

Felicia Fox: What kind of plan?

Will Rabbit: You need to think of a way to solve your problem.

Felicia Fox: I don't have a problem! Hank does!

Hank Hawk: What? It's your fault we got wet!

Felicia Fox: My fault?!

Will Rabbit: Hey, you two! You're arguing instead of making a plan. You need to go step by step.

Hank Hawk: What do we do first?

Will Rabbit: First, you talk about the problem. Then you say what you want to do, and you listen to what the other person wants to do.

Ask the children:

- What does Will say are the first three steps in making a plan to solve a problem? (Talk about the problem, say what you want to do, listen to what the other person wants to do.)

Felicia Fox: We know what our problem is. We both love floating on the raft, and we hate waiting to use it.

Hank Hawk: That's the problem, all right. What I want to do is float from this tree over to that tree.

Felicia Fox: Way over there? I'd never get to use the raft! What I want to do is float from my den to that riverbank.

Will Rabbit: Now you need to agree on a plan. That means that both of you need to give in a little.

Felicia Fox: Maybe we could both use the raft for a short time. Hank, you could float to that tree and then give me a turn.

Hank Hawk: That's not far enough. What about the tree down there?

Felicia Fox: That's too far. How about the tree in between?

Hank Hawk: Okay. That seems fair. And why don't you float from your den to that little hill? That's about as far as I'll be floating.

Felicia Fox: Yeah, okay.

Ask the children:

- What is the fourth step in making a plan? (Agreeing on the plan.)
- What does Will say Hank and Felicia need to do if they're going to agree on a plan? (Each give in a little.)

Will Rabbit: You're doing very well with your plan. I was wondering if you could share the raft.

Hank Hawk: Hmmm. I'll bet we could float on it together.

Felicia Fox: What if you take a turn, then I take a turn, then we float together for a while?

Hank Hawk: That sounds good.

Will Rabbit: Yes, your plan sounds very good. Are you feeling good about negotiating?

Felicia Fox: About what?

Will Rabbit: Ne-go-ti-a-ting. When you negotiate to solve a problem, you talk with the other person and come up with a plan that's fair for both of you. The last step in negotiating is to follow your plan.

Ask the children:

- What does Will say Felicia and Hank have been doing? (Negotiating.)
- What does "negotiating" mean? (Talking together and coming up with a plan that's fair for both.)
- What's the last step in negotiating? (Following the plan.)

Hank Hawk: Great! Let's start right away, Felicia. You can take the first turn.

Felicia Fox: Gee, thanks, Hank. I'm really glad we're going to stop fighting and start floating!

Ask the children:

- Why did Hank and Felicia need to negotiate? (They weren't having any fun, they were fighting, they weren't enjoying the raft.)
- How did they feel after they negotiated a plan? (Happy, friendly toward each other.)
- What steps did Will teach them?

Review the skill steps, asking the children to repeat each one:

1. Talk about the problem.
2. Say what you want to do.
3. Listen to what the other person wants to do.
4. Agree on a plan.
5. Follow your plan.

Be sure the children understand that negotiation means discussing a problem and agreeing to compromise ("give in a little"). Emphasize that without cooperation and compromise, negotiation won't work and problems won't be solved.

Present the following four approaches to negotiation:

Take turns: "You can swing two times, and then I swing two times."

Work cooperatively: "You use the green crayon, and I'll use the blue crayon. Then we'll trade."

Share: "We can both sit and look at the book together."

Select an alternative role: "If you want to play the pirate, I'll play the captain of the ship."

Invite the children to tell about times they've had problems that could have been solved if they'd known how to negotiate. Ask them also if they've ever negotiated a problem successfully.

You might explain to students that they have likely negotiated conflicts already without knowing they were using the skill. Negotiation can help children decide such matters as what to play at recess, what television shows to watch, where to go at lunch, and how and when chores will be done at home.

Display nonverbal communication Posters 1, 2, 3, and 4 to prompt discussion of the facial expressions and body language that are usually part of these skill steps. Emphasize the importance of speaking and behaving in a friendly manner while negotiating with someone to solve a problem. Display the posters during the remaining activities to prompt or cue the children as needed.

Negotiating is a complex skill that requires cooperation. As appropriate during practice and maintenance activities, review related skills such as listening, speaking assertively, agreeing on group rules, sharing materials, and taking turns.

PRACTICE

A Raft Problem Role Play

Materials

Three puppets (Hank Hawk, Felicia Fox, Will Rabbit)

Give the puppets to three children and ask them to role-play the events in the story: Will Rabbit tells Hank Hawk and Felicia Fox about negotiation as a way to solve their problem about using the raft. Hank and Felicia negotiate a plan to take turns and share the raft. Will compliments them on their plan.

After the role play, discuss how the skill was presented. Then ask the players to exchange puppets and role-play again. As time permits, allow every child an opportunity to practice with a puppet. When all have participated, have various children role-play negotiating conflicts, this time without using the puppets. They might use the story events or devise another scenario. Encourage the class to offer the players feedback on the way they presented the skill.

Group Solutions

Materials

Stickers

Have students role-play negotiating conflicts in the situations listed below or in others they suggest. Make clear that neither insisting on having everything your own way nor giving in to the other person on every point is negotiating. The goal of negotiating is to decide on a solution that is mutually agreeable. Remind children of the four approaches to negotiation and of the skill steps, telling them to watch for the steps in the role plays. As each group of players negotiates, ask the other children to observe. If the group has trouble arriving at a plan, ask the observers to assist.

Give a sticker to each student who performs the skill steps adequately. Tell students who do not earn stickers that they will have other opportunities to practice the steps and receive stickers.

Sample situations

1. Sheri and Ron got a new book as a gift. They both want to read it at the same time.

2. Mike and Tim share a bedroom. Mike likes to stay up late reading with all the lights on. Tim likes to go to bed early with all the lights off.

3. The teacher has a classroom aquarium. All the children like to feed the fish. Each morning, several students rush over to get the fish food.

4. Ruby, Arthur, and Jennifer are playing store. They all want to be the manager.

5. Emily and her brother Leon are on a two-day car trip. They've made their parents angry with their squabbling over who gets to play their music.

Nifty Negotiator

Materials

Blackline Master 4 (Badges); stickers

Preparation

Use the blackline master to make badges, writing "Nifty Negotiator" or drawing a picture on each. Attach double-stick tape to the backs.

Show students the Nifty Negotiator badges. Explain that throughout the week, if students have a problem that needs negotiating, you will choose an uninvolved student to wear a badge and be the Nifty Negotiator. The Nifty Negotiator's job will be to listen to the problem and help the students think of solutions. Examples of problems needing negotiation: Two or more students want to be first in line, want to use the same game or toy, want to distribute class materials, or want to feed the fish.

Monitor the negotiations, coaching students as needed and reminding them to follow the skill steps. Commend the children for listening, offering solutions, and accepting compromises.

Give a sticker to each student who performs the skill steps adequately. Tell students who do not earn stickers that they will have other opportunities to practice the steps and earn stickers.

Adaptation

As children become capable negotiators, offer their services to other teachers or classes.

MAINTENANCE

Negotiating Conflicts Every Day

Materials

Stickers

Observe students daily for opportunities to recognize and compliment those who negotiate conflicts. As appropriate, ask the children to tell you when they have used the skill and to describe what they said and did. Give a sticker to each student who uses the skill.

Negotiating Conflicts in Literature

Materials

Classroom books and stories such as these:

Cosgrove, Stephen. *Little Mouse on the Prairie*. Los Angeles: Price Stern Sloan, 2001.

Crary, Elizabeth. *I Can't Wait* (2nd edition). Seattle: Parenting Press, 1996.

Crary, Elizabeth. *I Want It* (2nd edition). Seattle: Parenting Press, 1996.

Crary, Elizabeth. *I Want to Play* (2nd edition). Seattle: Parenting Press, 1996.

Crary, Elizabeth. *My Name Is Not Dummy* (2nd edition). Seattle: Parenting Press, 1996.

McCain, Becky. *Nobody Knew What to Do: A Story about Bullying*. Morton Grove, IL: Albert Whitman, 2001.

Meiners, Cheri. *Talk and Work It Out*. Minneapolis: Free Spirit Publishing, 2005.

Schenk de Regniers, Beatrice. *How Joe the Bear and Sam the Mouse Got Together*. New York: Lothrop, Lee & Shepard Books, 1990.

Select stories that discuss or feature characters negotiating conflicts. After the children have read or listened to a story, discuss how negotiation was important to the characters.

Negotiation Corner

Preparation

Make a sign that says "Negotiation Corner." Post the sign in an area with a table and chairs where students can go to negotiate. Title a bulletin board "We Negotiate."

Show students the Negotiation Corner. Explain that whenever a problem occurs, you'll ask the students involved to go in the Negotiation Corner to work out a solution. Problems requiring negotiation might include two or more children wanting to be first at something, wanting to use a game or material, wanting the next turn at something, or wanting to handle a classroom task.

Review the four approaches to negotiation and the skill steps. Tell the children that after each negotiation, you will ask the people involved to tell about their problem and solution. Then you'll post the children's names on the bulletin board. You may want to require that students agree on two or three possible solutions because many conflicts can be solved agreeably in several ways.

> *Note: In classrooms where conflicts occur frequently, be judicious in assigning students to the Negotiation Corner. Students who appear to be creating problems for the reward of using the Negotiation Corner should not be permitted to continue doing so.*

Adaptation

Ask children to write about or illustrate their classroom negotiations and put them in the Negotiation Corner. They might also compile a book of negotiations.

Negotiation Journal

Preparation

Label a manila folder "Negotiation Journal."

Tell students that each time they negotiate a conflict, they are to write, draw, or dictate what happened for inclusion in the class Negotiation Journal. Collect the papers in the folder. Periodically discuss the journal with students, asking for other possible solutions to the conflicts.

Remind students of typical conflicts that negotiation can help solve: disagreements about who will take the first turn, who will use a game or material first, or how an item or a task will be shared.

APPENDIX A SKILL NAMES AND STEPS

UNIT 1

Greeting

1. Look in the person's eyes.
2. Smile.
3. Say hello in a friendly voice.

Introducing Yourself

1. Look in the person's eyes.
2. Smile.
3. Say hello and tell your name.
4. Ask the person's name.

Listening

1. Look in the person's eyes.
2. Think about what the person is saying.
3. Repeat what the person has said.

Joining a Conversation

1. Listen to what people say.
2. Wait for your turn to talk.
3. Say what you think.

Starting a Conversation

1. Go up to the person.
2. Smile and say hello.
3. Ask about what the person is doing or tell about what you are doing.
4. Listen to the person's answer.
5. Say something else.

UNIT 2

Naming Feelings

1. Remember that "happy" is how you feel when something really good happens.
2. Remember that "angry" is how you feel when someone is mean or unfair.
3. Remember that "afraid" is how you feel when you want to get away.
4. Remember that "sad" is how you feel when you lose something or do something wrong.

Naming My Feelings

1. Think about what just happened.
2. Think about how you feel about what happened.
3. Remember the emotion words.
4. Choose one of the emotion words.

Naming Others' Feelings

1. Look at the other person's face.
2. Look at the person's body posture.
3. Listen to the person's words.
4. Listen to the person's tone of voice.

Sending Messages

1. Think of the message you want to send.
2. Think how your face should look.
3. Think how your hands and body should look.
4. Send your message.

Controlling Temper

1. Stop what you are doing.
2. Take five deep breaths.
3. Count to 10.
4. Think about the right thing to do.
5. Do the right thing.

UNIT 3

Making Positive Self-Statements

1. Think of what you like to do.
2. Think of what you can do well.
3. Tell someone.

Making Positive Statements to Others

1. Look at the person.
2. Find something nice about how the person looks or what the person is doing.
3. Tell the person.

Expressing Feelings

1. Think about how you feel.
2. Think about who needs to know your feelings.
3. Tell the person how you feel.

Speaking Kindly and Using Courtesy Words

1. Think of what you want to say.
2. Think of a way to say it kindly.
3. Use a nice voice.

Speaking Assertively

1. Think about what you want.
2. Think of a way to say it calmly.
3. Say what you want.

UNIT 4

Respecting Others' Property

1. Ask permission to use someone else's property.
2. Handle it carefully.
3. Return it promptly.

Sharing Materials

1. Think of what you want to do.
2. Think of how you can do it together.
3. Agree on a way.
4. Do it together.

Accepting Individual Differences

1. Think about the ways people are like you.
2. Think of the good things about people.
3. Treat people as you want to be treated.

Joining a Group Activity

1. Go up to a person in the group.
2. Make eye contact and smile.
3. Ask politely if you may join.
4. Check that the person has understood you.

Mediating Group Rules

1. Think about whether the rules are fair.
2. Think about how the rules might be changed.
3. Offer new rules.
4. Ask what others think.
5. Make sure everyone agrees.
6. Use the new rules.

Offering and Giving Help

1. Think about what people are doing.
2. Think about what you could do to help.
3. Ask if you can help.

Giving and Accepting Criticism

When telling someone about something they have done wrong:

1. Use a nice voice.
2. Use kind words.
3. Help the person do the right thing.

When someone tells you about something you have done wrong:

1. Listen politely.
2. Think about what the person is saying.
3. Let the person show you their way.
4. Thank the person for helping you.

UNIT 5

Taking Turns

1. Find out when it is your turn.
2. Wait for your turn.
3. Play when it is your turn.

Putting Materials Away

1. Check what needs to be put away.
2. Check where it goes.
3. Put it away neatly.

Playing Group Games

1. Ask permission to play.
2. Learn the game rules.
3. Follow the rules carefully.
4. Take your turn.

Helping Others Participate

1. Ask if the person wants to join.
2. Explain the rules.
3. Check to see if the person understands.
4. Demonstrate the game.
5. Let the person practice.
6. Say something nice about how the person is playing.

Following Game Rules

1. Learn the rules.
2. Watch others play.
3. Ask to join when you know the rules.
4. Take turns during the game.
5. Try hard when it is your turn.

Winning and Losing

When you win a game:

1. Say "Thank you!" when congratulated.
2. Smile.
3. Shake hands.
4. Say something nice to the other player.

When you lose a game:

1. Say "Congratulations!" to the winner.
2. Smile.
3. Shake hands.

UNIT 6

Ignoring Aggression

1. Don't look at the person.
2. Don't talk to the person. Think about other things.

3. Think about good things that will happen if you don't look at the person or say anything to the person.

Getting Away from Aggression

1. Don't look at the person.
2. Don't talk to the person.
3. Walk away from the person.
4. Go to a safe place.

Asking for Help

1. Go to a safe place.
2. Find a trusted adult.
3. Explain your feelings.
4. Ask for help.

Responding Defensively

1. Try to stay away from the person.
2. Try to run away.
3. Yell for help.

Negotiating Conflicts

1. Talk about the problem.
2. Say what you want to do.
3. Listen to what the other person wants to do.
4. Agree on a plan.
5. Follow your plan.

APPENDIX

B PUPPET MASKS

CARLA BLUEJAY

From *Taking Part: Introducing Social Skills to Children—PreK–Grade 3 (2nd ed.),* © 2009 by G. Cartledge and J. Kleefeld, Champaign, IL: Research Press (800-519-2707, www.researchpress.com)

BENNY FROG

SHELLI SQUIRREL

HANK HAWK

WILL RABBIT

FELICIA FOX

APPENDIX

C   POSTERS

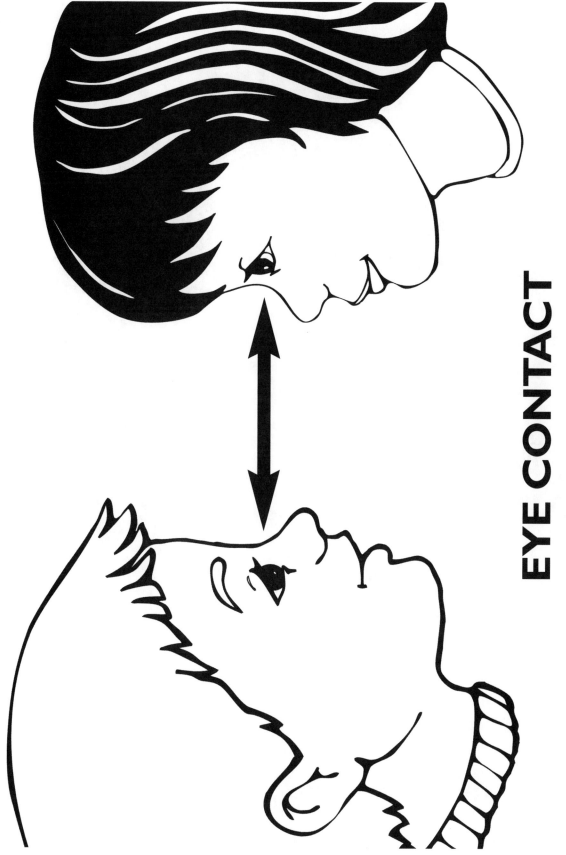

EYE CONTACT

From *Taking Part: Introducing Social Skills to Children—PreK–Grade 3 (2nd ed.)*, © 2009 by G. Cartledge and J. Kleefeld, Champaign, IL: Research Press (800-519-2707, www.researchpress.com)

FACIAL EXPRESSION

TONE OF VOICE

POSTURE

From *Taking Part: Introducing Social Skills to Children—PreK–Grade 3 (2nd ed.)*, © 2009 by G. Cartledge and J. Kleefeld, Champaign, IL: Research Press (800-519-2707, www.researchpress.com)

D BLACKLINE MASTERS

INDIVIDUAL SOCIAL SKILLS CHECKLIST

Name: _____

		Needs Instruction	Shows Some Competence	Mastered	Comments
Unit 1 Making Conversation	Greeting				
	Introducing Yourself				
	Listening				
	Joining a Conversation				
	Starting a Conversation				
Unit 2 Communicating Feelings	Naming Feelings				
	Naming My Feelings				
	Naming Others' Feelings				
	Sending Messages				
	Controlling Temper				
Unit 3 Expressing Oneself	Making Positive Self-Statements				
	Making Positive Statements to Others				
	Expressing Feelings				
	Speaking Kindly/Using Courtesy Words				
	Speaking Assertively				
Unit 4 Cooperating with Peers	Respecting Others' Property				
	Sharing Materials				
	Accepting Individual Differences				
	Joining a Group Activity				
	Mediating Group Rules				
	Offering and Giving Help				
	Giving and Accepting Criticism				
Unit 5 Playing with Peers	Taking Turns				
	Putting Materials Away				
	Playing Group Games				
	Helping Others Participate				
	Following Game Rules				
	Winning and Losing				
Unit 6 Responding to Aggression and Conflict	Ignoring Aggression				
	Getting Away from Aggression				
	Asking for Help				
	Responding Defensively				
	Negotiating Conflicts				

From *Taking Part: Introducing Social Skills to Children—PreK–Grade 3 (2nd ed.)*, © 2009 by G. Cartledge and J. Kleefeld, Champaign, IL: Research Press (800-519-2707, www.researchpress.com)

My Taking Part Sticker Collection

Name: _____

From *Taking Part: Introducing Social Skills to Children—PreK–Grade 3 (2nd ed.)*, © 2009 by G. Cartledge and J. Kleefeld, Champaign, IL: Research Press (800-519-2707, www.researchpress.com)

Blackline Master 2

Blackline Master 3

Badges

Blackline Master 4

We're All Ears 1

Blackline Master 5a

We're All Ears 2

Blackline Master 5b

Talk-Starter Bugs

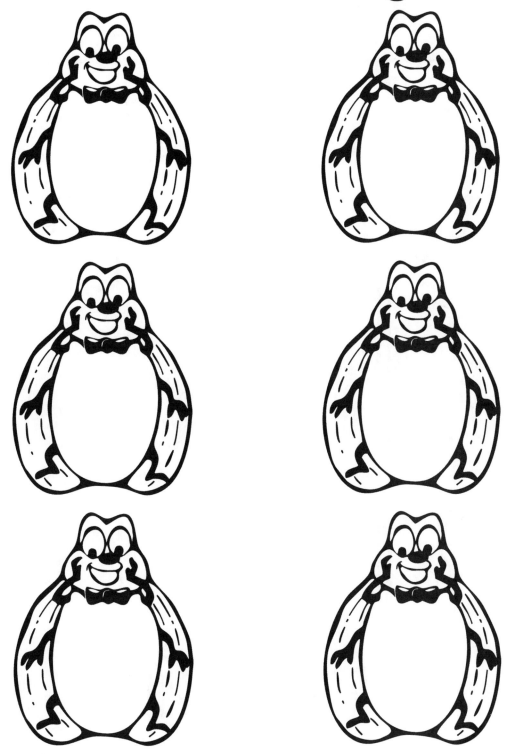

From *Taking Part: Introducing Social Skills to Children—PreK–Grade 3 (2nd ed.)*, © 2009 by G. Cartledge and J. Kleefeld, Champaign, IL: Research Press (800-519-2707, www.researchpress.com)

Blackline Master 6

357

How Do Feelings Look?

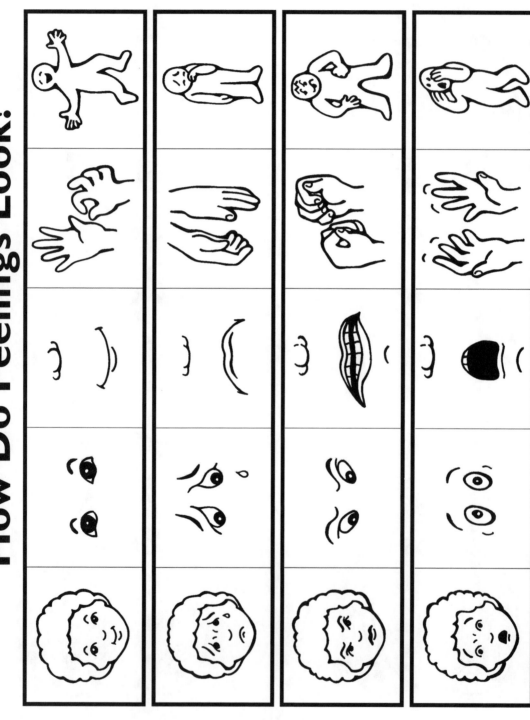

From *Taking Part: Introducing Social Skills to Children—PreK–Grade 3 (2nd ed.)*, © 2009 by G. Cartledge and J. Kleefeld, Champaign, IL: Research Press (800-519-2707, www.researchpress.com)

Blackline Master 7

Feelings Faces

Changing Faces

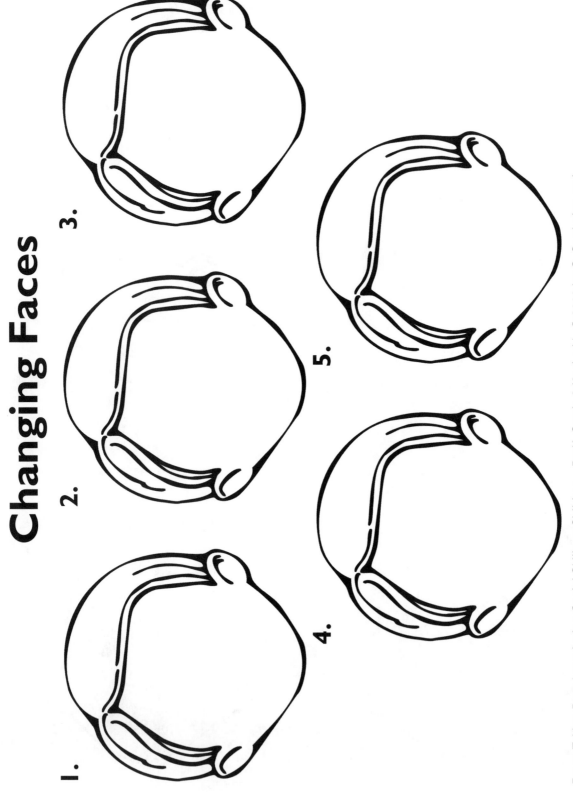

1.

2.

3.

4.

5.

From *Taking Part: Introducing Social Skills to Children—PreK–Grade 3 (2nd ed.)*, © 2009 by G. Cartledge and J. Kleefeld, Champaign, IL: Research Press (800-519-2707, www.researchpress.com)

Blackline Master 9

Straight Talk

Straight Talk

Mean Talk

Weak Talk

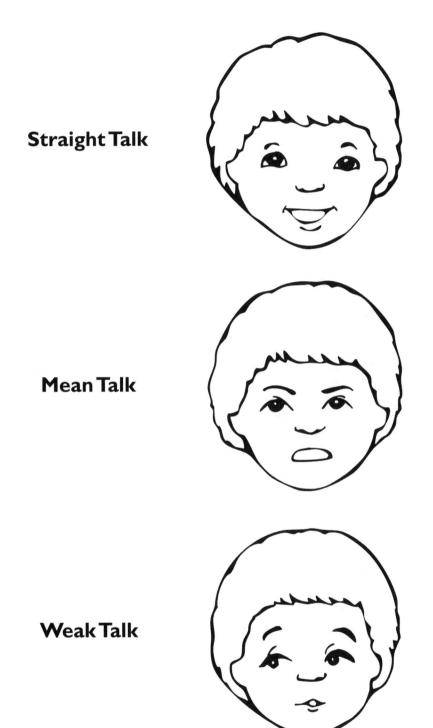

From *Taking Part: Introducing Social Skills to Children—PreK–Grade 3 (2nd ed.)*, © 2009 by G. Cartledge and J. Kleefeld, Champaign, IL: Research Press (800-519-2707, www.researchpress.com)

Helping Hand

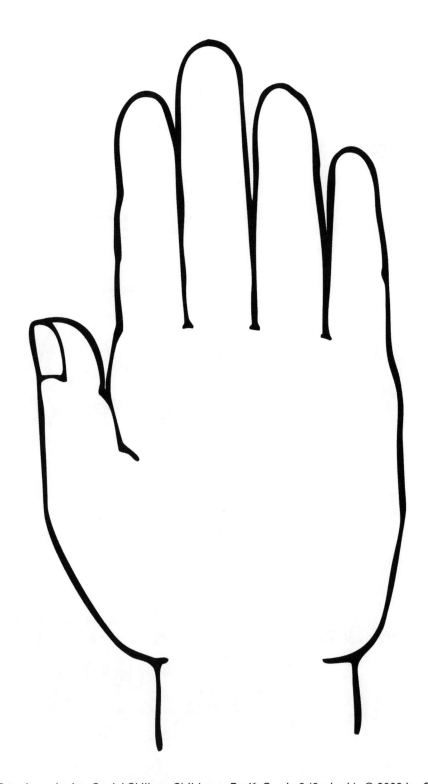

Blackline Master 11

From *Taking Part: Introducing Social Skills to Children—PreK–Grade 3 (2nd ed.)*, © 2009 by G. Cartledge and J. Kleefeld, Champaign, IL: Research Press (800-519-2707, www.researchpress.com)

Friendly Face

Blackline Master 13a

Unfriendly Face

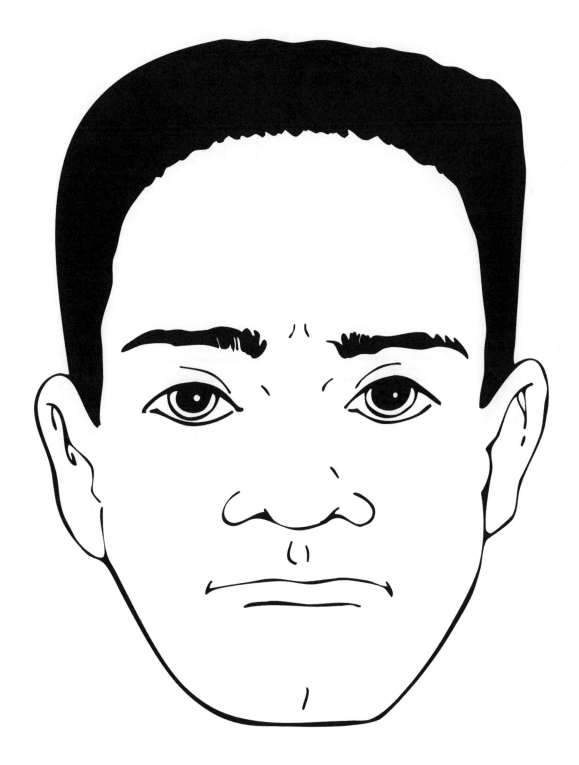

Blackline Master 13b

365

I Can Handle It

Help Me

From *Taking Part: Introducing Social Skills to Children—PreK–Grade 3 (2nd ed.)*, © 2009 by G. Cartledge and J. Kleefeld, Champaign, IL: Research Press (800-519-2707, www.researchpress.com)

Blackline Master 14

It's Okay

Defend Myself

From *Taking Part: Introducing Social Skills to Children—PreK–Grade 3 (2nd ed.)*, © 2009 by G. Cartledge and J. Kleefeld, Champaign, IL: Research Press (800-519-2707, www.researchpress.com)

Blackline Master 15

ABOUT THE AUTHORS

GWENDOLYN CARTLEDGE, Ph.D., is a professor at The Ohio State University, School of Physical Activity and Educational Services, special education programs. She documents an extensive teaching career in both the public schools and higher education. A faculty member at OSU since 1986, her professional teaching, research, and writings have centered on students with mild disabilities, the development of social skills, and early intervention and prevention of learning and behavior problems through effective instruction. Her scholarship includes four coauthored books: *Teaching Social Skills to Children and Youth* (3rd ed.); *Cultural Diversity and Social Skills Teaching: Understanding Ethnic and Gender Differences; Teaching Urban Learners;* and *Diverse Learners with Exceptionalities.* She has also published social skills curricula and numerous articles in professional journals.

JAMES KLEEFELD, M.Ed., has taught students from kindergarten to postgraduate level for Cleveland Public Schools and Cleveland State University. He has written 10 books for the entertainment field and is a regular contributor to several magazines. Currently he is the Managing Editor of *Funny Paper Magazine.* In addition, he regularly presents educationally significant programs on character and antibullying in elementary schools. He resides in Avon, Ohio.